AT THE CRACK OF DAWN

AT THE CRACK OF DAWN

Sannsibble

Library of Congress Control Number: 2011916421
ISBN: Hardcover   978-1-4653-6461-6
                  Softcover   978-1-4653-6460-9
                  Ebook   978-1-4653-6462-3

This book was printed in the United States of America.

To order additional copies of this book, contact:
Xlibris Corporation
1-888-795-4274
www.Xlibris.com
Orders@Xlibris.com
90151

DEDICATION

This book is dedicated in the memory of my mother Jane, my father Walter, and my grandparents Lolita and Alfred who taught me the basics; and to my children who inspired and supported me, and my family and my friends who shared with me along the way. T*eamwork –living in the love of the common people.*

To: Huong Vo

Best wishes ♡

From: Jannsibble – 2016

ACKNOWLEDGEMENTS

T O ALL WHO participated directly and indirectly in all of the events, allow me to say "*A World of Thanks*. Every effort has been made to include all of our team members, all participants, and every cooperating organization and supporters in the manuscript. Our programs evolved over an extended period of time and was conducted in different phases, but none the less our momentum was ongoing. It was during those different phases that we each shared in our vast wealth of diversity of cultures, people and organizations. All in all, it was one moment in time. T H A N K Y O U !

CHAPTER 1

W E WERE ORDINARY citizens from all walks of life. Our motto and creed was "People at work laying the foundations for a lasting peace." Our activities were often low-keyed. The majority of our chapter members were seniors who were eager and willing to transfer their knowledge by volunteering to do chapter work, and by sharing their experiences with our members and our community. In 1991, I was elected president of our Greater Miami chapter.

At that time, I knew very little about the organization, but as a lifelong volunteer, I willingly accepted the role. Community leadership and volunteer work was not new to me. From my youthful days I had served as president of our 4-H Club, served in Young Christian Leadership groups, provided leadership in debating clubs, public speaking groups, and a whole host of other community and civic organizations. I have also chaired several committees in church, college, and other community organizations in my adult life. So community leadership was not new to me by any means. I was a die-hard grassroots learner and worker.

Our vice president was a member of the organization for over twenty years. Ethel has served the chapter in numerous leadership capacities. When I was elected as the president, Sam Brenner, one of our board members, asked me about Agnes Crabtree. I did not know who she was. Ethel provided me with information about Agnes Crabtree. Ms. Crabtree was the founder of the Greater Miami Chapter of the United Nations Association, which was founded over thirty years ago. I was delighted to be provided with historical information on the chapter. I wish I knew more about the organization but figured the gaps will be filled in as I go along. I was eager and willing to learn more about the organization and the people with whom I will be working. It did not take me long to realize, however, that I have seen those people before. The commitment and dedication of volunteers, their faces are the same that one sees everywhere, the ones who without hesitation always say "I will" whenever something needs to be done. Those people by no means fit the "Mickey" profile; because they are conscious, proactive, and will go any lengths for a good cause, especially if it means a peaceful existence with respect for all. They are people like me.

My spirited enthusiasm in undertaking the leadership of the chapter was due mostly to the fact that I believed in what the organization represents; furthermore, I welcomed the opportunity to increase my volunteer activities. I was in the process of getting a divorce, and I thought it would be a wonderful opportunity to engage my children and myself in community activities as a way of escaping the drudgeries of the divorce. So we wholeheartedly embraced the work that we were doing for our chapter. I performed administrative roles in the planning, development, and the execution of activities. Soon after I was elected president I realized that my team mates had the profile of the same people who wherever one goes across the globe, are the same people who willingly show up to do volunteer work. They were truly dedicated and committed to community work, and in helping to make the world a better place.

Many of our chapter members like me shared our volunteer efforts over a wide spectrum of activities. Many of us plan volunteer work strategically at different phases in our lives. One of my volunteer portfolios at one point in my life was being a soccer mom and coach. I coached minor league boy's soccer for over six years. I did not set out to be a coach. I took my son to his minor league soccer practice. A turn of events on the soccer field on the third day of practice inducted me into coaching the youths for over six years.

On the field that evening, the young men looked very stunning in their green shamrock jerseys, white shorts and black soccer cleats. Their teenage coach walked off the field and never returned. The boys including my son were all between the ages of six and seven years old. We felt very disappointed and just could not standby and watch our young players huddled in the middle of the soccer field waiting for the coach to return. To rescue the moment all of the mothers and me did a quick survey of who among us knew the game. I was volunteered to lead the young men and that was how I wounded up coaching soccer for over six years.

As far back as I can remember, I have always been involved in some form of civic or youth volunteer activity. Volunteerism has been a lifelong enriching experience. The participation factor gives one a sense of belonging, of being a part of, and the satisfaction of having contributed. However, of all the volunteer work and leadership roles that I have performed, the most challenging was the leadership of the local UNA-USA Greater Miami chapter.

My initial involvement with the organization was intended only to be on a limited basis. I was introduced to the chapter by its former president and board member, Professor Carlos Watson. He invited me to one of the chapters' potpourri dinners. The meeting was held at the Coral Gables Congregational Church. The guest speaker was the chairperson of UNIFEM. The Coral Gables Congregational Church was a typical venue for chapter meetings. The chapter makes a small donation to the church for each meeting. It was a very good and practical arrangement. The members had the use of the kitchen for the reheating and serving of meals. The location was also very nice, it was very spacious and quietly nestled in a coconut palm grove.

I arrived at the meeting before Professor Watson. I was welcomed by Ethel and the chapter members. I looked for Professor Watson the entire meeting but he never came to the meeting. I apologized to Ethel for the non-show of Professor Watson but Ethel would not have it, she told me that she should be the one who apologizes for him not showing. She explained to me that it was not unusual of Professor Watson to be a non-show. She said he had a habit of inviting guests and then not show up at the meeting. Professor Watson was the president emeritus. The members welcomed me, and I felt at home even though I was a bit uneasy because Professor Watson, my host, did not show up for the meeting.

So here I was, after attending three meetings, and becoming a new member of the chapter, I am elected the president of the organization. It is no wonder that Dora and Jess, who by the way are twins and were also senior board members, would continually whisper among themselves, then surfaced with the same question over and over: "Sylvia, do you know how long it took before Professor Watson, Ethel, and others were elected as president of the chapter?" Sometimes I wondered if that was a trivia question or whether it was a question to drive home a message. I took it that they meant how long each of those individuals had to be chapter members before they were elected to leadership. My membership in the chapter was less than six months. I attributed the honor of the new role as president of the chapter to my willingness to participate.

I assisted the chapter in the planning and executing of a town hall meeting on the issues in Haiti a few months before I was elected to the post. I also pledged resources from my workplace to assist with the chapter's work as needed and when available, but I did not foresee that I would be promoted to chapter president. I had no idea of what laid ahead, but when I became the chapter president I hopped into the pilot's seat after I was shown the way to the cockpit. The crew and passengers were willing to let me fly the plane.

The majority of our members are retired seniors. They are a wonderful group of people. I considered myself fortunate to be working with that much talent and experience, not to mention the grace and "un vrai savoir-faire en matière de vivre'. They knew about life and had the knowledge and life skills of dealing with people. Perhaps my sentiments and respect of working with seniors are deeply rooted in the fact that I was raised by my grandmother who was very wise.

I have tested the faith of this class of people time and again, and I have found a wealth of resource that has helped me throughout my life. They take the time and patience to respond to my genuine inquiries. Working with seniors reminds me of the old saying that "a new broom sweeps clean but the old broom knows the corners". I say that with a "much respect, big up, and honor" if you get my drift.

Some of our more senior members take naps during meetings. It was not unusual for some members to also take naps after having their meals. Dora and Jess, our twin board members were famous for nodding in our meetings. I sat beside them most times. It was usually after awaking from their nap that they would hold caucus between themselves before turning to ask me if I knew how long it took other members to be elected to be president of our chapter. I could never figure out how both ladies take their naps and awake at the same time. It must have been synchronized napping. That they were twins made it even more beautiful and breath taking. But they knew their stuff, no one could put anything over on them. They were smart ladies. In the pictures at the back of the book find the lady that is standing holding her dress with her left hand and pointing her raised right arm toward the stage; she is my friend Dora.

My son accompanied me to some of our meetings. He noticed the nodding of our members during the meetings. Actually, it was not too difficult to notice the condition since it also came with the occasional rounds of snoring. Watching our members sleep in a meeting is hardly something that an active teenager would ignore. Teenagers are very observant, and nothing misses their scrutinizing eyes. My son asked me why is it that so many of our members sleep during the meetings. I wasn't sure if his question was a sign of protest of having to accompany me to the meetings or because he was more accustomed to energetic interaction as would be in soccer or Pop Warner football.

Members who sleep in meetings are definitely not his cup of tea. He preferred members who are awake, alert and who would engage him in small discussions on issues that were being discussed in the meetings or even talking about his football games or their youthful sports activities. I explained to my son that many of our members are retirees, and it is not unusual for seniors to take a nap during the course of the day, although almost everyone junior or senior takes a nap after a meal.

I also told my son that people also sleep in meetings because of boredom with the topic that is being discussed. Sometimes people sleep in church during the service which could be because they are bored or tired. He accepted my explanations although I did not believe he bought them. Perhaps my example of people sleeping in church was not a wise choice. I had a recent experience when I visited Professor Watson's church only a couple weeks before.

I was invited by Professor Watson and accepted his invitation to visit his church. During the service the Pastor used visual images as illustrations. At the end of the Pastor was the first person to exit the church and he waited at the door to shake hands with the congregation. When I shook his hand he asked me if I enjoyed the service. I told him no because of the negative impact of the visual images. Professor Watson, his wife Rose and I went to the Sunday school session after the service.

The Pastor came and asked me what did I not like about the service. I told him that I should have felt inspired and uplifted according to Jesus's word. He told me that I need to get saved. I told him that I was already saved. I was baptized at a ripe age of twelve years old in the Baptist Church when I accepted the lord as savior.

Professor Watson and Rose joined the discussion and said they felt the same way I did. The Pastor asked the entire congregation in the Sunday school how they felt about his sermon. They all felt the same way I felt. The Pastor and his leadership were very proactive. He told the congregation that he will change the way in which he uses the visual images. He asked the adults in the congregation why they had not spoken up about the impact before. They told him that they knew the word so the moment would have passed. He then asked what about the children and young adults who were sitting in the front pews; who speak for them. I told him I did, that was the reason why I brought it to his attention.

On our way home Professor Watson said to me that it was a wonder the Pastor did not ask where was my fork. I happened to be wearing a red long sleeve dress, red stockings and a pair of red granny boots that day. Rose was amused with her husband's comment. I was too for a brief moment, but was more concerned that I did not intent to start an issue.

My son knew of the experience so when I used boredom in church as an example of why people sleep during the service, the way he lowered his chin and looked at me when I mentioned boredom in church, I knew what he was thinking. He also knew that it was Professor Watson who introduced me to UNA-USA. My son accompanied me to our meetings because I would not leave him home alone. That wasn't because he was irresponsible, but because we were involved in all aspects of our lives; it was a learning experience.

The sharpness of wit and wealth of resource of our senior members through their life experiences cannot be underscored. Many of our members were like walking history books. They were firsthand witnesses to the Holocaust and World War II. Most of our senior members were over the age of sixty; thus, even for our organization, United Nations Association of the USA, they had knowledge of its development as well as of the United Nations. The wealth of knowledge that was transferable by our senior members was valued and appreciated. We understood that they may have a need to take a nap now and again between speeches and after meals. It was a small price to pay in return for the valued experiences.

Our napping members usually awake with a burst of energy. Anyone who attended our meetings—be it an annual meeting, a regular monthly meeting, or a board meeting—would recognize that although we had a napping problem in our meetings, we conducted ourselves with strict protocol. We took pride in ensuring we had a quorum at our meetings by conducting a roll call. Our members also paid special attention to the reading of minutes of previous meetings, and to the correction and amendments of those minutes for accurate record keeping. We crossed the *t*'s and dot the i's.

Proper conduct and ethical practices were observed on all occasions that called for those behaviors. That is not to say that as humans not prone to errors, because we were, but even in those instances where we made errors or when our behaviors were less than desired, it was handled gracefully. There were times, however, when things were quite out of order, but the gavel ruled no matter how many times it took to pound into the table.

All of our meetings were conducted in a formal manner. Our board meetings were usually called to order by our chairperson. We opened with a brief moment of silence. We followed our meeting agenda, and each person who wishes to speak must address the chair, and do so in the fashion of their point, such as point of inquiry, etc. It was simply the civilized thing to do. For anyone who did not know how to enter the zone of earning the privilege to speak, like a guest or a new member, our education committee would tacitly assist our newcomer by informing him or her of our protocol.

We conducted ourselves democratically by using Robert's Rules of Order as a guide. Before any decision is made on any issue, we engage a rigorous debate, and then vote on the outcome in order to accept, reject, or table the matter. Our chairperson usually maintains a tie-breaking vote in case any vote is equal on both sides of the debate.

The Congregational Church hall was our main meeting area. We sometimes change our meeting place depending on the type of meeting. Sometimes we held our meetings at a local restaurant. We may go Chinese or Italian dining depending on the preference of our members. There were times when our decision was based solely on the price of the meal. A discounted price is always attractive. Many of our members had limited budget due to their fixed retirement income.

Other members who did not have fixed retirement income had limited disposable income and therefore could not support expensive eating activities. Some members did not mind either way, but they preferred to donate in the support of other chapter activities and programs instead of expensive meals.

Some members actively paid the cost of introductory membership dues for students and for others with limited income. An introductory membership ranges anywhere from ten to twenty dollars annually.

To raise funds for our programs we conduct numerous fund-raising activities throughout the year. Our fund-raising activities include but are not limited to yard and book sales. Our members used creative and innovative ideas for fund-raising. We strived for a zero-cost approach just so that all funds raised would be used for our chapter's programs and sponsorships. The items for our yard and book sales are donated by chapter members, well wishers and community supporters. We depended on donations and likewise we made donations or provide sponsorships to other organizations. We also proactively recognize and give awards to citizens in our community for their humanitarian services, and or for good deeds that they performed.

We are a grassroots organization, so we do everything at the grassroots level. Well! That was the way things were up until the time we hit the limelight with our historical activities that began in 1994. A fiftieth anniversary is a benchmark for everyone. It does not matter if it is an individual celebrating a fiftieth birthday, a wedding anniversary, or the fiftieth anniversary for any organization. Half a century of existence and survival calls for a big celebration. And so it was for the United Nations. The year 1995 was the fiftieth anniversary of the world organization, and it was time for a celebration.

So here I was, the president of the local chapter of United Nations Association of the USA—Greater Miami, the one to lead the fiftieth anniversary celebration in the vast ocean of public awareness in our community. I willingly accepted the role even though I did not know quite where it was headed. It did not matter however, because my team members had experience and knew something about the course. I could see through their eyes while I am learning and getting a handle on things.

I was elected president in the fall of 1991, but my role officially began in late spring of 1992. In the interim, I was given a president's handbook to read. I browsed through the pages of the guide leisurely during the weeks leading up to the time when my role would become official. It was very difficult to absorb all the information in the handbook. As I tried to absorb the information I thought to myself that I should have read the handbook before I accepted the role as president. It appeared that a chapter president had more responsibilities than what I had imagined. The intricacy of the organizational structure of chapters and divisions, council of organization, national headquarters, and relationship to the United Nations and the United States government seemed complex and monumental.

I read the introduction of the president's handbook which was "A Word of Welcome." This section was a congratulatory note on being elected president of the chapter. It outlined the importance of the position. As president of the chapter, I was expected to lead the board, committees, and volunteers in assisting others to understand the United Nations, issues on its agenda, and the role of the United States in this organization.

"Wow!" I uttered to myself. This appears to involve politics, but I am not a politician, I thought. What do I do now? I asked myself. My thoughts began drifting in the direction of exit strategies. None of the considerations solidified in my thinking. I have already accepted the role and it was not within me to back out without a pressing reason. Therefore I must face the challenges ahead I reassured myself. To convince myself that I could handle it and relieve my anxiety, I resolved that the role would be an on-the-job learning experience.

I knew at that point whatever skills and knowledge I have must be complemented with the skills and knowledge of all of our members. The thought of teamwork gave me a warm feeling. I must engage team leadership and teamwork. There was simply no way that I could do all the stuff that was described in the handbook single handedly. I did not even know all there was to know about any of the organizations, much less to assist others to learn about them. Therefore we were all going to have to learn about them together. Thank goodness for our senior members and their knowledge. From my position they could nap all they need to; as long as they are there I knew I would get by with help from my friends.

One of the mandate as the chapter president is to help other citizens to make their voices heard in the public debate, and to help the world organization become more effective. That is a tall order for any volunteer community leader. The United Nations and its systems are intricately complex. The UN is an international organization that was founded in 1945 by fifty-one countries after the Second World War. Those countries were committed to maintain international peace and security, to develop friendly relations among nations, and to promote social progress, better living standards, and human rights. The date charted as the establishment of the UN is October 24, 1945. The unique nature and powers vested in the organization by its charter provides the opportunity to take action in a wide range of issues across the globe. Currently, there are 192 member states in the organization.

Membership in the UN is open to all peace-loving states that accept the obligations contained in the United Nations Charter and, in the judgment of the organization, are able to carry out those obligations. The provisions for membership are outlined in the United Nations Charter, chapter 2. States are admitted as members by decision of the General Assembly upon recommendation of the Security Council.

The United Nations is neither a state nor a government. Therefore, it does not possess the authority to recognize a state or a government. As an organization of independent states, it may admit a new state to its membership or accept the credentials of the representative of a new government. The procedures for membership include the submission of an application and a letter formally stating the acceptance of the obligations under the United Nations Charter to the secretary-general.

The Security Council considers the application; any recommendations must receive the affirmative votes of nine of the fifteen members of the Security Council. If any of its five permanent members—which are China, France, the Russian Federation, the United Kingdom of Great Britain and Northern Ireland, and the United States of America—vetoed the application, it cannot move forward. If the Security Council recommends admission, the recommendation is presented to the General Assembly for consideration. A two-thirds majority vote is necessary in the assembly for admission of the new state. Membership becomes effective the date the resolution for admission is adopted.

Member states are expected and are assessed dues to the United Nations. The criterion that applies to member states through the General Assembly is the member states' capacity to pay dues. Factors that are taken into consideration are the country's gross national product (GNP) and a number of adjustments, including external debt and low per-capita incomes. The percentage shares of each member state in the UN budget are decided by the General Assembly.

The methodology and range are from a minimum of 0.001 percent to a maximum of 22 percent and a maximum of 0.01 percent from least developed countries. The United States is a top contributor to the United Nations at the 22 percent level. In 2005 for example, the top ten contributors and respective percentage levels were the following: United States, 22 percent; Japan, 19.47 percent; Germany, 8.86 percent, United Kingdom, 6.13 percent; France, 6.03 percent; Italy, 4.89 percent; Canada, 2.81 percent; Spain, 2.42 percent; China, 2.05 percent; and Mexico, 1.88 percent.

Since the assessments are based on gross national products (GNP), richer countries generally pay more and poorer countries pay less. To calculate the dollar amount of contribution for 2005, all one needs to do is to look up the gross national product of the country for that year and figure out the percentage to arrive at the amount of dues in dollar amount.

It is not unusual for some member states to fall behind in paying their dues. Some member states fail to pay dues simply because they can't afford to pay because of poverty, and sometimes failure to pay and payments withheld are used as a way of exerting political pressure or to make a political point. Chapter 2, article 19 of the United Nations Charter has a provision for member states who do not pay their dues, and it states in part, "A Member of the United Nations which is in arrears in the payment of its financial contributions to the Organization shall have no vote in the General Assembly if the amount of its arrears equals or exceeds the amount of the contributions due from it for the preceding two full years." The General Assembly, however, may allow a

Member State that is in arrears to vote if it is satisfied that the nonpayment is due to "circumstances beyond the control" of the Member State.

The United Nations System is large and complex. Although the organization has charted its establishment on October 24, 1945, its development can be dated back to the Atlantic Charter of 1941. In that year, US President Franklin Roosevelt and Britain's Prime Minister Winston Churchill sought to ensure security and economic opportunity for all nations with the Atlantic Charter peace proposal. Later in 1942, the document was signed by forty-seven nations in support of the Atlantic Charter. President Roosevelt suggested the term the *United Nations*. A meeting of representatives of the United States, United Kingdom, Soviet Union, and China, dubbed the Dumbarton Oaks Conference in Washington DC in 1944, provided the blueprint for the United Nations. The organization was hammered out at the Yalta Conference in 1945, and later that same year at the San Francisco Conference, fifty nations gathered to complete a charter for the United Nations. The charter was signed on June 26, 1945, and put into force on October 24, 1945.

Poland, which had not yet formed a postwar government, could not attend the conference but they signed the charter later as an original member, thus making the fifty-one member nations to the founding of the United Nations. In attendance at the signing of the charter were forty-two non-governmental organizations; among those were the American Association for the UN, who attended the conference at San Francisco as advisors to the US delegation. The American Association for the UN is the predecessor for UNA-USA.

The UN system consists of its main bodies, subsidiary organs created by the General Assembly, and specialized agencies and related organizations. The six main bodies to the United Nations are the General Assembly (GA), the Security Council (SC), Secretariat, Economic and Social Council (ECOSOC), Trusteeship Council (TC), and the International Court of Justice (ICJ).

The General Assembly is the main deliberative body of the organization. This is where representatives of governments meet for about three months each fall. Here, considerations are given to reports from the five other main bodies. The General Assembly makes recommendations on a wide range of international issues, approves the UN budget, and apportions expenses. Each member of the assembly has one vote. Most decisions are made by a consensus of the majority vote rather than submitting the matter to a vote. The General Assembly appoints a secretary-general upon the recommendation of the Security Council.

The Security Councils' primary responsibility is to maintain international peace and security as provided by the UN Charter. This is the body of the UN that alone has the power to back up its declarations with actions to ensure compliance with them. There are fifteen members in the Security Council, five of which are permanent members. The permanent members are the United

States, Russia (which, in 1992, assumed the seat held by the Soviet Union), United Kingdom, France, and China. The other ten members of the Security Council are elected by the General Assembly to each serve a term of two years. In order for a resolution to pass in the Security Council, it must receive nine "yes" votes, including those of the five permanent members. A "no" vote, otherwise called a veto, by any of the five permanent members defeats the resolution.

The Secretariat is headed by the secretary-general. This body provides services to the UN's main bodies. It administers the policies and projects that are established by the main bodies. The Secretariat has a staff of over fifteen thousand international civil servants, both men and women, from over 150 countries. Those staff members work at the UN Headquarters in New York, in offices in Geneva, Vienna, and elsewhere across the globe, serving as technical experts and economic advisors. The secretary-general is appointed for a five-year term and is eligible for reappointment.

Former secretary-generals include Trygve Lie of Norway (1946-1952), Dag Hammarskjold of Sweden (1953-1961), U Thant of Burma (1961-1971), Kurt Waldheim of Austria (1972-1981), Javier Perez de Cuellar of Peru (1982-1991), Boutros Boutros-Ghali of Egypt (1992-1997), and Kofi Annan of Ghana (1997-2006). The current secretary-general of the United Nations is Ban Ki-Moon of South Korea, who, in 2007, succeeded Kofi Annan.

The Economic and Social Council (ECOSOC) coordinates the economic and social work of the UN, its specialized agencies, and its related institutions. It oversees five regional economic commissions, a number of functional commissions responsible for specific issue areas such as human rights, the status of women, population, and sustainable development. It also coordinates works for a few standing committees involving programs coordination and non-governmental organizations. ECOSOC has fifty-four members who are elected by the General Assembly for a three-year term. This main body of the United Nations usually holds a four- to five-week session each year, alternating between New York and Geneva.

The Trusteeship Council has a roster of permanent members who are identical to the members of the Security Council. The Trusteeship Council was originally given jurisdiction over eleven former colonies. Its agenda shrank as the trust territories achieved independence or merged with neighboring independent countries. The last territory attained its independence in 1994. The Trusteeship Council suspended operation on November 1, 1994, with the independence of Palau, which was the last remaining United Nations trust territory, on October 1, 1994. The council amended its rules of procedures to drop the obligation to meet annually and agreed to meet as occasion required, but its decision or the decision of its president or at the request of a majority of its members or the General Assembly or the Security Council.

The sixth member of the main bodies of the United Nations is the International Court of Justice (ICJ), which is also known as the World Court. This body decides legal disputes between countries that agree to accept its jurisdiction. It can also issue advisory opinions at the request of the General Assembly and the Security Council. The court's fifteen judges elected by the General Assembly and the Security Council for nine-year terms are chosen on the basis of qualification. Judges are not selected based on nationality, although the principal legal systems of the world must be represented.

The ICJ is located at The Hague in the Netherlands. Over the years, the General Assembly, in response to a variety of economic and social needs, has created a number of special bodies to deal with those issues. Some of those bodies are funded through the UN regular budget while others are financed by voluntary contributions of governments and sometimes private citizens. All the subsidiary organs created by the General Assembly reports to the ECOSOC and the GA.

The foregoing discussion and information are the reasons why I mentioned in previous paragraphs that the mandate of the chapter president to help other citizens make their voices heard in public debate and to help the world organization become more effective is indeed a tall order. Already by describing the primary structure of the organization, one may discern the complexity of the UN system. The subsidiary organs of the General Assembly, specialized agencies, and related organizations will be discussed later.

I continued to read UNA-USA's chapter president handbook to further discover what my role was. I created a short list of the steps that I need to take to become oriented to the role. I was reassured as I continued to read the welcome notes. There was a short paragraph that stated it did not matter whether I was a longtime community leader or a newcomer, and even if I did not know much about global issues and the United Nations, I wouldn't be the first chapter president in this predicament. How to get a handle on the organization was the first concern. I was familiar with leadership because I have been there done that, but those were on a straight line, meaning that I was a leader in different specific organizations at different times, but never for any organization that was so complex with intricately interwoven relationships across government and non-governmental organizations.

When I first learned about the organizations and their works, everything appeared to be a muddle of relationships. In order to get a handle on what they were about and what it was that I need to do, conceptually I began to separate them, find out what it was that each organization did or was doing, and then re-conceptualize the relationship between them. It was very difficult to wrap my brain around that; it was almost enough to give one a mental hernia. That is how complicated it was connecting the organizations and their inter-relationships; but I pressed on. I did not know much about the United Nations, but I knew a bit about UNA-USA on the chapter level.

UNA-USA is a large organization that works like an umbrella that serves different constituencies of community-based members such as local chapters, activists, affiliated organizations that came under the grouping of council of organizations, business leaders, educators, academic, and foreign policy specialists. Its primary mission is to educate the public about the United Nations and also to mobilize public opinion of the UN and to engage constructive US leadership in the world organization.

I did not know much about the structure or how the United Nations conducts its operations, I knew the body was made up of over 190 member states. It was elementary, therefore, that in my new role as chapter president one of my first considerations should be the diversity of cultures of the organization based on the number of its member states. My Bachelor of Arts degree in geography came in handy as an important tool. That degree was conferred by York University in Downsview, Ontario, Canada. I received my Bachelor's degree over seven years ago but I kept pace with new developments around the globe. When I initially went back to college while working and taking care of my family, I started the process enrolling in the faculty of education. One of my first passion was teaching, but later I switched my major to geography. It was one of those majors that could be classified as art or science. My educational journey from elementary school had the tendency of leaning more to science courses. The courses that lead to the switching from education to geography were "Science and Technological Change" and "Changing Roles of Women and the Family". I wanted to know where we were heading. Some of my other courses including human geography, urban geography, population geography, physical geography, and a whole host of history courses spanning the globe, I figured will now come to play in the task at hand. The way I figured it was I had some knowledge of where people, places and things are on the globe. I am aware of the global environment in terms of physical spaces and human dynamics, and I enjoyed interacting with people of different cultures, so that was a plus.

I continued to learn about my role as chapter president and UNA-USA organization from the handbook. The more I read and learn was the more it became apparent that I may not be as far out in left field as I originally thought. I was beginning to believe that I may very well be equipped with the foundational knowledge and basic tools to navigate the leadership of our local UNA chapter. I was feeling less overwhelmed and began to take control of what it was I need to do. If it appears that I took my role seriously you are correct in thinking so. It wasn't for any personal gratification because the job does not come with a paycheck, but it was just the way I am. Regardless that I was doing volunteer work I was either going to do a good job and not do it at all. Besides if I did not do a good job I felt that my reputation would be at stake. My best approach therefore was to muster all the knowledge I could about what I need to do and get a handle on the organizations.

I made a list of the first steps I need to take. First on my list was what to get from the outgoing president. Those items included the bylaws of the organization. I need to know how the organization governs itself, and also to become familiar with it so that I can prepare for the orientation of our new board members. I reminded myself that where I fall short in knowing the bylaws my team mates will fill in the gaps for me. I valued of our senior members increasingly as I made new discoveries of what was expected of me. I also itemized on my list of things to collect from the outgoing president, files and records, such as financial reports, minutes of board meetings of previous years, and reports and correspondence of current and ongoing projects. I also made a note to collect chapter reports that were disseminated to the division and national office, as well as a list of board members for our chapter, and a list of board members of the national and divisional offices.

Our meeting for installation of new officers was scheduled for the spring of 1992. I totally missed that meeting. My family was experiencing a change and transition because of our divorce that was being finalized during the same time. During the last few months of 1991, I was briefly hospitalized for minor surgery, which was not a very difficult operation. Laser surgery was quick, and it took a shorter period of time for healing. When I recuperated from my surgery, I was back at taking care of my family, working in my profession, and being a community volunteer.

I totally missed the meeting for installation of officers because everything converged at the same time. I also screwed up the dates on my calendar. I used a new 1991 calendar instead of the New Year 1992. My days on the calendar were off by one day. Where the date should have been Tuesday, it was on a Monday. The meeting on the calendar was on the wrong day. The day I should have attended the meeting was also the day I took my son to his school program.

Everything collided, I did not want to wing my way through the meeting, but that wasn't the reason why I missed the meeting. I believed that I was sufficiently prepared after reading the handbook. It was just that there was a total meltdown where time, schedules and plans collided. Professor Watson called me after the meeting that evening. He wondered where I was, especially that I was the new president. He found it quite odd that I did not show up for the meeting. He was afraid that I was backing out of the role.

I apologized and assured him that I was not negating the role, but that my absence was due to a turn of events and circumstances beyond my control. I was informed that Ethel filled in for me and that everything went very well. He told me that he understood the circumstances especially those concerning the divorce realizing that it was a difficult time for the family. He said that he and Ethel figured that something must have been going on because it was unlike me not to show up for the meeting. We laughed at the confusion and I felt assured that I was still the local chapter president.

Our chapter programs and activities, like those of many other local organizations in our community, were totally wiped out by Hurricane Andrew. Our annual big events are usually held between the months of September and December, and are centered on the observance of UN day which is held in October. The earlier months during the year are focused on divisional and national activities of UNA-USA. Those events include the Florida Division annual meeting and the national convention. Sometimes we may have time sensitive projects and events, but from September to December of each year our works involve public outreach leading up to UN Day on October 24 and to follow with out take from those events.

The year that Hurricane Andrew struck was a total disaster. Everyone in the community was displaced. The magnitude of the ranked number 5 hurricane totally wiped out the community. It left a path of destruction that was indescribable. Turmoil, chaos, hardships, and severe trauma were our state of being, at the time. We could barely find ourselves and our possessions, so world issues were the furthest from our minds. The storm caught many of us off guard.

After the divorce was finalized in April, the three of us, my son, my daughter, and I decided to take a short vacation. We visited Jamaica in June 1992, at the end of the school year. We were gone for a month. We returned to Miami and began to re-establish a close-to-normal mode of living. It was now life after a divorce. One of the things on my calendar was to make good a promise of hosting a reception for my friend and neighbor, Colonel Daryl Jones. He was running for state senator. The reception was in support of and to provide an opportunity for friends and neighbors to meet and greet our candidate for state senator.

I had plans to paint our house and to change fixtures by putting up new ones. We thought a new look to our home would give us a new perspective on things moving forward with our lives. It was the opportune time to do the painting and improvements to the home before the reception. We contracted our neighbor, who was a painter and carpenter, to do the job. One and a half weeks later the house was painted, and new fixtures were in place. The tiles around our swimming pool were replaced; everything on the property had a bright new look. The lawn was cut and the brushes were trimmed perfectly.

We were ready to showcase the new look of our home. The reception provided the perfect opportunity to do so. Our friends, neighbors, and family will be visiting with us. We had no idea that a monstrous storm was on the horizon swiftly approaching our shores. Had we known that it was on its way, we would never have put all that money in home improvements, only to have our home blown to smithereens in a short period of time. But for the grace of god many of us would not have survived. It was a living hell.

I contacted Daryl Jones's office shortly after we completed our home improvement, I spoke with his receptionist. We discussed the protocol of the reception to ensure that we were observing the rules of campaign donations. The reception was held on August 21, 1992. Among our invited guests were members of the Caribbean Chamber of Commerce, United Nations Association of Greater Miami, members of our private club TOFF (Togetherness of Families and Friends), parents and coaches of our Perrine and Palmetto Pop Warner Association, business associates, friends, church members, and our neighbors. We had plenty of food and warm conversations.

Daryl greeted and met our guests. They had many questions for our candidate. Many of our guests, including the Hosangs and the Hastings, were delighted to meet Daryl Jones. We continued the reception for two hours after which Senator Jones left for another event. After the reception ended some of our guests stayed a while longer engaging political discussions. My children and I received compliments on the new look of our home from those who knew what it looked like before. It was eleven o'clock when our last guest said thank you and bade goodbye.

Toni, Ceejae, and I began cleaning up soon after our last guest said good-bye. It was close to 12:30 a.m. when we finished our clean up. All the food was eaten, so we did not have anything to put away, except to clean the dishes, pack them away, vacuum, take out the trash, and rearrange the furniture to the original order. The pool and patio area were fine except for the removal of the trash and to put them aside for our regular trash pickup day.

After all was done, my son and daughter went to their beds. I had a shower and decided to watch television for a while before I hit the sack. While I flipped through different channels on the television with the remote, I saw the news and broadcast of a pending storm.

Each of the television channels seemed to have the same broadcast. At first I thought nothing of it but as it continued I began to wonder what was going on, why was I seeing the same thing over and over? I selected one of the channels and settled down to watch the broadcast. It looked and sounded serious even a bit ominous intermittently. I could hear the anxiety in the broadcaster's voice. My eyes were glued to the television as I tried to connect the dots of what was going on. It reminded me of something I experienced some years ago.

Many years ago in Canada, while I was watching television, I saw a broadcast of a nuclear disaster. Many people including myself thought it was a real nuclear disaster because of the way in which the program was presented. We made telephone calls to the local news channel, and the government to find out what we need to do to protect ourselves. We discovered that it was not a real disaster; it was a simulation program of a nuclear disaster. People were scared stiff. We got angry that we were not informed of the program, but felt relieved that it was not real.

I continued to watch the broadcast of the storm. The anxiety was increasing in the voice of the broadcaster. I assessed the situation as I kept looking at the program but I was thinking about what I was seeing and comparing it to the program I saw in Canada. The simulation program that I saw in Canada was on one channel only. The storm was broadcasting on all of our local channels. I decided to call my neighbor Brenda to check if she heard news of any storm on the horizon. After I dialed her telephone number and the phone began to ring, I decided to hang up because on second thought I did not want to wake her from her sleep. It was too late at night or better yet too early in the morning. It was 2:00 a.m. but before I could hang up the phone to prevent a second ring, someone picked up the receiver. Brenda answered, she sounded alert; I am glad that I did not wake her up. "Hello, Brenda, I am sorry to be calling you this late," I said. "Hi, Sylvia," she responded "It is not a problem at all, you did not wake us. Lesroy and I are up." I felt relieved that I did not wake them with my phone call. "Brenda, have you seen the news and broadcast about a storm somewhere in the Atlantic?" I asked.

Brenda responded rather shockingly, and quietly raising to me in an alarming tone. "Where have you been? There is a huge storm coming right at us!"

"No kidding! I saw the news, but I thought it was a simulation," I replied. She began describing the protective measures they have taken so far in preparing their home for the storm. She also told me that they have purchased and were pretty much prepared for the storm. "Oh my god, I am behind the eighth ball. Brenda, I missed you at the reception. Your son called to tell me that you were working late and would not be able to attend. I was very busy with the home improvements and planning the reception. I have not been able to watch the television for a few days or perhaps for about a week, until tonight." I said to her. I told her that I sat down to look at television after the kids and I finished our cleaning up after the reception, and that was when I saw the broadcast, but I did not seriously because I though it was a simulation program. I told her that I had to go and hung up the telephone. I sat there for a few minutes looking at the television spaced out and frozen with my mouth open wide. The news had to sink in before I could move.

As I sat staring at the television listening to the moment by moment tracking of the storm, my thoughts were blank. I did not know where to begin planning and preparing for the storm. I knew I was behind the eighth ball from hearing what Brenda said about being prepared already. I quickly collected myself and shifted my thoughts to think of what I need to do to get ready for the storm, but it was so sudden. I stopped thinking about the reception and began searching for a note pad and pencil to make a list of things to be done.

The broadcaster was announcing things to do. I kept uttering the word *darn* as I searched for a notebook to begin making my list. It was a darn time to find out about the storm, a darn time to begin my preparation, and a darn time for this to be happening. I found a notebook and went into my office to get a pen. I sat down and began making a list of items I need on one list, and on another page a list of the things we need to do. The pen did not work; I tried moving the pen in a circular motion on the paper to see if this motion would encourage the ink to flow. The pen was no good, it did not work; I got up and started searching for anything that would write—a pen or a pencil.

I found pencils in the desk drawer. I checked to see if it had a sharp point. It did not have a sharp point, but there was sufficient lead at the tip of the pencil to write on paper. I am sure that I have pens somewhere but I could not think of where they were at the moment. I felt a surge of adrenaline as I made my list. I also enlisted the help of the broadcaster who was now naming the stores where supplies were available.

. As I jotted down the items that I need, I wondered why no one at the reception spoke of the storm or even mentioned that one was on its way. I brushed the thought aside, thinking perhaps no one knew about it or perhaps they thought that I knew about it, and planned to make preparations after the reception. I thought of calling some people who were at the reception to tell them about the storm, but on second thought I figured that by now everyone knew about it. I was perhaps the last one to have found out about the storm; only if I was not so busy doing everything else, I would not feel so pressured to get moving now; but it was a very good reception.

Toni and Ceejae were up; I heard sounds coming from both ends of the house. They saw me sitting on the couch in the family room with sheets of paper scattered around me. I had pages on the floor, on the couch, and to my left; every bit of space had papers all over the place, I did not realize that I had used up so much paper. I was sitting at the right side of the couch so I could use the armrest for support while I was writing. I had the remote control somewhere buried between the seat cushion and the armrest.

"Mom, did you go to bed last night?" Ceejae asked as he entered the family room, towel in hand, drying water from his face. Toni entered the kitchen through the living room and was reaching for a glass in the upper cupboard. "Yes, Mom did you get any sleep last night?" she asked repeating Ceejae's question. I shook my head to say no, biting on the pencil that I held between my lips as I turned to a fresh page in my notebook. "No sleep. I have to get this done," I said with a sense of urgency.

Ceejae sensed that something was not right he walked up to the side of the couch and peeked to see what I was doing. Toni joined us as I pointed to the television. "That is what is going on," I said. "There is a giant storm heading our way." Toni and Ceejae picked up some of the loose pages off the couch, and both sat down to look at the television.

We discussed the possibility that it may never hit our community because so many storms were forecasted in the past, and in the end, they changed directions or did not come at all. Nevertheless, we continued with our preparation plans. We finalized the list of items that were needed. We went over the things we need to do. By the time we got through with the list, it was time for Toni to return to her campus. She was a student at Florida International University, North Campus. She also had a job on campus and was to return to work that morning. She came home to help with the reception. She left for campus while Ceejae and I headed to the store to purchase supplies.

Our next-door neighbor was putting up plywood on the back windows of his house. I went over to talk with him a little to see what he could do to help us. John was very kind; he offered to help us with whatever we need to do. He said, no problem; he would help us to put down the shutters, put plywood on those windows that do not have shutters, and anything else that was needed to secure the property.

We spent the better part of the day shopping for supplies. There was no bottled water to be found anywhere. None of the local supermarkets or stores had water. The store shelves were empty, except for a few canned goods distributed in small groups on the shelves. We picked up a few canned vegetables and other canned goods from those that were left on the shelves. We did not bother to check the contents label on the stuff we picked up as we normally to there was no time for that because we were hurrying to get things done before the storm I still had the gut feeling that I was behind the eighth ball in getting things done. I was perhaps too late in doing my shopping, had I known about the storm sooner I would have shopped for my stuff a long time ago.

Ceejae was very understanding; he reassured me that we had plenty of canned goods in the pantry at home. He also reminded me that perhaps the storm will pass over us like those other ones before, and all this work would have been for nothing. He told me not to worry about it, but I could see the concern on his face as we mingled with the other customers who were also very busy looking for supplies.

Some people had a strange sense of calmness in their demeanor. They engage small conversations about the storm and looked as if they did not have a care in the world. I could not understand what they were so calm about. They were laughing and making light of the situation. It reminded me of Noah and the Ark. Some people just don't get it. "We will get everything done on time, Mom," Ceejae said watching me fidgeting in the line while the customer ahead was wasting time talking with the cashier.

We headed to Home Depot to purchase nails and plywood. We did not expect to do any better in finding supplies than we did in the supermarket, but we hoped for the best. Home Depot's parking lot was congested with traffic, as was everywhere else. People in pickup trucks, cars, and vans were loading up with supplies. We drove into the parking lot at a crawl trying to get closer to the entrance of the store. Some of the customers were wheeling carts, bobbing in and out between the moving vehicles. There was a commotion that brought the traffic to a stand still. A cart loaded with two-by-fours spilled its contents obstructing the flow of traffic.

We were relieved to discover that Home Depot had ample supplies of plywood. *Smart operation*, I thought. The store was trucking in supplies as fast as they were being sold. Plywood and other supplies were stacked outside of the store. It was very easy and convenient to pick up the items that we needed. The store had plenty of nails. I stood in the aisle picking out the nails, a woman yelled "Mike, Mike! Where are you?"

"I am over her with the nuts, honey," replied an elderly gentleman who was standing about three feet away from me. I looked at him, he looked at me, and we cracked up with laughter. "Nuts and honey, this must be a cereal alley" I said as I gave him another look from the corner of my eyes and moved on. The moment of laughter was a perfect antidote, for a while I forgot about the storm.

We loaded up the car with our supplies. The sheets of plywood were packed in the car trunk hanging half-in and half-out. The store assistant tied a piece of red cloth on the plywood that hung out of the back of the car. "We do not have far to go," my son said to the store assistant as they both worked at securing the plywood with ropes. We double checked to make sure that everything was secured tightly, and then we joined the slow procession of vehicles leaving Home Depot's parking lot.

Our next stop was at Radio Shack. We purchased batteries and a shortwave radio. The store did not have too many customers. We moved quickly through the check out. We bought a large amount of batteries all of different sizes. We also bought a couple of large flashlights. My son picked up a compass, I am not sure why we would need one, but it may be useful, one never knows what to expect with a storm the size of the one that was on its way. Our last stop was at Winn-Dixie, it was only three doors down from Radio Shack.

Winn-Dixie had more supplies on the shelves than the first supermarket that we went to. We found candles and more canned goods. We bought a whole box of candles, chocolate bars, potato chips, cookies, and baked beans. We moved quickly through the check out, stacked the bags on the floor in the back of the car, and headed home.

We pulled into the driveway loaded with supplies. Marco and Austin, two of the Ceejae's friends, came over just as we pulled in. "Hey! What's up?"

They greeted each other with hands clutching, touching shoulder to shoulder, and the works. "Can we help?" Marco asked as they moved to the back of the car to unload the plywood. In no time all four of us removed all the stuff from the car. We placed the plywood on the lawn, the rest of stuff were taken inside the house.

We sat down on the patio, Marco and Austin filled us in on what their parents did at their house to prepare for the storm. I offered the young men soft drinks. I had not eaten all day. By now I was absolutely hungry. We snacked on potato chips and cookies. I pulled the list of things that need to be done from my pocketbook. First on the list was to put down the hurricane shutters on all of the windows to the bedrooms. Marco, Austin, and Ceejae tackled that job. It wasn't too difficult to do. All that had to be done was to loosen the screws, pull down the shutters, and bolt them in place.

I took a few minutes to make a phone call to Ethel. I reminded her of our scheduled UNA-USA meeting for that weekend; I asked her to call the others and cancel the meeting. We were working on our global policy project. The meeting was scheduled for Saturday evening. She told me that it was already taken care of. She called Farrokh Jbavalla earlier and cancelled the meeting when she heard about the storm. She said she figured no one will be prepared for the meeting because of all the preparation that everyone had to do before the storm; they probably haven't even read the chapter for this week's meeting, she commented. That was great, Ethel always thinks ahead.

Farrokh Jhabvala was one of our board members; he was also the chair of our Global Policy Studies Committee. Ethel and I did not stay on the telephone for too long. We chatted briefly about our storm preparation. We were satisfied that we were both preparing for what was ahead. She told me that John Brennan, her companion, did almost all of the work already. "Take care of yourself and the kids and stay safe" she said to me, "you and John do the same" I replied, before I hung up the telephone.

I resumed my work. We took all the movable objects from the lawn and placed them in the garage. Some of the stuff was placed in the shed at the back of the house. Marco, Ceejae, and Austin moved all the furniture from the pool and patio area and placed those in the garage. Some of the items were put in our family room. We were busy as bees moving right along getting things done.

Ceejae, Austin and Marco became very good friends since we moved in the neighborhood four years ago. The three young men are of the same age but they attended different schools. At the end of their school day, if neither one of them have extra curricular activities, they meet at our house for snacks and video games. Most school days in the fall Ceejae has Pop Warner football practice. The boys rotated sleep over on weekends.

Ceejae came to me for *the things to do list*. We went over the list again to make sure that everything was done. Ceejae read the list and checked things off when the other boys answered "check". Garbage cans, lawn chairs, flowerpots, hoses, soccer ball, basketball, football, baseball bat, dartboard, tables, shovels, fork, mats, and all other items on the list were called out.

Our garage was packed from top to bottom. There was hardly any room to move anywhere, but I had a good feeling that we accomplished the tasks we set out to do, and we still had time to spare. We were not quite finished yet, however. We still had the two huge glass windows to cover. The window in the living room needs to be covered with plywood, and the one in the family room needs to be covered with the hurricane shutter. Ceejae asked Austin to help him with the family room shutter that was leaning up against the back of the shed.

It was a huge shutter with dimension of approximately six by four feet. Several hands were needed to put up that one. That shutter was taken down originally to prevent obstruction of the walkway in the pool area. We did not want anyone bumping their heads on it. We had difficulty putting the shutter in place. The sheer size of it made it very heavy. It was build of zinc or some other form of metal. John, our next door neighbor, saw that we were struggling with it and came over to help. We had the shutter secured in place with his help. He was much taller and bigger than all of us, and he is experienced with this kind of work.

John continued to help us with the living room window. He promised that he would cover our glass window in the front with the plywood. We had no hurricane shutter for that window. I did not know what became of the shutter. When we bought the home in 1988, before we closed on the purchase we checked for hurricane shutters for all windows. We did this because we knew that we were purchasing a home in an area that was frequented by hurricanes. All of the windows in the home had shutters but there wasn't one for the huge living room window. John used all three sheets of plywood to cover the window.

The nails that we bought at Home Depot to fasten the plywood in place did not work. John walked over to his house to fetch his toolbox. He returned with a drill and his tool box. He searched in the tool box and selected a handful of nails. He showed them to me; a bunch of flat-headed nails. "These are the nails for concrete" he said, turning them over so that I could have a better look at them. It took him about thirty minutes to cover the windows.

John checked the front entrance door to see if we need to do something for it. He opened the door and felt along the wooded frame. He used the back of his hand to tap the frame a few times. He took a close look at the material in the frame of the door. It was a beautiful front door that looked like a stain glass design, but it was not made from glass, although one could not tell that from a distance. John said the door was made of a very sturdy Plexiglas. That material is very strong and it is able to withstand any hurricane force wind, he told me.

John walked around the entire house and checked the work we did. He was satisfied that we did a very good job. We too felt satisfied that we completed the storm preparation on time. He did not have time to stop for refreshments when I offered him a cool drink. He had to return to continue working on his own storm preparation for his home. We thanked him for helping us and told him to call us if he needed any help, I am sure there was something that we could do to help him, even if it was to hand him his tools.

The summer heat did not make it any easier for us. We pressed on with our preparation. The fear of the storm was much greater than the fear of the heat. Almost everyone in our neighborhood was busy securing their home. Some people took different approaches to prevent damage from the storm. We took the traditional and old fashion way by using plywood and hurricane shutters. Some people simply applied duct tapes to their windows and sliding glass doors. The duct tapes were placed on glass doors and windows in the shapes of Xs.

Other people did not even bother to do any storm preparation, the simply packed their family and pets in their vehicle and left the community heading north. One would think that with all the history and data that have been accumulated on storm damages over the years, that similar to building standards, hurricane preparation would have been standardized. I could not imagine how effective duct tape on glass windows could be in protecting a home and its occupants; I certainly did not think it could do any good; not with the size of the storm that was forecasted.

Our external preparation was completed. It was time to take care of the internal preparation. It was very dark inside the house. The only sight of daylight was from the small window in the laundry room. We intentionally left the shutter up so that we could see outside. The window overlooked the driveway; we could see our neighbor's house from that window. If we climb on top of the washer and dryer and get a close up view, we could see the northern section of our street.

The television was on; we turned up the volume so that we could hear updates of the storm from any location in the house. We only had one television set, a huge one in the family room. That was the way we wanted it. It was just a family policy. I called my daughter to find out when she would be coming home. She told me she was helping with the storm preparation at her workplace on campus, and that she will be home as soon as she is finished.

My son and I began to work with our internal storm preparation checklist. We started working on the first thing that was on our internal preparation list which was check and secure our important documents. We took our important documents from the file drawers, place them in plastic bags and replace them in the file cabinets. Next we removed our wall decorations including paintings, pictures, and wall hangings; we placed them in large plastic garbage bags, and put them on the floor underneath heavy furniture. We did this for each room in the house.

We continued working on our internal preparation. All vases, porcelains, and artifacts on tables, countertops, and desks were removed put inside plastics bags and placed in the corners of each room where those items were displayed. Some were place behind large pieces of furniture if they could be fitted into those spaces. By now we were tired and overwhelmed with the amount of work that we did and still had more to do. It is no wonder some people may take the easy way out of simply leaving town to ride out the storm. But even if we chose to do that, we still would have to protect our property before we could go anywhere.

It may not have been such a good idea to keep the television on such a high volume. I heard everything that was said about making preparation for the storm. I kept doing things that weren't even on my list because of what the broadcaster was saying. Ceejae and I were in high gear moving at a fast pace. It is not easy climbing on ladders to remove wall decorations, and removing and wrapping fragile objects then to place them in a safe area in the house. If the entire house is blown away by the storm then what good was it doing all this work? Taking the time to prepare for the storm provided us with a psychological advantage. We were gearing up to meet the storm and we were not going to take it lying down doing nothing. We were being proactive by making preparation.

We moved to our most important documents. Those we arrange in small piles then put them in zip lock plastic bags, and then we put all the zip lock bags in triple garbage bags. Everything was important. We decided that documents such as our passports, insurance policies, birth certificates, and some other things like baptismal certificates, diplomas, etc., were very important. We plastic bagged those documents and placed them in one of our inner closets. There were too many photographs and photo albums, so we just stashed those in the metal file cabinets.

"Forget the clothes, there is nothing we can do with those" my son said as I made a move to the clothes closet. We were satisfied that we took care of all we could with documents, wall hangings, and loose glass objects. All the good that preparation did for us; you will see later that even with all that preparation the storm will get you one way or another. If the house is not blown away then mildew and fungus will overtake the home if there is no air conditioning or electricity.

We were literally storming through the house taking preventative measures to protect our property and belongings. We had a whirlwind of activities. We started a round-robin of boiling our water to store for drinking purposes. The supermarkets ran out of bottled water our alternative was to boil our own water.

Our drinking water was supplied by Zephyrhills on a weekly basis, but they weren't doing delivery that week; and even if they did two bottles of water would not be sufficient for drinking and cooking. We have to consider the possibility that we may not have any water supply what so ever after the storm. At least that was what the broadcaster suggested on the news. The announcement was that we should consider making preparations for water supply after the storm.

This was our first time preparing for a storm. We have never done or experienced this before. We di everything by the book. We had one full bottle of water on the floor and the half bottle that was on the cooler. We boiled enough water to fill two large empty water bottles. The capacity of those water bottles was five gallons each. We filled as many empty containers as we could with water including filling up one of the bathtubs.

The announcer repeatedly mentioned that we may be without electricity for a while. I decided to cook because our stove used electricity. I figured that doing a roast and some fried chicken was a great idea, and that was just what I did. I had stuff in the freezer. I took out a roast and some chicken thighs. I poured hot water over them in the kitchen sink for quick thawing. While the roast and chicken were thawing, I started peeling potatoes for the potato salad; I also put some red kidney beans on the stove to boil.

The announcement of the storm on the television was now reaching a fever pitch. It was a certainty that we were going to be hit the question was how hard will it hit us. We completed our storm preparation and was now slowing down to a wait and see pace. It is real and it is going to happen. It was a terrible feeling to be totally at the mercy of a storm and just to sit and wait to see what will happen. We did all that we could.

I finished cooking the roast beef, fried chicken, rice and peas, and potato salad. I placed the potato salad in the refrigerator while the beef, chicken and rice and peas sat on the kitchen counter to cool. I dished out three plates of food for our dinner and set those aside. All the lights inside the house were on. It was very bright but we had the feeling of being totally battened down, totally shut off from the outside with the exception of the sounds that came from the television.

It was Sunday evening, time went by quickly but yet it felt like time stood still. We were very sublime. Toni was still on campus assisting her department with preparation for the storm. She called to say she would be home later that evening. Ceejae and I sat down to plan where in the house we would stay to ride out the storm. The announcer said to stay in a location that has inside walls.

We walked through the house still checking to make sure that we took care of everything, at the same time we were scouting for the best and safest place to ride out the storm. We took another walk around the house. There were a few old tires behind shed. We removed them and place them inside of the shed. We secured the storage shed with the padlock.

It was so quiet outside one could hear a pin drop. There was no one insight. The sky had a strange translucent green orange color. Not even the clouds were stirring, there was a sense that something was about to happen. It must have been the calm before the storm. We went indoors still trying to decide where in the house is the safest place to stay.

We took into consideration what the announcer said of find a place in the home with inside walls. We had four bedrooms. All our bedrooms were on the same wing of the house. The two bedrooms in the middle had three inside walls each, but there was also one external wall for each of them. All bedrooms had hurricane shutters on all windows and were secured tightly. Ceejae's bedroom, one of the two rooms in the middle, had a wall-to-wall bookcase on its external wall; we listed it as one place where we might stay to ride out the storm.

Toni arrived home while we were still contemplating where in the house we were going to stay. She noticed that the shutter to the window in the laundry room was not put down and asked about it. Ceejae went and put the shutter down. We were now sealed in the house; all the hurricane shutters were down. Ceejae return inside and reported that no car or any living person was in sight on the streets or anywhere. "Everywhere is quiet", he said to us.

We sat down to have our meal. The food was cold because it was dished out hours ago, we ate it anyway. The telephone rang. Ceejae picked up the receiver and answered the call. "Mom, it's Richard Rigg, the call is for you." Richard Rigg was a family friend. He and his family lived in Country Walk. I have known Richard, his father, and his siblings for many years since childhood.

I took the phone from Ceejae to speak with Richard. He implored us to come over to ride out the storm at his house. He felt that Ceejae, Toni, and I should not be alone. He believed that we would be much safer staying at their place. I assured him that we did all the preparations for the storm, and I believe that we will be safe where we are. We chatted for a while on the telephone. I asked him about the family members and how they were doing considering the storm on its way. He told me that everyone was doing fine. We wished each other's family well and exchange prayer thoughts.

The telephone rang again; this time it was my sister Maxine. She lived in Miami Gardens. She was concern that we were alone to ride out the storm. She invited us to come and stay with her and the family at their house. I shared with her all the work we did preparing for the storm. I assured her that I believe that we would be safe right where we are. I asked her about her preparations. She too assured me that they believed they will be safe where they are. She asked if I saw the sky. I told her that it looked like a fluorescent glow of green the last time I was outdoors. We exchange thoughts and prayers and wished each other well and to be safe riding of the storm.

We considered going someplace else to ride out the storm, but we felt that we would be safer at home. The house was built in 1961 and is located in the Palmetto Golf and Country Club Estates. When we purchased the home we did some research on the property and subdivision. We also looked up the developer and from what we found it looked like they were very good at what they do; build homes. The home was purchased while were still living in Canada.

We took special care in researching the property before the purchase was finalized. We considered the possibility of being hit by a hurricane and whether or not the house could withstand that type of disaster. We knew we were moving to a place that was frequented by hurricanes. Unlike being able to check a flood map to see the likelihood of our home being affected by a flood; we had no guidelines or reference as to whether or not the home could survive a hurricane. We had no technical sense or guidance in this area, all we had was our common sense in making our decision to purchase the home. All the external walls were thick, solid concrete blocks. All of the houses in the neighborhood were built by the same construction company, at least that was what we were told when we purchased the home.

At 10:00 p.m., people were still leaving the area. Some of our friends called to say they were going farther north. We were about a mile away from the coast. Those who lived near the coast were ordered to evacuate, and had done so over the past few days. No evacuation was ordered for our immediate area. We each had a shower and dressed for the storm. How does one dress for a storm? It is anybody's guess.

We imagined it would be a very rugged environment if we were ever blown outdoors with flying debris, falling trees and all that chaos, so we dressed in long-sleeve clothing and leather boots. We did not discard our winter boots that we wore in Canada, it was a good time to put them to use. We made two survival kits and in them were ropes, scissors, chocolate bars, flashlights, batteries, pocket knives, and first aid medical supplies, and other items that may be useful in an emergency. We also had helmets to protect our heads from injuries.

We removed the shelves from one of the closets in the hallway close to the bedrooms. We planned to use that location as a backup safe room. We place one of our survival kits in that location. We decided to stay in our guest room. We set up our short wave radio, brought in our lanterns, and place a survivor kit in the guest room.

I was standing in the kitchen making a cup of tea; it was 11:45 pm. All the lights in the house went off and on four times. It stayed on for a while then it continued to go off and on for period of time. I lit a candle and finished making my cup of tea. I picked up the cup to take a sip then the lights in the house died taking the television, and all appliances with it. The lights didn't just go off suddenly; it was a long slow drawling sound. It was ominous and the show of force was about to begin.

Ceejae turned on one of the flashlights and focused the beam on one of the electrical outlets. He unplugged the electrical cord for the lamps then walked through the house and did the same for every electrical outlet ; he unplugged all appliances and everything that was plugged into an outlet and covered each socket with a plastic gadget, I do not know what they are called—they had two prongs like an electrical cord—we had a whole bunch of them. He ran short of a few gadgets and used plastic duct tape to cover the left over. It is amazing how the sounds of plugged in appliances add to the buoyancy of liveliness. It was so quiet you could hear a pin drop. I wondered why did we not leave the area like some people did instead of facing this danger, but it was too late now we had to stay put.

Toni lit the lantern, and we retreated to the guest bedroom. Krissy, our cat, crawled under the bed. Ceejae curled into his comforter on the bed. Toni curled up in hers beside him. I sat on the carpet and began tuning the shortwave radio. I found a station that was broadcasting information about the storm. I placed the radio on the carpet then pulled a pillow from the bed and stuck it under my head as I stretched out on the carpet with my ear close to the radio.

We prayed and stayed where we were listening to the radio. The announcer described moment by moment what was happening as the winds picked up speed. It was very close. I could tell from the sound of his voice that he was anxious and afraid. I thought about him, no not the announcer, I thought about him as a person; I wondered when was he going to get the hell out of where he was and take cover. We too were scared but we remained calm and placed our trust in God. We stayed where we were and we waited.

The last words we heard from the announcer on the radio was "you are on your own, take care of yourselves". Then the radio died and all that we heard was a bunch of static wave sounds. The damn storm took out the weather station. "Darn, Mom! It is here" said Ceejae, as we looked at each other. We started a round of communications with our eyes. We looked at each other, we saw our fears and anxieties, but behind it all was the consolation that we are together and were there for each other. I have seen those looks before. When my mom passed away my older brother and I looked each other in the eye, we saw each others soul. We read each others thoughts and knew we are there for each other and our younger siblings.

The storm landed between SW 152nd Street and Eureka Drive, a category 5 storm packing winds in excess of 160 miles per hour. It was the third most powerful storm that ever landed in the United States. On Monday, August 24, 1992, at the crack of dawn, all hell broke loose in our community. The ferocious Hurricane Andrew slammed into South Florida, wreaking havoc and destruction in its path. Homestead, Florida City, Miami, and other areas were totally wiped out as if hit by an atomic bomb.

Entire communities were flattened. People struggled to survive the impact. We heard screams outside. Ceejae broke the silence by saying, "Mom, I hear screams. Should we check to see if anyone is out there and let them in?" I looked at him, shaking my head in the negative. We were no match for the force and whatever it was out there, no way were we going to open the doors to even look at it. I had no intention of letting any part of that monstrous storm in the house by opening the door. That thing out there was alive and angry.

Our home was battered. It sounded like a train was moving through; it roared, and there was no end to the sounds, and time stood still. There was a brief moment of silence, then it awoke with a raging thunderous engulfing uproar, a catastrophic gut wrenching howl from the depths of hell; then one, two, three loud explosions as the sounds of giant trains barreled through. What ghastly monstrosity; it was a living hell outside. We heard every sound, all hell had broken loose. We were calm. We prepared for the monster. We sat calmly, breathing deeply and on the look out for the first crack in any of the walls.

We were ready to spring into action. We placed our trust in God and we were ready, willing and able to help him with the job of our survival. We knew we were protected. It felt like our house was caught up in a vortex. We listened quietly as the storm wailed and roared. We maintained our calmness and serenity. We looked at each other and without uttering a word acknowledged what we heard. I knew from the look on the faces of my son and daughter that they we were mobilized and ready to take any action necessary for survival. We each had the resolve that there was no way we would go down without a fight in the storm. We were prepared.

We were a ferocious threesome, if Andrew took our home it wasn't going to find us sitting down. Our backs were covered by the Most High—the one who walked on water, the one who rebuked the storm and calmed the seas. We were entrusted with the first order of self preservation and survival. We were prepared to survive, even if it did not work.

The assault continued; we sat there listening, waiting, and ready for action. The storm ran its course. It was now whistling. The walls of the house were at rest. Intermittently there were lashes of debris against the walls outside. We relaxed our position. We tuned the radio and found a station. The broadcast was clearer. The announcer warned about the eye of the hurricane. He cautioned to be careful because of the back draft.

We maintained our relaxed position. It was too soon to go outdoors. We opened the door of our safe haven. Water was everywhere. The floors looked liked a washed-up coastline. Seaweed and sand littered the floors on the western wing of the house. Water dripped from the ceiling. Overhead fixtures hung lifelessly from the ceiling. Everywhere that the flashlight beam was pointed was damaged.

The home was flooded. We waded through the water across the family room and opened the door to the pool and patio area. The entire domed screen of the pool patio area was gone—gone with the wind. The patio frames were missing. The patio screen door was still standing. The door remained closed in its frame. Wow! How did that happened, and was it suppose to have a meaning?

The swimming pool was filled with furniture and debris. There were couches, tables, stools, garbage cans, tires, and all other sorts of things and objects, none of which belonged to us. Everything in our path of vision was destroyed. The two cars in the driveway were wrapped with electric wires. Our uprooted orange tree lay on top of the wires. All the electrical wires, transformers, and the posts that supported them were strung across the backyard. The storage shed was gone, so were all its contents, only the concrete foundation remained. Our neighbors did not fare any better. It was worse than a demolition derby.

We proceeded with caution walking to the driveway. The street and our front yard were under water. It was flowing like a river. From where we stood the water appeared to be waist deep judging by the gradient of the front yard to our street. Trees and debris littered the river. We looked up and southward and could see forever; the sky was low, very low and the land rose to meet it in the distance. Not a bird was insight; it was the calm after the storm. I suggested that we return indoors for fear we were in the eye of the hurricane. We were left absolutely speechless.

To say the community was hit severely would be an understatement. We returned indoors and closed the door behind us. We waded through the water back to our safe room. There was nothing we could say because it is what it is. We knew it was bad news for everyone everywhere in our community. Without mentioning it to either Toni or Ceejae, I anticipated reports of massive destruction and loss of lives. I checked the telephone and there was a dial tone.

What we saw and heard was unbelievable. We knew the storm was fierce and harsh, and from what we heard and saw, we expected the worse but we hoped for the best for everyone in our community. We knew it will be bad news community-wide. We remained in our safe room and continued to listen to the radio. We heard the names of the cities that were hit severely but it was too soon for the reports to come in. Time went by but I did not know what time of the day it was. We were locked in a time warp surrounded by destruction. What time of day it was did not matter it would all be the same. We sat and waited until we heard the sound of voices outside. We emerged from our shelter for a second time.

I unlocked the door to my Cressida, put the key in the ignition and turned it, and the motor started. I tuned the radio to find a station. I heard Country Walk was totally wiped out. It was the community where our friend Richard and his family lived. I prayed that they survived the storm. We listened as one by one the destruction of cities in the region was announced. Andrew came, it reaped havoc on our community, the wind have passed, but now were faced with the storm of life.

The next few days were spent trying to locate our friends and relatives who lived in the community. There was no water or electricity. Camps providing shelters and food were set up for everyone in need. We worked at getting the water out of the house, and made room for our friends and their children who lost their homes. The entire community came together. We comforted and consoled each other and shared what we had. We teamed up sharing supplies, a place to stay and lending a hand to each other. We embraced each other as some body and none of us was any body. We were in it together.

We shared stories of how we survived through the hours of the storm. Richard and his family had a horrific experience. They survived by covering themselves under a mattress. Their house was blown away. When I heard how they survived I did not regret turning down the invitation to ride out the storm at their house, but I was sorry to hear how horrific their experiences were. Horror stories were abundant, and some people lost their lives. It was a very sad and traumatic time but we could not look back, the only direction we could go was forward.

Our community was transformed instantly. Some of our residents and businesses embraced the laborious task of rebuilding, while others moved to other regions. Some moved farther north to Fort Lauderdale, Palm Beach, and other surrounding areas, while others totally and permanently vacated the state. A large number of people temporarily relocated to other communities while their homes were being rebuilt. There was a large inflow of people from other regions within the state as well as from out of state. Many of them were contractors who came to rebuild the community while others came simply to look for opportunities.

Damages from the hurricane were estimated at over $26 billion. It was a hard-knock life for us living in the disaster zone. We did all we could to help our neighbors and ourselves. We were pressed down and out with all that had happened. We went for weeks without running water and electricity. The water in our swimming pool served our neighbors well. They bailed out buckets to manually flush their toilets as we did too.

After weeks of basic survival, we decided to relocate from the area. We hired a contractor to put protective covering over the exposed roof of our home. Our insurance company came to our rescue. I was very anxious about the claim process. I did not take the time I should to read over the policy when I bought it. I knew I was covered but the truth is I did not check all the details. I had intentions of doing so but never got around to it. I never imagined that I would need to use it.

Now that the event has occurred I wondered if I knew all there was to know about my insurance policy and if I had everything covered. I was almost sure that I had nothing to worry about but I also knew that I should not feel so sure about it. Everything was in a state of chaos and confusion. Faced with a disaster and living the harsh realities of it, I wondered if my insurer was a reputable company. I found the address of the company. It was a local address in Coral Gables. I took my policy and went to visit them. It was very difficult to reach them by telephone. We had a dial tone immediately after the storm, but later that too died. I could not contact the company by telephone, so I decided to go to the office in person. It was perhaps better that way.

I arrived at the office still traumatized from my experience. I had no idea how long it will take for me to tell them all that had happened. The damages were so extensive. I wanted to say all that there was to be said in one word, or simply just sit there and stared without saying a word; hoping they could feel what I wanted to tell them. I said to the person at the desk "I am totally wiped out. I have this insurance policy, I believe that it is with your company, and I believe that I am in the right location. The damages are so huge, I don't even know if you can cover all of it. My policy says right here that if any of these event occur, you will pay for replacement and other things, can you afford to pay and can you do it quickly?" There was a gentleman standing by a glass window with a golf club in hand, He was putting into a cup. He must have overheard what I said to the person at the front desk. He walked over to where I was and introduced himself. He said he was the manager. He ushered me into his office and offered me a cup of coffee.

My appearance was not in the usual form that I would have presented myself. Our clothes closet was filled with water during the storm. Every bit of clothing was damaged. Mold and mildew was everywhere. I salvaged a pair of slacks and a tee-shirt. I brushed them down with my hands, but I was still looking like raggedy Anne in comparison to the manager and other members of staff in that office.

I was wearing the same outfit for two days. I straightened my slacks as I walked into the manager's office. I knew I was on auto pilot, because nothing was the way it was supposed to be. Perhaps it was just a reaction to the manager's appearance; he wore a finely tailored suit. I am used to carrying myself we but now I looked like a raga muffin.

While I was sitting in his office waiting for my coffee he began humming and I recognized the tune. He took a notepad from the right hand drawer of his desk and placed it in front of him. The song he was humming was the "Battle Hymn of the Republic." I mentally hummed the song while he tapped the beat with the pen on the notepad. I did not want to get too comfortable, so I repeated what I told the receptionist when I first arrived. The manager said,

"Mrs. McLeod, I realized that you have been traumatized. I am here to work with you, and to assist you through this process."

A lady entered his office with a cup of coffee. She stretched out her hand with the coffee towards me, "Mrs. McLeod, here is your coffee. Would you like cream and sugar?" "Not thank you" I responded, as I accepted the coffee from her. I felt a bit more at ease but the entire process was weighing on me. The manager set up the claim. Before I left the office that day I was presented with a check for emergency accommodation.

The manager went over all aspects of my policy with me. He told me that the process would continue over several months, but an adjuster would visit the property before the week ended. I sighed with relief because I knew I was in good hands. I have been an insurance professional for many years. I have sold insurance protection to many people, but the value of having insurance protection never meant more to me than at that moment.

Disasters have a way of exposing our humanity; it shows how vulnerable we all are. It can happen to anyone anywhere and at anytime. We are truly blessed to live in a society where more fortunate ones can run to the rescue of those who are caught in time warps. Hurricane Andrew changed our sense and perception of time. Every thing was rolled back. We were traumatized and struggling to survive.

We decided to relocate to Fort Lauderdale. It was very difficult to find accommodation because of the disaster. Thousands of people need a place to live but houses and apartments were scarce because of the high demands. We were looking for rental or a lease with an option to purchase. At the same time we were looking for a place to live, we were also working with a contractor to repair the damaged house.

After searching for a couple of months, we found a condominium in Shaker Village, Tamarac. We leased the condo with an option to purchase it within four months. Our home in the disaster area was still being repaired. Before we could occupy the condo it needed a paint job and new carpets. It was left to us to find a contractor to do the job. Since the time we vacated our damaged home we have been staying at hotels.

During the interim while working on the repairs of our damaged home and finding a new place to live, Ceejae was registered to attend St. Thomas Aquinas High School in Ft. Lauderdale. He was originally registered to attend Columbus High. We had to make those changes because of the turn of events after the storm. It was his first year in high school. Toni continued to attend Florida International University, there was no interruption of her program.

The new home was painted and ready for occupancy in November, 1992. We took occupancy of the condo as soon as it was ready for move in. We did not have much to move in with, just ourselves. We had no furniture, only the stuff we salvaged from the damaged property. After we moved into the condo we began the process of purchasing new furniture and other stuff.

After the repairs were completed on the damaged home. we put the house up for sale and sold it. The minister who bought our home had a very difficult time finding a mortgage company to provide a loan for his purchase. There was a moratorium on mortgages in the disaster area. To complete the sale we agreed to hold a money-purchase mortgage on the home. Our attorney drew up the papers and completed the sale. The minister lost his home during the storm. He was in urgent need of a home for his family. He told us he planned to use the swimming pool for baptismal purposes. We were both motivated by the urgent need.

We settled in the new condo and tried to move forward with our lives. There was still a great deal to do. We were returning to some form of normalcy but not quite there yet, we were in a better position to provide more assistance with the rebuilding process in our community. It was a team effort working with friends and families through the rebuilding efforts. I commuted back and forth in the disaster area. Everyone was doing the best they could to get back on track. It was obvious that some changes in the community will be permanent. It was too soon to tell if the changes would be for better or worse.

My office was still located in Coral Gables. All of my clients were displaced; and were homeless, waiting on their homes to be rebuilt, or relocating to some other city. Hurricane Andrew was my first experience of a major disaster. I developed a greater and deeper understanding of how disasters impact the lives of people and their community. From that experience I learned that it was insufficient to prepare for the prevention of damages alone; one must also consider the worst scenario and have alternative back up plans. The possibility of relocating must be considered when faced with catastrophic disasters. Had we considered that possibility before the storm we may have pre-select a community where we would have liked to relocate. It was extremely difficult to make those kinds of decision in a traumatized state.

It is also very important to become aware of community emergency management policies and processes. Do not wait until after a disaster occur to find out how the process works. It is difficult to gather information when nothing is normal and everyone is on the same page of chaos. Fortunately we were in close proximity to other communities who were operating normally. In those communities their ATMs, department stores, telephone service, electricity, running water and other services and amenities were fully operational.

As time went by I read about disasters around the globe. Some of those disasters were due to natural causes, while others were caused by political unrests and instability. Because of my personal experiences with Hurricane Andrew I look at disasters through a different set of lenses. I slowly began to reactivate my volunteer activities with UNA-USA. We emerged from Hurricane Andrew with a deeper and keener awareness of the impact of disasters on human lives, and I have developed a great appreciation of the works of the American Red Cross, the Salvation Army, the United Nations, and other organizations that provide humanitarian services when disasters occur at home or abroad.

CHAPTER 2

W ITH ALL OF the changes brought by the storm or as a result of it, commuting was proving to be more difficult each day. After our relocation to Broward County, I leased a small office space on Oakland Park Boulevard. The intentions were to use this small office as a satellite office where I could work from, thus not having the need to drive to Miami daily. Since the storm traffic to and from Miami was horrendous. All roads leading in an out were congested with transportations taking building materials to the disaster zones or returning to get more supplies.

It took a long time to get to anywhere. My clients were now dispersed all over South Florida. The branch office for the company that I worked for was still operational in Coral Gables. Continuing UNA-USA volunteer work was a great challenge. It was just five months since the storm and everything was still very chaotic. Many of our chapter members had enough problems dealing with the after effects of the storm. Some of our members relocated to other cities and regions. I worked from the small office in Oakland Park because it eased the burden of travelling back and forth to Coral Gables. It also became the center of operations for our UNA-USA Greater Miami Chapter.

Operating in Broward County created confusion, as if things weren't confused enough already, Broward County has a chapter of UNA-USA. Our chapter was often mistaken for the Broward County Chapter. The Greater Miami Chapter and Broward County UNA-USA work very closely in joint and coordinated activities, but they are two separate chapters. There are no provisions in our bylaws restricting membership by any specific geographical location. If a new member submits a membership application directly to the national office, the director of membership will assign the new member to the closest chapter of the member's residence, if a choice of chapter is not indicated on the application.

Activities began picking up in the summer of 1993 when the vice president and I attended our state annual meeting. The meeting was held at the Langford Hotel in Orlando, Florida. At that meeting our chapter was designated to host the state annual meeting for Florida Division UNA-USA 1994. In UNA-USA, the term *Division* has several meanings. However, for the purpose of this discussion, the term *Division* is a structural model. UNA-USA has twenty-three units that are called Divisions. Those Divisions fall into four categories.

The type 1 Division operates like an umbrella that serves chapters in a state or part of a state. Most of the Divisions of UNA-USA fall into this category and perform service functions. They stimulate and facilitate contact among chapters, encourage the formation of new chapters, conduct statewide business, and maintain contact with state officials.

Type 1 Divisions include Arizona, Connecticut, Florida, Illinois, Iowa, Kentucky, Michigan, Nebraska, New Jersey, North Carolina, Ohio, Oregon, Texas, and Wisconsin. Southern California, Northern California, and Southern New York State were also type 1 Divisions, but they were a special subcategory in that they serve only a portion of the state specifically rather than statewide.

Type 2 Divisions perform similar functions as type 1, but they also function as chapters in a metropolitan area. Type 2 Divisions include Colorado Division in Denver, Hawaii Division in Honolulu, Minnesota Division in Minneapolis-Saint Paul, and Utah Division in Salt Lake City.

A type 3 Division functions as a state or territory chapter. Delaware and Puerto Rico are type 3 Divisions. So are Alaska, Arkansas, Maine, Maryland, and Wyoming. Those serve as chapters for the entire state.

Type 4 Divisions serve an area beyond their state of district borders. The National Capital Area Division for example serves as a chapter in the District of Columbia as well as the DC suburbs in Virginia and Maryland.

Division activities primarily fall under the umbrella of a type 1 Division. Generally, type 1 Division operations include meetings for chapter leaders, which are usually held on a bimonthly or quarterly basis. At the meetings, a forum is provided for chapter leaders to share news and plans for cooperative activities.

Some Divisions such as the Florida Division have extensive statewide conferences annually to which all members in that Division, as well as leaders from other Divisions are invited. Other activities of type 1 Divisions include the distribution of newsletters, coordination of UN Day including working with the governor on the appointment of a UN Day chair for the state, and a state UN Day proclamation. All other Divisions perform the same function in their respective locality. Type 1 Divisions are also the logical unit to maintain contact with non-governmental organizations at the state level.

Some Divisions, such as Florida and Southern California, actively build a council of organizations, which is a function that is usually performed at the national headquarters level. Other functions that are performed by Divisions include skills training (which is usually conducted at Division meetings in the form of workshops on membership recruitment), fund-raising, programming, and board development.

Training for the implementation of the Global Policy Project is also another aspect of Division functions. The Division level also helps to develop governmental relations, outreach to members at large, formation of new chapters, and formation of contact groups in areas where there are too few members and leaders to form a chapter. Although a Division has specific functions, it was not unusual to find chapters functioning at Division levels, because it is the leaders of chapters that are often on the board of Division levels.

The entire structure of UNA-USA chapters and Divisions is an intricate network of leadership that shared resources, skills, ideas, and in essence, is a cross functional team structure. Membership dues were shared between the chapters, divisions, and the national office.

It was no coincidence, therefore, that at our state annual meeting in the summer of 1993, it was also decided that because of the proximity of the Greater Miami and the Broward County chapters, both chapters were to work jointly on coordinating the annual state meeting for 1994. Dr. Blanca Moore-Velez, the president of Broward County chapter and I accepted the responsibilities to host the event.

The 1993 annual state meeting was my first event in the capacity of president of Greater Miami chapter. I learned the role as I go along. U N Day 1993 was held in Coral Gables on October 22, 1993. The annual observance of UN Day is usually held in October of each year. It was the first time since the hurricane that our members met in the same location.

We talked about the disaster because it was still the focus of everyone's attention. I was not surprised to find that the experience of the disaster had similar impact on our members. The experiences of the disaster gave everyone, who engaged in the dialogue, a sharper focus on the role of the world organization in assisting displaced populations across the globe.

UNA-USA believes that effective international organizations are essential to deal with a host of global issues. Those issues may involve peace and security, the environment, sustainable development, the scourges of disease and narcotic drugs, the wise use of resources, and disasters. The UN has an essential role in addressing international issues. The world organization has a commendable record of achievement. But like all human institutions, the UN has problems and could do its job even better.

UNA-USA acknowledges those problems and offers constructive solutions. But while the association supports the UN, it is not an uncritical supporter.

UNA-USA is a constructive critic that provides balanced information, and realistic recommendations for a stronger United Nations system. UNA-USA is a nonpartisan organization. It draws leadership from both major political parties. An effective UN should not be identified with support from any one political viewpoint.

UNA-USA seeks leaders and members of all ages, from all racial and ethnic groups, and all economic and social backgrounds. The organization takes pride in its reputation as a credible source of objective information serving several different audiences including students, academics, the media, government and business leaders, and the general public.

The position taken by UNA-USA is a call for constructive and creative U.S. participation in cooperative efforts with other nations, and with non-governmental organizations to realize the ideas of the United Nations Charter. Similar to the ways in which UNA-USA provides constructive criticism, and support to the United Nations, the association also is a constructive critic of the policies of our government, and encourages the United States to use multilateral approaches, or cooperative action by several governments, whenever possible, to achieve its foreign-policy objectives.

The origins of UNA-USA can be traced to the League of Nations Association, which was founded in 1923 to encourage the United States to cooperate with the technical and humanitarian work of the league. After the creation of the United Nations in 1945, the League of Nations Association was reconstituted as the American Association for the United Nations (AAUN), a grassroots membership organization.

Eleanor Roosevelt, who was a U.S. representative to the UN General Assembly during the Truman administration, became a leader of the AAUN after leaving government service. In 1947, the U.S. Department of State took the lead in founding a second organization, the U.S. Committee for the United Nations, a coalition of non-governmental organizations. The initial purpose of the U.S. Committee was to coordinate the national observance of United Nations Day.

In 1964, the AAUN and the U.S. Committee for the U.N. merged to become the United Nations Association of the USA. The associations' policies are set by its board of directors, which is made up of forty-five members who meet four times each year. The composition of the board are nine members who are elected by chapters and divisions on a regional basis—two elected by the Council of Organizations, seventeen elected by the National Convention, and seventeen elected by the board itself. The board has a committee structure, including a chapter and division committee composed of the nine chapter/division-elected members of the board and up to eight others appointed by the chair of the association.

The officers of the association are the chair, secretary, treasurer, and president and CEO. Our officers were John C. Whitehead, chair of the association; Shirley S. Quisenberry, secretary; Christopher Brady, treasurer; and Alvin P. Adams Jr., president and CEO. These officers served for the 1997 term and may have even served earlier or later.

The National Convention meets in alternate years. It elects seventeen members of the board, and six of the eleven members of the nominating committee make recommendations to the board. An open meeting of the board is held at the time of the convention. Voting delegates represent chapters, divisions, and affiliated organizations. Members of the National Council and the board of directors are also delegates.

Another part of the structure of UNA-USA is the Council of Chapters and Division Presidents (CCDP), which is composed of the presidents of each chapter and division. The purpose of the Council of Chapters and Divisions is to facilitate communication among chapters and divisions, to assist with their activities, and to provide a forum for chapter and division leaders to meet.

The National Council, which is yet another sector of the association, is a group of up to two hundred distinguished association leaders, and other prominent Americans. The National Council assists the association in a variety of ways. The national headquarters of the association is located in New York City. That is where the executive office and departments are, and it staffs approximately thirty-five members. UNA-USA also has an office in Washington. That office represents the association in the nation's capital, monitors executive and legislative branches, and directs the association's advocacy on U.S.-U.N. relations.

The national programs consist of several modules, including education programs, Council of Organizations, Global Policy Project, and Advocacy on U.S.-U.N. Relations, United Nations Day observance, and Landmine Awareness Project. In our education programs, UNA-USA provides materials and services for the sixty thousand students and educators, who participate each year in the Model United Nations.

The association also sponsors a national high school essay contest, and produces curricular materials on the U.N. Chapters and divisions often sponsor or work with Model U.N. conferences, do essential work to implement the essay contest, and conduct U.N. education seminars for teachers. UNA-USA Council of Organizations involves work with over 145 other non-governmental organizations. Members of the Council of Organizations include religious groups, trade unions, service clubs, and women and youth groups.

Each year UNA-USA sponsors a study or action project in which members study a global issue, and prepare recommendations to strengthen the U.N. in dealing with this issue. A briefing book for the project is issued in September, with final recommendations due in the spring. Our advocacy on U.S.-U.N. relations involves the coordination of information supplied by our Washington office. Chapters and divisions maintain contact with their members of congress through letters, telephone calls, and personal visits. The land mines project is a special initiative to mobilize the U.S. public opinion in support of the elimination of land mines.

UNA-USA's relationships with the United Nations are both formal and informal. Formally, the association is associated with U.N.'s Department of Public Information, and is on the roster of the Economic and Social Council. UNA-USA is often accredited to the U.N. conferences. Informal connections are numerous and significant. UNA-USA leaders and staff have continuous contact with key members of the U.N. Secretariat, and with members of the diplomatic community, particularly through policy studies programs.

UNA-USA also maintains contact with many U.N.-specialized agencies. UNA-USA's relationship with the United States government is a complex matter. Although the association is nonpartisan in nature, UNA-USA does try to develop and suggest constructive policy options to U.S. leaders. Many of UNA-USA's national leaders have served in government, and provided special access to U.S.-government decision makers.

The third set of relationships comes from the Council of Organizations that consists of over 145 non-governmental organizations, including professional groups, service clubs, religious organizations, and groups serving the needs of women, children, and youth, labor unions and public-interest groups. These diverse organizations share a common commitment to international cooperation. At the national level, UNA-USA has strong ongoing activities with many of the churches, the American Association of University Women, the National Education Association, Lions International, the World Federalist Association, the U.S. Committee for UNICEF, and the League of Women Voters, to name a few. This networking is replicated by chapters and divisions at the community level.

UNA-USA is one of several hundred national and international non-governmental organizations. We regard the NGO community a valuable partner in our work. UNA-USA also cooperates with umbrella organizations, such as the National Council of World Affairs Organization. UNA is as member of the International Campaign to Ban Landmines, and NGO coalitions for the fiftieth anniversary of the Universal Declaration of Human Rights (1998), and the International Year of Older Persons (1999).

Finally, UNA-USA enjoys a growing set of mutually beneficial relationships with other national U.N. associations, and with the World Federation of United Nations Association (WFUNA). Our association has strong bilateral ties with several UNAs, particularly those of Russia, Canada, and the United Kingdom. A number of our chapters and divisions are "twinned" with UNAs in other countries. WFUNA provides a framework for these relationships. Based in Geneva, WFUNA encourages the formation of new UNAs, helps existing associations especially in developing nations, and seeks to create a worldwide "people's movement for the U.N." WFUNA holds a plenary assembly every two years; UNA-USA sends a strong delegation to each plenary assembly.

UNA-USA is a nonprofit organization with annual revenues and expenses of approximately $5 million. These funds are raised from fund-raising, corporations, individuals, and members. Every program area is expected to be self-supporting. The Policy Studies Department is supported primarily by foundation grants, with some earmarked corporations, and individual gifts. Corporate Affairs derives its income from donations, corporate memberships, and the sale of publications. Administration and Finance Development is supported by corporate contributions, interests, and general contributions from individuals. Public outreach programs are supported by membership dues, fees paid by the groups in the Council of Organizations, sales of publications and program materials, and foundation grants.

Membership dues constitute 14 percent of the association's income. Abut 40 percent of the dues' income from the membership of chapters are returned to the chapter and divisions. The remainder is used by the national office to cover services provided to chapters and divisions, including membership services, the Council of Chapter and Division Presidents, the quarterly mailing and other informational mailings, field visits, and relevant staff salaries and benefits.

UNA-USA does not accept funds from the U.S. government, and accepts only occasional minimal funding from the United Nations. In recent years, the U.N. has provided UNA-USA with small amounts of money designated for special projects, for example, support from the UNDP for the National High School Essay Contest. Amounts of money provided to UNA-USA by the U.N. are usually less than $10,000. In addition to membership-renewal notices, UNA-USA sends annual giving appeals to all members. The association also encourages planned giving, especially bequests and gifts of life insurance.

UNA-USA has a tax-exempt status under federal Internal Revenue Code section 501(c) 3. This determination exempts UNA-USA from federal or state income tax on all forms of income derived from exempt purposes. According to section 501(c) (3), an organization must be "organized and operated exclusively for religious, charitable, scientific, and testing for public safety, literary or educational purposes." Under this determination, UNA-USA is not to conduct substantial political lobbying or engage in political campaign.

This is interpreted to mean than not more than 20 percent of the association's budget is devoted to lobbying. The 501 (c) (3) statuses do not relieve the association of the requirement to file tax returns for informational purposes. Any chapter or division whose gross receipts are normally in excess of $25,000 must file Form 990, the Return for Organization Exempt from Income Tax, and Schedule A of that form by the fifteenth day of the fifth month after the end of their accounting period. Chapters and divisions with paid staff are responsible for filing the quarterly federal employment tax deposits (FICA) to IRS and W-2 forms at the end of the year.

A chapter carries out the mission of UNA-USA at the community level; that mission is to strengthen the United Nations system and the United States participation in it. The chapter is a community-based group of members dedicated to informing and educating citizens of all ages about the United Nations system and the role it plays in world affairs.

Chapters collaborate with other parts of the association to develop policy positions and to examine critically U.S. participation in the U.N. system. Chapters also enlarge a diverse constituency in support of constructive United States participation in the United Nations. There are prerequisites for obtaining a chapter charter. When the national office is satisfied that the prerequisites are met by a chapter seeking a charter, including having a well-defined area that does not already have a chapter, a charter is issued.

The prerequisites include having a minimum of twenty-five current members, an elected board of directors (including a president, treasurer, and such other officers as may be necessary as well as one or more representatives to the division), and chapter bylaws that must be consistent with a model bylaws provided by UNA-USA. Chapters are required to conduct activities related to the work of the United Nations system.

A minimum of two board meetings per year is required, and as many meetings of the executive committee, if any are needed or as necessary. Other requirements of chapters include an annual membership meeting, which may include a community-related program to conduct the business of the chapter. Chapters are required to submit annual reports to the national office as well as provide a copy to the division where applicable. In addition to prerequisites and requirements, chapters have specific goals in order to become an increasingly active and effective community organization.

Chapters are encouraged to seek goals for their work, such as the following: development of significant financial support above membership dues; reaching the public media about the work of the United Nations and UNA-USA; contact with elected officials to inform them about the work of the United Nations and UNA-USA. We were also required to have systematic involvement of the community in chapter programs; periodic contact with chapter members through a newsletter or other form of correspondence; issuance of a program calendar outlining future UNA activities; establishment of an information and publications UNA Center with listed telephone number, through which the public can learn about the work of the U.N. and UNA.

Another chapter requirement was the cooperation with local libraries to establish U.N. and UNA information centers, which are easily identifiable Chapter presidents are required to attend or designate a representative to attend division board meetings, and attendance by delegates, and members at annual division membership meetings; and attendance by the president or a designated representative of the chapter at annual meetings of the Council of Chapter and Division Presidents, and National Conventions.

Chapters are expected to comply with the requirements and goals. Our chapter's goals were very ambitious, and in view that many chapters did not have a central administration office from which to conduct activities. Some chapters have administrative offices; those chapters usually have five hundred or more members. Many chapters were operating from the president's home or workplace. Some of our chapter leaders run operations from their business. Events and activities are scaled based on the chapter's resources. Our chapter, Greater Miami UNA-USA, averages two hundred members for the period 1991-2000.

The 1994 National Convention was held in New York City. It was my first time attending a national convention for the organization. Ethel and I were delegates to that convention. We were happy that New York City was chosen as the location for the convention because we would have the chance to visit the United Nations and possibly our UNA-USA headquarters.

We arrived in New York City for our national meeting. I had not been to New York City since December of 1988 when we stopped over while we were moving from Canada to Florida. The City has such a remarkable presence, it is almost like a signature. The only setback that prevented mobility was the amount of ice that was everywhere in the city. The region was experiencing an unusual assault of ice storms that began in mid January shortly before we arrived. Those ice storms sent temperatures below zero over the entire region. When we settled in to participate in our annual meeting, one of the things on our agenda was visiting the U.N. headquarters. We were able to sit in on a few sessions in the General Assembly, and had a grand tour of the U.N. Headquarters.

Ethel was very experienced in attending and participating in UNA-USA national conventions. She coached and guided me in all the sessions. Her assistance in completing information on our chapter's business was awesome. Ethel is one of our retirees' board members, but no one would believe that Ethel was past the age of seventy years old. She was full of energy; I could hardly keep up with her as she moves from session to session in the national convention. Because of her experience at these kinds of meetings, she navigated her way through the maze of issues on the national agenda with ease. I admired her proficiency and was happy that she was my coach. I was very comfortable working with her.

One of the tasks I was asked to perform at the national convention was to make a presentation in one of the workshops. The topic of that presentation was *How to raise funds for the upcoming fiftieth anniversary celebration of the United Nations.* The objective of my presentation was to assist chapter leaders in developing fund raising ideas for their U.N. 50 events and programs.

I pooled ideas drawing on my professional background as a financial advisor, and chose to speak on corporate sponsorship. The purpose was to share ideas, skills and techniques of how to make direct contact with decision makers, and how make attractive presentations for corporate sponsorship. I prepared my presentation before I left for New York.

I went to retrieve my materials for the presentation from my hotel room but I could not find them. I did not want to let my team down by not being able to make the presentation; I need the materials to do it. The workshop was due to begin in one hour. Ethel suggested that we call my office in Miami to check if it was left behind. I made a telephone call to my office in Oakland Park. I was relieved when my assistant picked up the telephone. I feared that she may have already left for the day. The presentation package was in the office.

I looked for Ethel, I thought she was still in the room but she wasn't. I did not know where she went. Suddenly, she burst into the room, paper in hand with a fax number. My assistant faxed us the presentation pages and one set of handouts. Ethel requested that our workshop be move back by one presentation slot to allow time to make copies of the handout. The hotel staff assisted us in converting the faxed pages to overhead transparency while Ethel and I worked at making the copies for handouts.

A number of different organizations were having functions at the hotel that weekend. The entire place was buzzing with people, events, and activities. The sub-zero temperature in New York City seemed to have driven everyone inside. The weather channel said it was one of the coldest temperatures recorded for that date. Ethel and I weren't sure we could make all the photocopies we need on time. We were making one hundred copies. We pulled a few ranks to get the job done. The photocopying machines were in high demand. Nonetheless we got the job done. I was ready to do my presentation in the workshop.

I was looking forward to making my presentation. I felt privileged to be able to share fund raising ideas with other chapter leaders. It was not the same as sharing ideas with my peers at work, but I was willing to take the time to explain the ideas in such a way that everyone could understand them. I believed that these ideas will be helpful to chapter leaders in developing programs for UN50.

The meeting room was packed to capacity. Over 200 people were seated and ready to share in the workshop. Each attendee was provided with a handout. I took my position on the podium and was introduced by the moderator. The presentation lasted for twenty minutes then we went right into the questions and answers session. The chapter leaders and representatives welcomed the ideas that were shared, but there was one attendee who did not seem to like any of the ideas.

The basic element of the approach to fund raising that was presented encouraged chapters to adopt a team approach with those companies who are responsive to request for funding. I emphasized the mutually beneficial aspect of *what is it for me, and the how will it help me* effect. One of the suggestions that I gave in my presentation—a thinking outside of the box scenario—was to enlist the company's participation in such a way that a direct link can be made to the company's operations.

I provided a number of examples in our handouts for the audience and chapter leaders. One of the examples that I provided was related the use of demographic data for marketing purposes. Actually, that was nothing new but the mentioned of it in the forum and especially as it referred to the United Nations led to something that I did not expect. Wow! That sets off a very heated debate. The member in the audience stood up and shouted "You cannot do that!"

The tone and passion of his words did not escape anyone in the room. To be quite honest, I was not prepared for the outtake, but the debate was welcomed. I looked at the panelists to my right and left on the platform; searching their faces for someone or anyone who had any level of expertise on the subject to jump in, and lead in these new developments. I anticipated all sorts of questions for my presentation but I did not expect to be challenged in this fashion. It was taking too long, no one volunteered; so I carried on.

I clarified the information that I presented. By this time he moved from the back of the room to the front row. I previously covered how donations are handled in terms of tax deductions, UNA-USA and its chapters are 501(c) 3 status, and I even spoke a bit about business expense deductions. The time in which to do the presentation did not permit detailed taxation discussions but the general idea was presented. I discussed how chapter leaders may get beyond the gatekeepers to reach decision makers; how and what kind of information to provide to decision makers; how to observe protocol during the sponsorship request process, and even how to draft letters when making their requests for funding.

I was not an expert on the United Nations or its agencies, neither did I know all there was to know about UNA-USA. I was a *new kid on the block.* I stepped to the front of the raised platform; *Snagglepuss*—this is the perfect time to *exit stage left*, I thought to myself, "*Heavens to Murgatroyd*" No, I could not do that, I need to respond to the question or statement. The easy way out of the situation would have been to invite a one on one discussion with my challenger after the workshop ended. I scanned the room and all eyes were on me. It would not have been proactive to take the easy way out. UNA-USA members are stimulated by dialogue and debates. I knew the eyes were saying "come on Sylvia, do not let this one go take it on".

I briefly recapped my presentation stating its purpose. It was intended to provide an innovative approach to fund-raising for UN50 activities. I took a winning approach for chapters and their sponsors. At the same time getting corporate sponsorship is a great opportunity of creating public awareness of the works of the United Nations.

UNA-USA chapters operate locally in communities where there are businesses that operate locally, nationally and internationally; those businesses may either be for-profit or not-for-profit organizations. Regardless of the type of organization or its structure, organizations are people businesses. Information such as population dynamics, demographics, customs, and culture are key elements that are important to any business decision maker.

"Mr. Jones, thank you for your comment. I do respect your view, but I am not suggesting that the United Nations open the database of the Security Council. The data that I am referring to are those that pertain to population dynamics such as customs and culture, political environment, and any such information that will help those who conduct business globally to improve the process of marketing or in making business decisions. Another aspect to consider is how the United Nations conducts its business and the way in which providing this information to business leaders may improve the operations of the United Nations in its procurement process." That was my long answer to the question or statement.

The short answer to the I provided to the attendees was to the effect that the United Nations system is not limited to the main bodies only. There are specialized agencies, regional commissions and whole host of related organizations dispersed all over the globe. Those commissions, specialized agencies and related organizations collect data globally. UNA-USA chapter leaders and national headquarters have access and knowledge of information that could be useful to business leaders and professionals in their community. I was not specifically referring to the Security Council which is a part of the main body to the United Nations. I was referring to specialized agencies such as the Food and Agricultural Organization of the United Nations (FAO); World Health Organization (WHO); United Nations Industrial Development Organization (UNIDO); International Labor Organizations (ILO), just to name a few. Many decision makers in businesses are unaware that they can tap into the wealth of information that is available in the UN system. Thus my presentation was geared to showing chapter leaders how they might attract sponsorships from the local businesses in their community. I paused for a moment to see if my response was accepted. The audience loved my response. They stood up and clapped their hands. It was a great moment of relief. The audiences requested more handouts and the opportunity to contact me later for more details. We also accepted requests from chapter leaders who would like assistance in developing their corporate sponsorship programs.

Ethel and I paid close attention to our speakers who were from the United Nations. We were on the lookout for potential speakers for our Greater Miami chapter's future activities. The camaraderie in the convention was astonishing.

We collected and shared resources. We moved through the convention halls very quickly, everything was moving at a fast pace; we had lots of grounds to cover between events. More than one hundred UNA-USA chapters participated with exhibits; other organizations and NGOs 'also participated.

We attended luncheons, dinners, and plenary sessions. Ethel and I did not miss one beat; we kept up the pace, and took in as much as we could. The featured speaker at one of our luncheons was a former assistant secretary-general under the leadership of Javier Perez de Cuellar; who was the former secretary-general of the United Nations. Perez de Cuellar's term in office was January 1, 1982, through December 31, 1991.

John C. Whitehead, chair of our association, introduced the speaker Giandomenico Picco. "Wow!" I said, turning to Ethel, who was seated to my right at the table. "Ethel, He looks great. I did not know such fine, debonair specie of men worked at the United Nations." She gave me a wide smile with a nod as if to say "yes! We turned our attention to the speaker.

I checked out the speaker as he walked to the podium. He received a warm welcome with applauses from the audience. His posture and demeanor were perfect. He wore a finely tailored double-breasted navy suit, complemented with a white shirt and red-and-navy-striped-silk tie. He stood at about six feet five inches. First impressions are lasting, and it can be a deciding factor whether or not the audience will listen to what is being said. *Well, I thought, I believe that I am going to enjoy this speech.*

Giandomenico Picco spoke about the Lebanon hostage crisis. He told us a bit about his work at the United Nations. It was more than I expected—what he told us, I mean. He was very knowledgeable of the topic, and sharing his personal experiences brought us face to face with hostage crises, the negotiations for release of hostages, life and death issues, and the impact on human lives. I made notes during his presentation. I gave him five stars. I place a note beside his name as someone I would like to invite as keynote speaker at one of our chapter's events.

After the luncheon Ethel and I compared notes on the speaker. We were on the same page; we both felt that it would be neat to invite Mr. Picco to speak at our chapter. Our members strongly believe in the power of dialogue. It never hurts anyone to engage dialogue as a way of getting their point across. One of our members, Dora, has a beautiful way of demonstrating the power of language in communication. She made this point over and over that it never hurts anyone to talk about their problems even if they were to talk until the face turns blue; it never hurts to talk and at least something can be achieved in the exchange of words.

Language has a powerful effect of equalizing and stabilizing situations. Words whether spoken or written can be an effective way of persuading others to change an opinion, even if it takes a long time. There is another larger and more profound statement to the power of words. In short it goes "In the beginning was the word." I leave the rest of the phrase to the imagination or for recollection. Another cliché to the use of words is the one that says the pen is mightier than the sword, but it is not the pen that matters, it is really the words that are written with that pen.

The Lebanon hostage crisis was a systematic series of kidnapping and hostage taking that involved ninety-six hostages from twenty-one different national origins. The crisis occurred between the periods 1982 and 1992. Some of the hostages were murdered, some died from lack of proper medical care, and some died because of ill treatment. From what I have read on the hostage crisis, people were taken as hostages not because of any involvement in political activities but because of their country of origin.

A UNA-USA membership provides us with a window to our world, and the numerous issues on different aspects of issues that one way or another affect our daily lives. Our chapter members are interested in learning more about terrorism and how those atrocities affect and impact the lives of innocent people. Other issues that our members were eager to learn about are world hunger, world health issues, human rights, child labor, and a whole host of other issues. So getting good speakers with first hand experience of any of the world issues was very important to us.

Ethel and I met with Mr. Picco after the luncheon. We thanked him for sharing his experience with us. We expressed our interest in having him as one of our speakers sometime in the near future. He welcomed the idea. We took a few photographs, and then we moved along to mill with the crowd.

Another speaker at the national meeting was the secretary-general of the United Nations, Boutros Boutros-Ghali. He was the keynote speaker at one of our dinners. This was a special event. It took a long time to enter the ballroom. The line moved very slowly because of security clearance that was necessary to enter the hall. On this day the entire building had a pumped up security. We entered with passes but they had to be checked before we could enter the ballroom. We did not mind the wait; we were looking forward to meeting the secretary-general. Ethel and I sat at the same table. The pageantry began; soon all officials including the secretary-general were seated at the table on the raised platform.

The room buzzed with activities. I looked around the hall. It was too huge to see every angle. At the tables that were in view, everyone was engaged in conversation. There was more buzz than the usual at other luncheons and dinners. I assumed it must have been the presence of the secretary-general that was creating the hype. William J. van den Heuvel, chair of our Board of Governors, welcomed the U.N. secretary-general Boutros Boutros-Ghali, and introduced him to the audience. Our table was located in the middle of the room, so we had a very good view of the secretary-general as he left his seat and approached the podium.

Boutros Boutros-Ghali is a petite man. His black horn-rimmed eyeglasses looked slightly oversized but they looked good on him. The secretary-general addressed the audience. He had a resounding quality to his voice. His words came across deep and solid as he gave intermittent smiles throughout his delivery.

Mr. Boutros-Ghali spoke eloquently about the United Nations, his role, and the challenges that the world organization faced in its current state. He spoke many languages. His grandfather was the prime minister of Egypt from 1908 until he was assassinated in 1910. Boutros Boutros-Ghali served the United Nations from January 1992 until December 1996. He was preceded by Secretary-General Javier Perez de Cuellar, and was succeeded by Kofi Anan.

Mr. Boutros-Ghali's political career began in his home country, Egypt, where he served as a member of the Central Committee of the Arab Socialist Union from 1974 to 1977 under the presidency of Anwar El Sadat. He was also Egypt's Minister of State for Foreign Affairs from 1977 to 1991. He has a PhD in international law. He was also a professor of International Law and International Relations at Cairo University.

Mr. Boutros-Ghali had a very impressive biography. It showed all of his lifetime accomplishments. His biography was included in our program brochure. His tenure at the UN was not without controversies. The secretary-general came under fire during his term in office for several controversial issues. He submitted an Agenda for Peace about how the UN could be more responsive to violent conflicts but was criticized for the United Nation's failure to act during the genocide in Rwanda. The genocide took place some time in 1994. Over one million people died in the Rwandan genocide.

Other global conflict that plagued his administration—for which he was criticized for either inaction or failure to act effectively—includes the crisis of the Yugoslav wars after the former Yugoslavia disintegrated. One of the larger controversies that Mr. Boutros-Ghali was faced with during his administration was the bigger question of the effectiveness of the U.N. system, and the role of the United States in the U.N.

Boutros-Ghali was nominated for a second five-year term in 1996, by ten members of the Security Council. His nomination for a second term was vetoed by the United States. Poland, South Korea, Italy, and the United Kingdom did not support the resolution of the ten members of the Security Council, but the four nations voted in support of Boutros-Ghali after the United States declared the intention to veto the second term in office for Mr. Boutros-Ghali. He was the first secretary-general not to be elected to a second term in office, but he was not the first to be vetoed. Secretary-General Kurt Waldheim was vetoed by China in 1981 for his third term in office.

Boutros-Ghali pleaded for assistance to increase public awareness of the work of the United Nations. In his speech he spoke of the upcoming U.N. fiftieth anniversary celebration, and the opportune time to increase public awareness of the role of the world organization. It was to be a year of activities in 1995; marking the fiftieth anniversary of the United Nations. He called on all UNA organizations to reach out to our communities to mobilize public support for the world organization.

We formed a queue at the end of the event to meet the secretary-general. The line was very long because many people wanted to meet him. Ethel and I moved a long in the line; we met him and shook hands with him. He was indeed a petite man. My thoughts as I shook his hand were "a small man to carry the world on his shoulders'. It was a pleasure to have met the secretary-general.

As my first national convention wound down to a close there was a final plenary session to attend. The organization's business that was taken care of in this session was the installation of new officers and new board members. After that session wrapped up we had a final round of mingling with other UNA-USA members, then everyone began to check out of the hotel to return to their respective chapters and divisions. We exchanged final notes, say our farewell and headed home.

I left the meeting with a sense of accomplishment. I did not expect that so many people would attend the annual meeting. We collected a lot of information to share with our Greater Miami members. I regretted that I did not get the chance to visit our corporate headquarters. It was only a short distance away, but we did not have sufficient time to do that, and the icy conditions in the city hampered our mobility. It would have been especially nice to have gone on the same airfare that took us to New York City. Ethel and I paid our way. Our chapter did not have sufficient funds to cover our trip. I plan to visit the national headquarters the next time I am in New York City.

The national convention of January 1994 was my very first national meeting as president of the local Greater Miami chapter. It was great to have so many chapter and division presidents, model U.N. groups, our corporate staff, officers and leaders of UNA-USA, and so many people from our council of organizations at the convention. It was a wonderful experience meeting the secretary-general Boutros-Ghali, former assistant secretary-general Giandomenico Picco, and other U.N. officials. We were extremely motivated to build on the momentum for our UN50 celebrations. Our participation in the annual meeting solidifies our connectivity by being a part of a larger body.

CHAPTER 3

S HORTLY AFTER RETURNING from our national convention Ethel and I sent a notice of a board meeting to our board members, it was already the end of January and we had a lot of work to do for 1994. We need to start working on our state annual meeting which is to take place sometime between the spring and summer of 1994. We need all of our board members on board as quickly as possible to get the ball rolling by creating the committees, and to start working on different aspects of the state meeting There were many considerations to take into account including speakers, activities, venue, brochures, and other good stuff.

Ethel and I compiled a report of the national convention. This report was included in our first newsletter for 1994 and mailed to our members. We announced the board meeting in the newsletter. Ethel also sent a separate letter to all board members announcing the board meeting. Our bylaws require a letter to be sent to each board member at least two week before the meeting is to take place, so we observed the protocol.

Before the board meeting took place, I made a pit stop to see my parish priest. I needed spiritual guidance. I had some quiet time since the annual meeting. I was able to settle down and process my experiences and the information that I collected. I enjoyed the annual meeting and learned a lot of new things while I was there. However, when I read the information I took home with me and realized the world I had entered, I thought it best to get some spiritual guidance, and it was also time for me to touch home base with my faith. It is not that I am not always in touch with my faith, but I figured I could use extra help.

I contacted the secretary of St. Andrew Catholic Church, Coral Springs, Florida, and made an appointment to see Father Mullins. We met one week later. We greeted each other as we met in the front office, then I followed his lead into one of the quiet offices for discussion. Father Mullins prayed then we recited the Lord's Prayer. After our prayers he asked me, "Sister Sylvia, what's going on?" I told him why I came to see him.

I told him that in addition to touching home base, I was involved with UNA-USA, and I am the local chapter president. The organization with which I am involved supports the United Nations although not an uncritical supporter. My concerns were not so much about the people with whom I was working, because I believe that they are good people, but it was about the external exposure to an environment where bad people did bad things to others. He asked me to expand on what I said. I put it straight to him and told him that although I do no mind leading activities in our chapter for our community, I did not wish or want to become corrupted. Therefore, I was seeking his guidance.

He looked me straight in the eyes and gave me a big smile. He was very empathetic. He understood the potential of becoming a corrupted leader. I told him that in my leadership role, I have no intention of becoming Jesus. I remembered having a similar discussion with my parish priest in Canada. My intentions were not to have a godlike leadership role but one of a team leader. Many people believe that by its very nature the United Nations is the most political institution in the world. My role as chapter president was not with the United Nations but with UNA-USA. I want to keep it real and not confuse the two organizations.

I once had a discussion with my parish priest about the role leadership in the family as well as in the community. I understood the responsibility and accountability of leadership, but at the same time I did not wish to have a godlike persona. The potential of leadership influence on others is an awesome responsibility, it is important to keep the experience real. To be unrealistic and overly inflated may lead people down the wrong path. It was my intention to stay clear of those practices. My priest and I laughed when he commented in the affirmative that Jesus tried to save the world, he was god, and he died a young man.

The moral of the comment was that it was not wise to adopt a godlike persona in leadership; effective leadership embraces honesty, sincerity, integrity, wisdom, knowledge, understanding, and applicable leadership skills, and in all instances I must maintain my humanity. We are prone to mistakes and shortcomings, so even though we may have high expectations of self and others, it must be balance with awareness of our limitations. My values are anchored in my faith because it is the essence of my being. We must inspire and motivate others to act appropriately in a correct manner, thereby encouraging changes and improvements where and when needed.

I have seen and heard of leaders who inspired their followers to do wrong that impact the lives of others in a destructive way. It is not unusual for any type of conflict to erupt during the course of our lives. Observing the DNA or root cause of those conflicts is a way of going about finding a resolution. In other words the solution is in the problem. At least for those conflicts that naturally occur from human interaction, regardless of whether they are of difference of opinion, or from transactional interchange; they usually have a DNA. The worst conflicts are usually the types that are manufactured. Those do not have DNAs and thus all that one is left to contend with is that the proof is in the pudding.

Manufactured conflicts usually arise from leadership, or better yet, the lack thereof. I have seen and heard manufactured conflicts stemming from pulpits and podiums usually having no base in reality, and in turn those types of conflicts may create a chain of destructive reactions and actions with the potentials of destroying people's lives. Bad leadership is power to abuse and it should not be encouraged.

. Father Mullins and I had a very good discussion. He helped me to mirror my thoughts and to sort them out in relationship to my faith. It was worthwhile to sit and discussed with him my new role and apprehensions. We talked about my family and how my children were doing. We discussed other matters relating to stewardship at church. Before our session ended he prayed for me and gave me his blessings. I left the church office still not certain of what lies on the horizon, but strengthened because I was anchored in my faith.

Our session ended, Father Mullins walked me to the entrance of the church, we said farewell to each other, and I went my way. I got in my car; started the engine, and drove out of the parking lot. As I drove onto the street, I hit the play button on the cassette player. *Good,* I said to myself. Paul Simon's song "*You Can Call Me Al*" started to play. *Graceland* is one of my favorite albums.

The day of our board meeting arrived. The president of Broward County Chapter, Dr. Blanca Moore-Velez was present. We sent her a letter announcing the board meeting. Since the primary focus of the board meeting was the state annual meeting, it was important for her to be present. The state meeting was a joint effort by both chapters.

We held a brainstorming session in the board meeting. We had a map of the activities that were usually expected at the annual meeting, but we did not know how to fill them. We came up with a lot of shared ideas. The first item on our list was venue. We toyed with a lot of ideas of where we want the event to take place. We settled on three locations. Ethel, Hyman Mally our treasurer, Dr. Blanca Moore-Velez, and I were delegated to visit the venues and make the final selection from among the three hotels.

Our treasurer must be present in any financial decisions. Florida Division gave us an advance of $500.00 for deposit for the hotel. All of our programs are expected to be self-supporting. The $500.00 was expected to be repaid to the Florida Division. We setup a planning committee for the annual meeting and delegated members to be on the committee. After the meeting we moved quickly to check out the locations that were suggested.

We were moving quickly to secure the place for the event because we did not want to loose out on our choices. It was the high-demand season for hotel bookings due to seasonal conventions, and high school proms, to name a few. We preferred an attractive location that was accessible, and one that would showcase our local community. Guests and attendees were expected to make their reservations for the entire three days of events. Therefore we need a location that provided some attractions and one that was close to everything.

We discussed our choice of locations and agreed that being close to the beach was definitely a plus. Another important consideration was a location that was somewhere between the Broward County and Greater Miami Chapters. This way all members would have ease of access especially for those members who would be commuting daily to the event. Some members may prefer to commute each day instead of paying the cost to stay at the hotel. We were a volunteer organization and must consider the cost of every activity to our members. Paying out of pocket for events and activities are additional expenses to our members' personal and family budgets. Team members care about each other in every way.

We visited the three hotels. We considered and assessed the costs, menus, and other amenities. The Marco Polo Beach Resort on Collins Avenue in Sunny Isle, Florida became our target. We had a grand tour of the hotel; we looked at the meeting rooms, grand ballroom, and its surroundings. It was a beautiful oceanfront resort located within proximity to the city of Miami and Broward County. It was close to everything. South Beach was a few blocks down the road from the hotel, Miami Bayside and its attractions were just across the bay. Fort Lauderdale was only minutes away to the north. The resort was right on the ocean. We decided on that location for the state annual meeting.

It was a family friendly oceanfront beach hotel. We negotiated price and flexibility. Mr. Mally who travelled with checkbook in hand drew up a check for the deposit to conditionally lock in the venue. The booking agent took preliminary information. We signed a conditional agreement. We agreed to meet in one month to finalize arrangements for the event. We turned in a copy of the agreement to the chair of the planning committee. One item on the list of things to do was now completed.

The planning committee worked on all aspects of the state annual meeting. The final product will be presented for final approval at the next board meeting. Some of Broward County's board members and officers were also members of the planning committee. It was a joint effort. The next consideration was pricing of attendance and registrations for the event. Program content was a work in progress. A list of speakers, panelists, workshops, and entertainment were in the works. Ethel, Hyman, Blanca and I started to work on a sponsorship list for events. Some of those events were luncheons, dinners and award ceremonies.

While we were in the process of planning for the state meeting, I received a telephone call from the national office. A request came from the national programs director that I serve as the U.N. observer at the South African poling station that was scheduled to take place in Miami. This was being done to accommodate South African citizens who were either travelling or living outside of their country.

"Wow! I do not know anything about being a U.N. observer" I said to Jim Olson. He explained to me that I will be provided with instructions, but I must choose one other member of our chapter to assist me.

I was honored to be asked to serve and to be a part of such a historic, and an important event. I did a critical assessment while I thought about the request. I found no reasons why I could not assist, so I accepted the role. I told Jim that I will await instructions on exactly what is expected of me.

In March 1994, the United States Department of State, Office of Southern African Affairs, in cooperation with the United States Federal Election Commission, developed an arrangement so that South African citizens living in the United States could participate in the election that was set for April 26, 1994. The arrangement also involved the South African Embassy in Washington, DC, the Independent Electoral Commission in South Africa, and the South African Mission in the United States. There were a total of fifteen voting stations set up across the nation in different states, based on the number of South African citizens residing in the locality.

There were five stations in New York City, three in Los Angeles, three in San Diego, three in Chicago, two in San Francisco, and one station in Philadelphia, Raleigh, Houston, Dallas, Miami, Washington, DC, Boston, Atlanta, and Phoenix. Information by way of press releases was put out by the South African Embassy in Washington, DC, stating where the voting stations were, and what documents were needed in order to vote. Among the criteria and documents needed to vote in the election were being South African, being eighteen years of age or older and living in the United States, and possessing one of the following valid South African documents: passport, dark-blue ID book, green plastic card, or small black/brown reference book. Voter registration was not a requirement, and the date for voting was set for April 26, 1994, from 7:00 a.m. until 7:00 p.m.

I chose Ethel our vice president, to assist me on the assignment. She was absolutely delighted at the opportunity. Ten days before the election was to take place, I received my information packet containing my appointment letter, instructions, and materials to assist in the assignment. I was instructed on protocol in dealing with the media and others, completing the process, conducting observation, behavior, and reporting. I was provided instructions to fax my report to the Independent Electoral Commission at the end of the day.

In addition to faxing the report, I was also required to make a telephone call to the National Operations Center of the Independent Electoral Commission to leave a duplicate verbal report. I was to identify the voting station, provide the number of ballot bags, and the number of seals that were attached to the inner bag. I was also to provide a narrative on whether or not the polling station seemed to have operated in a free and fair fashion.

On the day of the election, I was up at the crack of dawn. I got ready and was on my way to meet with Ethel as we planned. She is to bring peanut butter and banana sandwiches. It was our favorite and staple for travelling or when on assignment. I told her that I will bring fruits and drinks. It was a twelve hours assignment from open to close, and we figured an extra hour for the wrapping up of activities. We had no plans of taking a lunch break, but we figured if the voting traffic slowed down, we could take turns with a five minute break to have a bite to eat. It was easy to slip a sandwich, a can of soda pop, and a fruit in each of our pocket book.

Ethel and I arrived at our destination on time. She pulled into the parking lot ahead of me; I followed about two car lengths behind her. I looked at the clock on my dashboard. It was 6:30 a.m. I pulled into the spot beside Ethel's car. I parked the car, gather my pocket book and exit the car. We greeted each other with a hug and smiles. We stepped back, looked at each other, then broke out laughing.

Unknowingly, we wore similar outfits. We both wore blue suits of slightly different shades, white blouses, black shoes, and carried black pocketbooks. "We are wearing the same outfit and perfect for the occasion I see" Ethel said." So we are, great minds think alike" I replied. We briefly ran through our preparation. We recapped our prepared responses for media questions, and then walked to the entrance of the poling station. Our response to any media question was simply to state that we were there to observe that the election and voting process was conducted in an open and fair manner.

We entered the poling station, reported our presence, and signed in. Voting officers and agents wore armbands as identification. The hall was arranged to have a smooth flow of traffic, and to allow voters to cast ballots in secret. Signs, notices, and posters graced the hall. The polls open at 7:00 a.m. An usher guided the voters through the long lines, and ensured that each voter had proper identification, and necessary documents.

The voter's first stop was at the UV lamp operator, who checked to ensure that the voter had not voted before. In this process, the voter placed hands with palms down under the UV lamp to check if there were signs of ink stains on either hands. After the UV lamp check of hands, the next step was to move forward to the document check officer for the examination of documents and age verification. If the officer is satisfied that documents are valid, they were stamped and returned to the voter. After that checkpoint, the voter was directed to the marking officer. The voter's fingers on the right hand, including nails, were marked with invisible ink. The fingers were then wiped and placed under the UV lamp to ensure that the fingers were properly marked.

The voter's next step was to complete an affidavit indicating the province for which he or she wished to vote. After that, the voter was given his or her national ballot paper. When that was completed, the voting officer stamped and folded the paper. The voter is then showed to a vacant voting booth by an usher to mark his or her secret ballot, then refold the paper with the markings hidden, and placed the paper into the national inner envelope. The voter then returned to the voting table to follow the same procedure in the provincial ballot. Both ballots were inserted into a large brown envelope by the voter, and then it was deposited into the ballot box.

Disputes were resolved by the presiding officer, and may involve not having the correct documents, or the voter may have voted previously, or if the identification did not match the voter. Provisions were made to assist blind or physically disabled voters with assistance by the presiding officer. Considerations and provisions were also made for spoiled ballots. If a ballot was in error, the voter may return the spoiled ballot, and received a new one, but only after surrendering the spoiled ballot, that a new one was issued. All voting was done by paper ballots. The voters were instructed on how to cast their vote by making an X for the party of his or her choice.

Our role as U.N. observers was not limited to the inside of the polling station only. We also walked the grounds outside of the voting station, and conducted our observations. Ethel and I took turns to ensure that at all times one of us was inside the voting station observing the voters and the voting officials. We walked the grounds of the voting station periodically. The media was not allowed inside the voting station, but they were camped out on the grounds of the premises.

I was approached several times by the media when I walked the grounds. They made several inquiries on what is taking place. My response was the same each time they approached me. "We are U.N. observers and our purpose is to observe that the election is free, open, and fair." Ethel reported that she had similar experiences and was asked the same questions by the media when she walked the grounds. She responded to the media in the same fashion. Some of the media reporters accepted that response while others kept pressing for more information. Pressing did not help them any because they were given the same response at all times.

The voting station was closed promptly at 7:00 p.m. We observed the final procedures in handling all ballots and papers. Used and unused ballots were procedurally handled and finalized by the signing of statements, and placing seals on all materials to be returned to the Independent Electoral Commission. We waited until the courier arrived. The sealed bags were loaded onto the courier vehicles. The courier left for the airport where the bags were flown to their final destination.

Our work at the voting station was now completed. Before we left we took a few minutes to speak with the officials. It was the first since we greeted earlier that morning that we spoke with them. I smiled at the presiding officer and shook his hand. He looked at me then he laughed and said, "You were stoic. I did not know you would smile at me." I smiled again at told him that far from being stoic, it was the moment and the nature of the moment. Ethel and I said farewell to all then we left the premises.

It was indeed a historic day, one that was observed with respect, and reverence in silence. My role was not yet completed. I drove to my office to complete the reports. I took notes of information that I may need while completing the report. By the time I reached my office it was approximately 9:45pm. I went up the stairs to the second floor, unlocked the doors to my office and switch on the lights. I disarm the alarm then sat at my desk to complete the report.

I completed the report with all information according to the instructions that were given to me: the number of ballot bags, number of seals that were attached to the inner ballot bag, name and registration number of monitor, and a brief narrative of whether or not I observed a free and open election. I signed the report then faxed it according to the instructions that were provided in my information packet.

I also made a telephone call to the telephone number that was provided, and left a message duplicating the written reported as instructed. At all times while performing my functions, I was aware of the significance and nature of such a historic day. It was an honor to participate in the first universal franchise election of South Africa.

I contacted Jim Olson at our national office the next day, and on behalf of Ethel and myself, expressed our gratitude for the opportunity to participate in South African election as U.N. observers. A U.N. observer is not an unusual request for UNA-USA chapter leaders. It was unique because it was the first universal election for South Africa, but it would have been the same for any global issues involving the U.N. where assistance was needed with the implementation of any program.

Many of our chapter members have participated in different events elsewhere in the globe. Those events may concern economic development, sustainable development, or human rights issues. Those type of duties and performing them are above and beyond the call of chapter work, but our members are willing to provide assistance where needed. I discussed earlier that we are not "Mickey" but dedicated and committed volunteers who will go any lengths for a good cause. The success of our chapter is driven by teamwork. Whenever anyone is asked to perform above and beyond duties, our committee members carry on the work of such an individual to prevent any interruption of our chapter work.

By late spring of 1994 our two chapters Broward and Miami picked up the pace for our annual state meeting. The planning committee had a full list of activities, and workshops that were going to take place. Bear in mind that even though we were hosting the event, all activities include the participation of all of our chapters in the Florida Division. We also incorporated input from our Model United Nations, Campus Network, and our Council of Organizations. Our host chapters worked a considerable amount of hours to put the program together.

With an underlying credo of diversity across the board, we engaged an inclusive policy to enrich our programs by encouraging participation. Thematically, we solicited ideas and volunteers from all regions. Likewise, we sought and found speakers from a wide variety of interests for our audiences. With such diverse participation we expected to have five hundred people or more at the three-day event.

We were ready to finalize all arrangements for our state annual meeting. Hyman, Ethel, Blanca, and I visited the Marco Polo Resort hotel to meet with the booking agent. At this meeting we were to provide our final numbers for each segment of annual meeting; luncheons, dinners, workshops and so on. We were asked to estimate the number of rooms for guests so that a block of rooms could be reserved.

All of our logistics were ready and in hand. We knew the type of equipment such as overhead viewers, microphones, and how many we need. We were rolling right along in our meeting. We described what type of decorations should be placed on the tables and for which part of the event. We described how and where banners are to be placed. We supplied the banners and flags.

All details were completely worked out, and it was done in such a way to ensure equal display from both chapters and our sponsors. We did excellent in providing the logistics for each event. Not all of registrations were in as of yet, but by the numbers of members in each of our chapters in the state of Florida, and by preliminary commitments, we did a pretty good job of coming up with the estimates.

Well! We did very well up to the point where we had to provide the estimates for our last dinner. This was our "black tie" affair UNA-way. It was our celebratory and awards presentation event for our annual state meeting. The agent asked us what the numbers are for the dinner. We were going to have the dinner in the ballroom. Broward chapter had an estimated number and so did Miami chapter. After much discussion Ethel said we would probably have seventy five people. I shook my head to disagree with her and said I believe that it will be more like two hundred people.

Ethel said, "I do not know where two hundred people will come from, you are probably good at pulling a bird out of a hat". Are we heading to a faux paux, I thought to myself, but we were doing so well. We laughed at Ethel's magician inference. After much ado over the number of people for the award dinner, it was finally decided that because I had the final say by executive privilege, and 200 was the magic number.

Traditionally, the state annual meeting is somewhat low-keyed; however, in view of the changing times and the upcoming UN50 celebrations, and goals of increased public awareness, the state annual meeting was planned with those objectives in mind; we turned up the volume a notch just like our national convention. We expected a larger than usual attendance at the 1994 state annual meeting. We included several workshops and programs on global awareness. This in turn expanded our reach of audience. We finalized our arrangements with the hotel and provided all the information that was needed to get the venue ready for the event.

We had a board meeting to go over everything for the state meeting. Our speakers and panelists were confirmed. Soon after that we mailed out invitations and registration forms to all members of all chapters and to the Florida division. We continued to respond to any changes that occurred. Our board members and our planning committee were on the upbeat because everything was going well, considering the narrow window of time within which we put the annual meeting together.

I felt a strong sense of relief that every thing was moving along smoothly. The meeting was only weeks away. Registrations were rolling in. I just knew we were going to have a record attendance at the meeting. Our participants were looking forward to conducting their workshops and presentations.

Ms. Ernestine Ray, chairperson for our entertainment committee who was also the curator of the Dillard Museum in Fort Lauderdale, and a member of the Broward County Chapter, telephoned me and reported a big problem. I was sitting in the family room listening to the radio when Ernestine called. I turned down the volume so that I could hear her clearly. Ms. Ray said she had some serious concerns with the entertainment.

The entertainment as listed on the program was a fashion show to be accompanied with drum beating and singers. Now she told me that the fashion show included teeny weeny bikinis and that she just found that out. And that was not all; the drummer wore dreaded dread locks. I did not immediately see what the problem was with the fashion show. I asked her what the problem was. She said she had not preview the show before making the agreement but now wondered if it would be in good taste for the event.

Everything was set to go. All the programs were printed. We could not afford to hire entertainers. The board already signed off on everything. I asked her why it wasn't brought to our attention before now. She said that there was no place or time to have seen the show in its entirety before the annual meeting. I had not seen the group perform before, but I trusted Ms. Ray's professionalism, and her ability to choose an entertainment suitable for the dinner. Ms. Ray told us that the fashion show would be thematic with the accompanying bongo drums. There was not much that I could say right at the moment when she called. I told her to give me a day and let me see what can be done.

We did not have a lot of financial resources to pay for entertainers, but we agreed to make a small donation for our entertainers. Other mutual benefits would come from the exposure at the event. We often used mutual benefits, such as exposure, as a way to secure the services. Now it appears that we really are going to be in for real exposure. I understood her predicament. We only had a small window of time to develop the entire program. We operated in an trusting environment. I am sure she did her best in securing the entertainers, and it might have been a slight oversight by forgetting the entertainers to describe details such as the type of attire that will be paraded in the fashion show.

Our agreement was not a quid pro quo basis, but because we did not have sufficient financial resource, and the services were for a good cause, the exposure of the service provider on our brochures may generate more business to the group. It was even better if our attendees liked the entertainment, and expressed interest in using the same group for their events. Ms. Ray worked very hard to coordinate the entertainment for our dinner.

It was only a few days before out state meeting. It was very unlikely that we could arrange for a new entertainment at this last minute. I did not know if it was possible to exclude any part of the fashion show. The programs were already printed, and materials for the annual meeting were mailed out. It was too short a time to call a board meeting for discussion about the matter, and there wasn't enough time to get new entertainment.

I turned up the volume on the radio; I need an escape for a little while. Perhaps it will all go away, I thought to myself. I just could not think about it right now. Just at that moment I said thank you to Paul Simon: *When I think back on all the crap I learned in high school it's a wonder I can think at all;* Wow!, James Brown: *I am a soul man;* I slid across the floor of the living room, first to the right and then to the left as I clapped my hands. James Brown could not touch me in this one; Wow! Before I could stop it was Bryan Adams; to the rescue with the *Summer of 69.* The Bee Gees *Jive talking,* set the pace for my cooling down, but it was really Don McLean's *American Pie* that caused me to breathe in and out deeply.

Finally, I slowed down. I completed my work out. It was now time to deal with the issue. I turned down the volume on the radio and picked up the telephone to call Ethel. I told her about the problem with our entertainment. Ethel said she will call the chair of the planning committee. Most of our board members were also members of the planning committee. Ethel called me back a few hours later. She told me that she ran it by the planning committee and that the board members were also aware of the situation. "Sylvia, it is your call" she said to me. I told Ethel that I will sleep on it. I knew I had broken my commitment to myself. One of my personal commitments was that I would never take any issue concerning volunteer work to bed. I need to have a good nights sleep in order to function properly doing all the things I was doing.

I slept on it and made my decision the next day. I thought of seniors and youths, I thought of the audience being able to digest their meals properly, I considered all the possible scenarios. We were having an annual meeting, but it was an UN-oriented activity. We embraced diversity and inclusivity. There were no definitions or classifications as to what is meant by diversity or inclusivity. Therefore, I saw no reasons to exclude our entertainment from the program provided it is of good taste and was not offensive to the audience.

If I were to remove the entertainment from the program, then in fact, I would be acting on exclusion instead of inclusion, and that would be counteractive to our creed and motto. But then, I do not know what the entertainment is like, I have never seen the fashion show, I do not know if it is in good taste. If it is not in good taste then my UNA-USA Greater Miami presidency would go down in sleaze and dirt, I thought to myself.

I backed up a little; I did not particularly like that thought of sleaze and dirt. I am the team leader I thought, I was delegated to make the call. Therefore although I am the one who will make the call, we all will share the blame if there are any repercussions. With that thought I made a decision and hoped for the best; the worst that could happen was the beating of the bongos. I contacted Ms. Ray and told her that the program will stay as is, and wished the entertainers well. She was a bit apprehensive but was happy that we are going to proceed as planned with the fashion show.

The annual state meeting was an astounding success. One of the more popular workshops was presented by Professor Jeanne Kates of Florida International University. She presented the global classrooms and explained to the audience of over 150 people; how products sold in one country are assembled in another, having parts that are manufactured in different countries. The audience showed keen interest in the global interactive environment.

The dinner and award ceremony had a full house packed with more than 250 people. I told Ethel I pulled the rabbit out of the hat not the bird. The dinner was held in the main ballroom. We had a featured speaker from the United Nations representing peacekeeping operations. Jim Olson, our national programs chair, represented UNA-USA national office. Several local officials were in attendance, including the chairman of Dade County Commission, Arthur Teele.

As the chairman entered the ballroom one of his attendants entered before him and announced his presence. It was out of the ordinary, but no one minded a bit. Arthur Teele later followed with a grand entrance and pageantry that was befitted to a lord or duke. Linda Horkitz and other board members were in awe. They clapped and cheered till everyone joined in, we were simply having fun. We were also hoping to receive a grant for our fiftieth UN celebration from the Dade County Commission. Perhaps the cheering for the chairman was a precursory to our chapter getting some funds from the Commission. Jim Olson made of point of raising the question during his speech. Mr. Teele acknowledged, and publicly made a commitment that he would do everything in his powers to help us with the UN50 celebration.

One of the awards given was presented in recognition of good works, and contributions to our chapter's activities. The recipient was SGI-USA. The Soka Gakkai International is a Buddhist organization. Mr. Tony Sugano, who was the leader of the organization, assisted us by providing volunteers who served on a number of different committees. Soka Gakkai International is an NGO with the United Nations. When our board elected to present Mr. Sugano with an award, he asked that it be presented instead to Mr. Ikeda, the leader of the organization who was in Japan. Tony explained to us that presenting the award to the head of the organization was protocol and customary in Japan. Our board agreed to his request. The award was presented to Mr. Ikeda and accepted by Tony Sugano and his wife at the dinner.

Everyone enjoyed the festivities, presentations, speeches, and dinner. We had different menu selections, all this to ensure that all of our guests would be comfortable and have a good time. Special arrangements were made for those who did not eat anything on the menu. We created a warm and friendly environment. Our choice of location was the perfect setting, we knew this because of the compliments received from our guests.

The presentations of the awards were over. It was time to roll the drums and turn our eyes to the stage at the far end of the room. The stage created a bit of curiosity all evening sitting there with the curtains closed. No one knew what was behind those curtains. The golden curtains began to open slowly. The stage was laid out thematically with an African decor.

The drummers began to beat bongos. The lights on the stage came on and so did the fashion show. First was a show of casual wear. The beautiful young ladies walked to the rhythm of the drums. The audience silently looked on. The show progressed as different outfits for different occasions where modeled. The momentum of the fashion show continued to build, and so did the rhythms of the bongos. The applause by the audience increased with each presentation.

I continue to build up anxiety because I knew what was coming, so were Ethel and Ernestine. Then there they were, the women wearing their teeny weeny bikinis. I sat on the edge of my seat waiting for the big moan of disapproval.

Well! Guess what? It never happened. The audience cheered and led out a loud laughter of enjoyment. Laughter and applause was pouring out so much, the roof was almost lifted off the ballroom. It was wonderful to hear the applause. I took a deep breath and let out a great sigh of relief, and then I joined in the laughter. One may have thought that it would have been only the elderly gentlemen who would be cheering; on the contrary it was not so at all. Everyone was cheering and having fun. The teeny weeny bikinis worn by the models were the icing on the cake at our UN Day 1994. It was a superb grand finale to our festivities. Our entire planning committee shared the credits, we were a great team.

The *Sun Sentinel* in the next-day's paper dubbed the performance "*a cultural show with an African beat.*" It was a superb way of wrapping up our event. Our state annual meeting continued with our final plenary session on Sunday morning. Our Treasurer reported that all costs and expenses were covered and settled. He also reported that a check was drawn to repay the five hundred dollars that was advanced by Florida Division.

The Florida Division board members were very pleased and proud of the event and the way it was conducted. They liked the way the programs were developed and executed. All of our Florida chapters' leaders congratulated the Miami and Broward chapters for our hard work and a successful meeting. We were asked to turn over data and information collected to the Tampa Bay chapter to be used in planning the next annual meeting.

The board members of our chapter and the Broward chapter remained at the hotel while our guests departed. We stayed to collect all materials such as our flags, posters, and table decorations that were provided by both chapters. While we were collecting the flags and the floral arrangements, Ethel jokingly said two of our miniature flags were missing from the set. Hyman chuckled before saying that we will have to replace those flags as quickly as possible, because if we didn't we are going to face another conspiracy accusation at the next event.

Time and time again we have been accused of conspiracy because of missing flags. At some of our events unknowingly to us, some of our flags disappear from our miniature flag set. We do not know how the flags disappear because none of our members have ever witnessed anyone taking them; all we know is that somebody or people kept on taking our flags from the set.

We have never memorize the flag of each member state that is represented in the miniature set; all we do is count them to see if they are all there by the number of Member States to the United Nations. The one thing for sure is that if any one of our guests do not see his or her home country flag in the set we will be accused of conspiracy because of the missing flag. If a discussion develops around the missing flag, which is usually the case most of the time; it will go into deeper issues than just the missing flag.

The issues that sometimes develop around missing country flags on several occasions wound up being linked to US foreign policy and issues on the United Nations agenda. We do not like to be accused of conspiracy because it is usually not the case. Sometimes we explained that the flags are mistakenly removed for souvenirs, and we have not had a chance to replace the ones that are missing. Sometimes that explanation is accepted and at other times it does not hold water.

We are often faced with the tedious task of defending ourselves. We did not wish to accuse any our guests of stealing our flags, but that is just what happened most of the times. Our flag sets are expensive; we do not have the funds to be dishing out every time to replace missing flags. We are very careful with our flags. It was bad enough having to replace them but even worse to be accused of conspiracy Discussions of missing flags often lead to other issues or better yet the real issues that are on peoples minds. In situations like those, our board becomes very proactive and may invite the individual to present their issues in one of our meetings.

At the grassroots level depending on the issue, we may draft a resolution, which is then processed through our local debate. If the issue has sufficient support, we will act on it by sending letters to our congressional representative or prepare the resolution to be submitted at our national or state annual meeting to move through the processing rank.

Our chapter had one more major event for the year; 1994 UN Day observance. That event was scheduled for October 24, 1994. We had big plans for that U.N. Day. It was also the launching of UN 50 which will be a year long set of programs and activities leading up to the fiftieth anniversary of the United Nations. Although October 24 is the official date on which the UN Day is celebrated, some chapters may have their celebration either a week earlier or a week later.

The observance of UN Day is a tradition of UNA-USA. It is one of those yearly activities that encourages public outreach to all sectors of the community. Public outreach included providing information not only on the works of the U.N. but also those of UNA-USA, and to bring the public's attention to pressing global issues, and information on how our country participates with the world organization. An integral part of the program is to encourage youth involvement and outreach by providing speakers to those organizations in the community who are also observing U.N. Day.

A local chapter may select any number of themes for U.N. Day activities. Some chapters choose themes of international cuisine while others may have a U.N. Day luncheon with keynote speakers addressing topics about the United Nations. U.N. Day 1994 was important to our local chapter because it was our launching of UN50 and the point from where we planned to build our momentum for our year long set of activities and programs.

The history of U.N. Day began in the spring of 1945. Representatives of fifty nations met in San Francisco to finalize the drafting of the Charter of the United Nations, a document that would have far-reaching effect. The United States was a leader in the drafting of the document, which went into effect on October 24, 1945. Two years after the charter became effective, the General Assembly adopted a resolution sponsored by the United States declaring and designating October 24 as U.N. Day.

Since 1947, U.N. Day has been observed in nations large and small around the world. Each president in the United States, beginning with Harry Truman, has issued proclamation asking citizens to observe U.N. Day, reflecting on the importance of the United Nations to our national interest as well as to each one of us. At the time the United Nations Charter was drafted, almost one hundred US national non-governmental organizations were represented at San Francisco. They provided advice and support to the official U.S. delegation. United States Committee for the United Nations grew out of those organizations and was consulted regularly by the U.S. government on matters related to the United Nations.

One of the traditions in planning a U.N. Day program is the appointment of a U.N. Day chairperson. In 1961, President John F. Kennedy appointed Robert S. Benjamin, chairman of the United Artists Corporation, as the first National United Nations Day Chairman. Local chapters mirror national office U.N. Day activities by also appointing a local U.N. Day chairperson. In 1964, the U.S. committee for the Untied Nations merged with the Association for the United Nations to become the United Nations Association of the United States of America (UNA-USA).

Robert Benjamin was the first leader of UNA-USA, and later, other outstanding Americans took on the coordination and supervision of the National U.N. Day program, working closely with the national U.N. Day chairperson. The celebration of U.N. Day in hundreds of communities all over the United States has changed significantly. In the early years, U.N. Day observance tended to be symbolic events consisting of an international dinner in the town or in the town's high school. Sometimes the U.N. flag would be flown from an official building. Today's U.N. Day programs focus on world issues on the agenda of the United Nations that affect our lives. University campuses, city hall, and the governor's mansion have become sites for serious debates of issues before the U.N. and how to approach them through international cooperation.

The generation born after the founding of the U.N. in 1945 has come to realize that the U.N. offers no quick fix but is an instrument through which multilateral processes to solve global problems are made possible. The United

Nations Day Program will continue to offer the opportunity to succeeding generations to acquaint themselves with the activities and accomplishments of the U.N. system in the years ahead.

Our chapter's celebration of U.N. Day is a major interactive activity with our community. We look forward to direct interactions with our schools and colleges, the local media, flag-raising ceremonies, festivals, luncheons, dinners, cooperative organizations, and conferences in our community. Our levels of interactions are usually multilateral and diverse, involving people from all walks of life. We invite others to join us in celebration, and likewise, others invite us to participate in their events.

The production of a U.N. Day program is very similar to producing any other civic or community program. All effective programs have a common focus or a theme or issue that appeal to a wide audience. When the topic coincides with community concerns, it is even more appealing to a large audience; this allows the participation of a large number of people and organizations. The first step in producing a U.N. Day program is to form a planning committee.

A planning committee should be considered as a wide-area network. Efforts should be made to reach out to people of varied interests and talents. Some people who are sensitive to the issues or citizens' concerns will suggest ways in which the theme of U.N. Day can be made relevant to the community at large. Among those to be included in the planning committee membership forming a wide-area network are young people, students, teachers, school administrators, representatives of civic and other voluntary organizations, local business leaders, and government authorities.

The objective in having a broad-based U.N. Day committee is to help in attracting a broad-based audience. Once the planning committee has been established, it can then be broken down into smaller units or teams, thus being able to divide the work. Small groups or teams could be assigned to do program planning, publicity and media relations, fund-raising, invitations and speakers, program printing, and liaison with schools and community. The more diverse the planning committee, the more enriched the participation level will be and the more resources that will become available from the talent pool.

Publicity and media relations are very important in publicizing U.N. Day program. The newspapers and television and radio stations that service the local community can play a major role in the U.N. program because it can help in reaching a greater number of people. The key to obtaining the support and assistance of the media is to involve editors and station managers directly in the U.N. Day program and activities. Invite them to play a role, not just simply to publicize the event.

Working with the media is not a simple undertaking, but there are certain steps to take to make the effort less laborious. Assembling a press kit and doing press releases are some ways to overcome the challenges of working with the media. The press kit may include a copy of the mayor or governor's U.N. Day proclamation, a concise one-page press release describing the overall U.N. Day program, the prominent individuals who will be participating in the particular events, and the organizations that are cooperating in the effort.

A good press release answers the questions who, what, when, where, and why in its first paragraph. The press release should also bid for attention based on the importance of the theme or issue of U.N. Day and its timeliness as connected to current events. The unique nature of the program and the personalities who are participating can also help to capture the editors or media attention. Editors are likely to pick up on the story if the spadework is done for them, giving the titles that go with the names and the source of a particular piece of information or quotation.

Generally, gaining access to the print media is not difficult, and the cost is usually no more than what it would cost for a stamp or a phone call. Some techniques to accomplish this include writing letters to the editor about current U.N.-related issues that are not getting enough attention or about instances of inaccuracies or incomplete reporting. Sharing those concerns with influential members of the community and attempting to enlist those individuals as signers of those letters can also be helpful.

It is more difficult gaining access to the airwaves of commercial radio and television. Personal contacts can be helpful in opening doors. It is important to point out the need, benefits, and the devoting of time to "public interest" broadcasting. One technique in this area would be to contact the station manager and ask for greater coverage of international issues. Indicate that there is an audience for this kind of programming. Citing polling results may also be effective in stimulating the interest in the U.N. Day program. Citing a few names of prominent citizens who either agree or support the point may also be effective. Another way to gain access is to take advantage of call-in shows to raise the issue of the U.N. Day program.

Public radio and television stations have a moral and legal obligation to serve the needs of the community. The U.N. Day planning committee's role is to convince them that the U.N. Day program and U.N.-related international issues fill such a need. It is good to illustrate the mutually beneficial nature of the relationship by publicizing these stations' international programming in your newsletter, in advertisements, and in other outlets.

Cable TV provides a unique opportunity to reach your community. Cable systems are required to maintain at least one "public access" channel, with broadcast time available on a first-come-first-served basis. Don't be afraid to consider the possibility of producing a program on your own. It can be done inexpensively and well, even by nonprofessionals. Most colleges and universities have audio-video equipment, and some offer classes in video or film production. One note of caution, do not rely on having a website alone to draw an audience. Many people would not know that a website of the organization exists unless the event is first promoted and publicize then to advise of the website for more information.

Our U.N. Day planning committee coordinated an energetic program for U.N. Day 1994. The program's intent was to celebrate U.N. Day for October 24, 1994, and also to launch UN50 celebration. That was to be a yearlong set of programs and activities. We began building momentum at our annual national meeting and also at our state annual meeting with our programs for 1994. We laid the foundational work for 1995 programs.

A key success factor in our U.N. Day program is the caliber of our speakers. UNA-USA is the nation's leading center for policy and public education on the U.N. As such, the association has a wealth of resources that are available to each chapter for selecting good speakers. I spoke earlier of Mr. Giandomenico Picco, the former U.N. under-secretary-general, and his knowledge of issues that were of interest to our members. Working through our national office, we invited Mr. Picco to be our keynote speaker for U.N. Day 1994. Our invitation was accepted.

We involve local speakers with our chapter's activities and evens. Local universities and activist groups are good sources of speakers, which are very appealing where funds are limited. When we look outside of our region for speakers, financing, logistics, and timing take on special weight because our chapter will be responsible for the speaker's long-distance travel, accommodation, and meals. However, the other side of having an out-of-town speaker, especially one that is or has been affiliated with the United Nations, is the drawing of a large audience.

Another setback in having speakers from out of the region or those who have been or are affiliated with the United Nations is that sometimes the speakers are not available. Events that are held in places like New York where the celebration of United Nations Day takes place on the twenty-fourth of October may have a higher priority on speakers calendar. If we are lucky, we will get a speaker from that region for that date; if not, we have to plan our U.N. Day program close to the twenty-fourth of October to get an out-of-the-region speaker.

There are times, however, when the chapter's theme or issue is so important on the United Nations agenda that we will get the speaker of our choice as requested. The U.S. government and U.N. officials do not require honoraria. UNA-USA reimburses speakers for their expenses and nothing more. Speakers' expenses can either be reimbursed if the speaker pays for travel and accommodation and meals or be prepaid by the chapter.

UNA-USA supports airline tickets for speakers in coach class only. If the speakers wishes to travel other than coach, only the amount that is equivalent to the coach class ticket will be paid. Speakers are advised that a chapter member will coordinate ground transportation from the airport. If overnight accommodations are required, the chapter reserves a room for the speaker in an appropriate hotel. Once all travel and accommodations are arranged for our speaker, the next step is to provide our speaker with confirmation of all arrangements. The final step in arranging for our keynote speaker is to request a biographical sketch so that we can properly introduce him or her to our audience.

The celebration was held at the Sheraton Biscayne Bay Hotel in downtown Miami. Our board members suggested that Mr. Picco spoke on the topic *"behind the scenes at the U.N."* Gail Neumann was our master of ceremonies. The program came together with our hard work and dedication. Participants included Model U.N. from our schools, cooperation from our Council of Organizations, American Association of University Women, American Jewish Congress, Soka Gakkai International, National Association of Colored Women's Clubs, and National Association for the Advancement of Colored People, Lions Club International, and International Association of Machinists & Aerospace Workers, among others.

Our teamwork in creating the program crossed diverse boundaries without overlapping the functions of each organization or group. Follow the activities and notice that each group maintained distinct identity and functions. There was no erosion of uniqueness. The underlying current was a flow of ideas and the joint use of resources that enhances the effectiveness of each participating organization.

The U.N. Day program began with our welcome and opening remarks. It was appropriate that the proclamations from our local government officials were presented and accepted immediately after our opening remarks. There were no set policies for this procedure; it was simply that our board believed it was appropriate to do so. In some cases, we have more than one U.N. Day proclamation from different government officials. The governor usually sends a proclamation with a representative from his office, and other surrounding cities likewise do the same. Our chapter serves the Greater Miami area, so it was not unusual to have more than one proclamation. We may have one from the City of Miami, Dade County, and the City of Homestead, Florida City, among others. Our board welcomed all proclamation from all our cities. The more U.N. Day proclamations we get, the merrier our celebrations will be.

Some people do not understand the meaning and significance of having a U.N. Day proclamation issued by our government officials. This is because they hold the belief that the U.N. Day proclamation issued by our government officials is a sign that the United Nations intends to rule the world. It is not unusual for that debate to take place as a side caucus outside in the halls where our events are held. The prayer of serenity when invoked at times like those helps to boost one's tolerance level.

We respond and accommodate those who wish to engage discussions at our events because it is one way of increasing public awareness of the work we do and about the U.N. However, there are times when the occasion does not permit the time or place to engage in a lengthy debate on the subject matter. Neither does one wish to hop on or off the political incorrectness platform by resorting to short one-liners as a way of shielding or escaping the issue. Praying for a higher tolerance level is a way of surviving the moment and to garner a diplomatic belt.

The individual who raises the point or issue is sometimes invited to take up the discussion in one of our meetings. If we were good at what we do, then such a person may sooner become a new member in our chapter. U.N Day proclamations are simply acts to recognize and invite the participation of citizens in the day's activities and observance. The following is a sample of the wording of a U.N. Day proclamation:

> WHEREAS, the United Nations was founded in 1945, and the anniversary of its founding is observed each year on October 24: and
>
> WHEREAS; the advancement of human rights, including the rights of children, women, displaced persons, and indigenous peoples is a priority for the United Nations and its agencies throughout the world, and;
>
> WHEREAS, the United States was one of the founding members of the United Nations, and continues to be a leader in supporting democratic values, including
>
> The rights of citizens of all countries, and
>
> WHEREAS, if the United Nations is to continue its important work of advancing human rights, protecting the environment, preventing and resolving conflict, and promoting humane and democratic values, it must have support from both the United States government and American citizens, and
>
> WHEREAS, (Person's name) has been appointed Chair of United Nations Day in (location) to work with a United Nations Day Committee composed of community leaders to organize events and activities to educate citizens about the continuing need for the United Nations, and the importance of identifying human rights violations and seeking solutions to such violations, and
>
> WHEREAS, the citizens of (Location) are invited to participate in all activities related to United Nations Day,
>
> NOW, THEREFORE, I (Local Government Official) officially proclaim October 24 (Year)

As United Nations Day
IN WITNESS WHEREOF, I have set my hand and caused the seal of _____
To be affixed on this _____ day of _____ in the year _____

SEAL SIGNATURE

Proclamations are usually done on official stationery, and are presented to the president of the local chapter during the event. Our master of ceremonies for U.N. Day 1994 was Mrs. Gail Newman, a member and board member of our chapter. Our event was kicked off at the Sheraton Biscayne Bay Hotel in downtown Miami.

Ethel met our speaker at the airport and took him to the hotel. It was customary for one of our board members or myself to meet our speakers or invited guests at the airport, and takes our guests to the hotel where we booked their accommodation. It did not matter what the title or official capacity of our guest or speakers; we do the same for everyone. If our speaker arrives a day before the event, we may give them a tour around the city or take him or her to lunch or dinner on the day of their arrival. In those settings, we conduct briefings and information exchange.

U.N. Day celebration for 1994 and the launching of UN50 were held at Sheraton Biscayne Bay Hotel. We occupied more rooms than usual for this UN Day because it was also the launching of UN50. In one of the meeting rooms we had a continuous-looped video playing with historic profile of the United Nations and activities of our local chapter. Display tables were set up with information for making donations in support of UN50. In the halls we also had numerous display tables with information for our cooperating organizations, and brochures from UNA-USA.

We had large flags and small flags everywhere; of Florida, Dade County, the city of Miami, the United States, and the United Nations, and the miniature flag set of its Member States. The miniature flag set with all the flags of Member States was placed in front of the stage. We made sure that none of the flags were missing from the set. The podium was draped with the crest of UNA-USA. Our UNA-USA crest was created by having the crest of the United Nations and the seal of the United States placed side by side. Some of the pictures in the back of this book shows the UNA-USA crest. Beautiful floral arrangements graced the stage at strategic locations. The floral arrangements were visible but out of the way of traffic so as not to attack the feet of our participants. We took special care in ensuring the safety of our guests.

Each table had a centerpiece representing hours of work by Ethel and volunteers, who carved each centerpiece from scratch to thematically represent diversity in the United Nations. A huge banner announcing our celebration graced the background of the head table on the raised platform. As the dinner got on the way servers moved between tables pouring refreshments; while a host of other servers waited in the wing ready to begin serving the salads, and then the main course. Chicken and salmon were favorite dishes among a cross section of our audience at most of our events, and this is what was served at our luncheon for U.N. Day 1994.

Everyone settled down to have their meals. As the dinner moved into full speed, there was occasional clinking of glasses as attendees raise them to cheer the occasion at their respective tables. Giandomenico sat to my right at the head table. We enjoyed slipping in a few words and smiles as we dined. I like him, but not in the way you are thinking, He is a fine and respectable person. He understood our work and knew how difficult it is. We spoke mostly about our chapter work and UN50. He encouraged me in the work we were doing. I need him to put in a good word for the work that we are doing to boost the momentum of UN50 celebrations. Soon everyone finished eating their main course, and it was time for dessert, tea and coffee. Nothing beats a good meal and warm conversations in setting the stage for our UN Day observance.

After our meal, our master of ceremonies introduced our first entertainer for the program. It was a beautiful rendition by our pianist, who received a hearty set of applause from the audience. I was introduced as the president of the Association by our Masters of Ceremonies, Mrs. Neumann. After a few words to the audience I introduced our keynote speaker, Giandomenico Picco. He was affectionately received by our audience with a warm welcome. He has such a remarkable official stage presence. He looked better than when I first saw him at the national convention in New York earlier that same year.

Mr. Picco graduated from the University of Padua with a degree in political science. He obtained a Master of Arts degree in International Relations and Comparative Politics from the University of California, Santa Barbara. His career with the United Nations included assistant secretary-general for political affairs from 1973 to 1992. Some of his most notable achievements included the United Nations efforts in the release of Western hostages in Lebanon, and the negotiations that lead to cease-fire between Iran and Iraq.

We were delighted to have Mr. Picco as our keynote speaker. His knowledge and experiences at the United Nations tweaked the interests of our members and audience raising our awareness to a higher level on the subject matter. The levels of interest were easy to gauge given the in-depth question and answer session that followed his speech. Our wide eyed, jaw dropping, note taking audience captured every piece of information. The information that was provided in his speech brought us face to face with the issues.

Our members are constructive critics of the United Nations. It is no wonder that one of our board members stood up and asked Mr. Picco, that since he no longer works at the United Nations, what did he know about the current operations to be this informed? Well, speaking about poise and grace, then again it could simply have been diplomacy, and very manly too; Mr. Picco gave a very eloquent response. He said "I am a nobody and it does not matter who I am". The important thing, he assured Sandy Leon and the audience, is the information that he was sharing with us.

He shared first-hand information of his experience at the United Nations and in the field. The thing about having keynote speakers like Mr. Picco at our events is that the information shared is factual, and is different from those we receive from the media or from distributed memos. First-hand information is not polished for public presentation, but presented in the form that they were experienced. We prefer unfiltered information, this way we can do our own assessment of the issue and circumstances. Sandy's question set the tone of our question and answers session with Mr. Picco.

Mr. Picco helped us launch UN50; he spoke of the work we were doing as a chapter of UNA-USA, and our role in helping to increase public awareness of the role of the United Nations and U.S. leadership in the world organization. Before Mr. Picco completed his presentation he commended our chapter for the work that we were doing. He encouraged the audience to give us their support especially with our UN 50 celebrations.

I presented Mr. Picco with a small gift in appreciation of the time he shared with us. He was given a standing ovation. Ethel and I were satisfied that we invited Mr. Picco to be the keynote speaker at our UN Day celebration. Mr. Picco was not able to stay for the duration of our event because he had another engagement that same day in New York for which he had to return.

Mrs. Neumann, the master of ceremonies, continued the program while I left to speak with Mr. Picco outside the ballroom. Mr. Picco and I spoke for a while. He once again congratulated and encouraged me with the work we were doing in the community. I wished him good luck in his future endeavors. We both promised each other to keep in touch from time to time. Hyman Mally, one of our board members, came and told us that Mr. Picco's driver was ready to take him to the airport.

Ethel met Mr. Picco at the airport on his arrival but she could not take him back to the airport for his departure because of her continued participation in the program. She was the recipient of an award, and she was also due to make a presentation to our youth groups. Another board member took Mr. Picco to the airport. The majority of our board members are trusted souls for transporting and taking care of our guests. I say this because I know that some of our board members had a napping problem. Those who were nappers were never allowed to drive anyone including themselves. They are picked up by other members when they need to go to anywhere.

. We shook hands and said farewell. We wished him a safe travel and Mr. Picco left. Hyman Mally walked with him to his ride. I went back to the ballroom to continue my duties in the celebration of U.N. Day. Hyman Mally was quickly at my heels. Before I could take my seat he told me not to worry because Mr. Picco is in good hands. Ethel saw Hyman and I huddling in the back of the room; she approached us quietly to check if everything was o.k.

She asked Hyman who was driving Mr. Picco to the airport. Hyman told us that the driver was Sam Brenner.

"I wish I had known that before now," she said, raising an eyebrow.

"Why, what difference does it make, Sam is an excellent driver" I said.

"If I know Sam Brenner, he will fill Mr. Picco's ear with the U.N. getting an army and all that stuff", Ethel said.

I smiled, took her hand and told her not to worry because Sam was a very good driver, and Mr. Picco is a big guy and is quite capable of taking care of himself.

"Surely anyone who was able to negotiate the release of hostages in threatening, uncertain, unstable, risky environments can survive a twenty-minutes ride to the airport with Sam Brenner. Mr. Picco knows where he is headed." I said to her to help ease her anxiety. She responded in an unconvincing tone, "I hope so" and returned to her seat at the table.

Sam Brenner was one of our board members. He has served several terms on our board. He has also been a member of our chapter for many years. Sam and Ethel became UNA-USA members at about the same time. He has long been dubbed the famous poet laureate of our chapter and of Surfside. He has written numerous poems. Some of his works were presented to our chapter. He has written poems about UNA-members, and sometimes he entertained us with his poems in meetings and in other events.

Sam was a former mayor of Surfside. In addition to being a member of our chapter and our board, Sam was our area representative for the World Federalist Organization. It was not unusual that some of our board members are also board members for other organizations. Earlier I mentioned the same committed and dedicated people appearing everywhere as volunteers for a good cause. Sam Brenner is one of those people.

Gail Neumann, for example, was also a leader in Results, an organization that advocates against poverty. Our organization membership was made up of people who wore different and sometimes many hats. Therefore, Sam's board membership in UNA-USA Greater Miami, and also the representative of the World Federalist Organization were not unusual. He was a very resourceful board member. He is always ready and willing to assist in whatever way he can. His commitment as a board member cannot be underscored.

Ethel and Sam have a long-standing difference of opinion about the United Nations and how it could become more effective. The difference is not about what the United Nations is as much as what it should be. Sam holds the opinion that the United Nations could be more effective with its own military force. He believes that if the U.N. had a military force it would be better equipped to carry out its global functions.

Ethel on the other hand does not see it that way. She believes that the United Nations does not need to have its own military force in order to carry out its functions. Ethel makes the point that the nature of the organization does not allow or give it any authority to have a military force. She often reminds Sam that the United Nations is not a sovereign state; therefore, it cannot have an army or military force; The U.N. is not a state or country, neither is it a nation with a territory to protect.

Other members join the debate whenever the opportunity presents itself. Sam uses every opportunity to raise the subject and press the matter. It developed into a long-standing difference of opinion between Ethel and Sam. So it was no wonder that when Ethel heard that it was Sam who drove Mr. Picco to the airport, she knew that Sam would raise the issue, and discussed it with Mr. Picco. She knew Mr. Picco would be a captive audience for Sam. Ethel feels the same way with any new members or guest in our chapter. She tries to prevent Sam from having undue influence.

Dr. Keith and Mrs. Erma Bennett, Mrs. Norman Hill, and Mr. and Mrs. Alvin Malley are the most senior members of our chapter, being members since 1960. These fine people who are also board members understood the development of the difference of opinions between Mr. Brenner and Mrs. Felts, who both have been members of the organization since the early 1970s. We admire the respect and tolerance Ethel and Sam have for each other regardless of their strong differences of opinion of how the United Nations should function.

Ethel and Sam are exceptional role models in our chapter. The fact that they have a difference of opinion on one issue does not mean that the same difference is carried over on all issues. In fact they sometimes share the same side and views of other issues. We debate many issues in our organization. It would be counter productive if any or everyone were to allow any disagreement or differences in opinions on any one issue to carry forward on all issues. If that was the case we would not be able to get anything done. Furthermore, those types of behaviors would dismantle our teamwork.

I might add however, that most of our chapter members share Ethel's point of view that the United Nations is not a sovereign state, and therefore it cannot have its own military force. In our global policy study, for example, whenever we discuss topics of atrocities and blatant disregard for human rights which are committed by member states against their own population, the short answers have the tendencies of siding with Sam Brenner, that the United Nations should have its own military force to act immediately. But cooler heads prevail and upon re-examination Ethel's point of view holds that the United Nations cannot have its own military force, because it is not a nation and neither is it a country. It is comprised of its member states, and can only act based upon the U.N. Charter.

Our U.N. Day '94 was one of our more successful events. We recognized community members with awards; members of our Model U.N. were credited and recognized for their participation in Model U.N. programs. Local students were presented with awards for participating in the national essay contest. Special thank-you and awards were given to Anne DelaCamera's students, who spoke passionately about the rights of children. Ethel received an award for her years of dedication to the association.

We kicked off the celebrations for UN50 which could not have been introduced any better than with the assistance of Mr. Giandomenico Picco. UN50 was launched on a grand scale. The added value our activities for 1994 were the people who joined our chapter becoming new members. We worked hard and learned a lot of new things. We accomplished all that we set to do and then some. We had no idea that I would have been called on to participate in the first universal election of South Africa, but Ethel and I did, and what an honor and experience that was. We were now looking forward to our UN50 activities.

CHAPTER 4

W E WERE SIMPLY ordinary people who were doing extra ordinary things. Teamwork was one of our core values. We were diverse in all aspects of skills, talent, education, age, gender, ethnicity, religious and non-religious affiliation, socio-economic backgrounds, to name a few. But the very fabric that made us resourceful and held us together, our diversity, was the very element that could divide us.

The agreement to disagree and the strong differences of opinions between Ethel and Sam was a cornerstone in our chapter which exemplifies respect and tolerance. Those characteristics—respect and tolerances—were another of our core values. Arguably, one cannot understand the value of respect without first being tolerant, and likewise cannot exercise tolerance without respect for others. It is a yin and yang effect where one cannot exist without the other.

It was those core values that helped our members to navigate the wide disparity of opinions on the numerous issues that were discussed in our meetings. No one was every certain of when a difference of opinion may surface or on what issue, but suffice to say that when the moment arises, the experiences of Ethel and Sam became our guiding light.

Each and every member of our chapter in addition to individual uniqueness, were accompanied by background experiences, an added element of who we are. Some of us had different customs and different religious affiliation. We all do not look the same way or think the same. We are a diverse people. Because we behave differently and think differently was no reason why we could not get the work done as a team. In addition to respect and tolerance for each other, working as a team allow us to gain new perspectives. Throughout the many years that I have worked as the team leader in our chapter, I have silently observed and learned that in several instances it is not so much the way things are as much as it is having a new perspective on things that propelled us in moving forward.

We found that differences in opinions often lead to more concise evaluation and resolution of issues. Whether an opinion is accepted or rejected by the decision of the vote, our members demonstrate respect and tolerance with each other, regardless from which side of the debate. The policy was simply an agreement to disagree. What I also learned, however, is that an agreement to disagree does not necessarily mean that opinionated differences will end with a majority voted decision. Sometimes those differences can develop into advocacy. Whenever that happens it is not unusual for research lines to be drawn thus enabling re-introduction of more evidence in support of a defeated motion.

Tolerance and respect are gauges to the limit of madness, allowing the consideration of new issues, and a way to resolve them. We strive to have a new perspective on things. An issue that has been resolved and settled by majority vote of the board or our membership may at any point in time resurface and be revisited with a new set of persuasive arguments by any member who chooses to press the point.

We practiced tolerance and respect even when dealing with external situations. We have invited numerous guests to share their experiences with us. We had citizens of Bosnia and other regions come to our meetings to share experiences and stories of survival. Some of those survival experiences took place on the backdrop of embroiled conflicts in our guests' homeland. Our chapter members are always eager to learn more about the issues in our world. At all times tolerance and respect guide our way even through gut wrenching issues.

One example of respect and tolerance at work that I would like to share concerns two of our board members and their ties to the external community. We invited the representative of the Taiwan Cultural Association in Miami to be our luncheon guest. After the invitations were sent to everyone to join us for a luncheon meeting, a difference of opinion between our two board members and our guest surfaced. It was a pre-existed difference of opinion. Our meeting took place at one of our local Chinese restaurant. The reason we held the luncheon at that location was because the cost of our lunch was less than five dollars per person, a great deal for our individual budget.

Fine dining at low cost is always welcomed by our members. I have stated before that we were pros at looking for low costs in all of our activities; we are volunteers and do not have a lot of money. Dining at the Chinese restaurant was very good especially on an all you can eat basis. You may wonder how we managed to have a luncheon meeting in a restaurant that serves a buffet.

Well, it not too difficult. We contact the restaurant owner and advise him that we have seventy five people for lunch on a specific date and time. We request a special section of the restaurant to be set up for our members and guests.

Our section was set up with a rectangular head table that seats eight people facing a set of round tables that seats six to eight people each. I am giving all these details so that if your volunteer organization or chapter is on the look out for low cost dining this is a good way to go. Our members and guests did not have to leave their tables to self serve from the buffet because the dishes were duplicated and placed on each table. When the dishes on the tables ran low, the server replaced them with new servings. We enjoyed specialized buffet at a low price while having our meeting; it was just another way that being creative helped our budget. It was low cost, low maintenance, low planning all the way, which is simply unbeatable at any cost. The only thing we took was ourselves, and our U.S. and U.N. flags that were to be placed at each end of the head table.

The invitations for the luncheon were mailed to our members. No registration was required; all that a member had to to was to respond by phone call saying that he or she will attend and how many people will be in his or her party, this way we have a head count of the number of people who will be coming. Everyone pays for his or her meal with the exception of our invited guest and an accompanying party. The cost of our meal was four dollars and fifty cents each. We asked each member to be prepared to pay five dollars each because we factored tips for the servers.

Soon after the invitations were sent out for the luncheon a buzz developed among our members about our invited guest. The information through the grapevine suggested that there were difference of opinions about having our guest at the luncheon. It grew and escalated to the point where Ethel and I received telephone calls about the matter. Ethel and I tried tracing the source of the conflict. We discovered that the source of the problem was a long standing issue between China and Taiwan that has led to a difference of opinions between our guest and board members.

Two of our board members are originally from China. Our guest was the representative of Taiwan Cultural Office in Miami. There was an ongoing difference of opinion. Lily Lu was a member of our board. Her father, Dr. Lu, was also a board member, and he was also a former Chief at the World Health Organization. Both Dr. Lu and his daughter Lily are dedicated board members. They are always ready and willing to assist in every call of duty. Their contributions to the association are valued. We respect them greatly.

Ms. Endo from the Taiwan Cultural Office in Miami insisted that Lily Lu not be present at the luncheon when the representative arrives. Ms. Lu, on the other hand, insisted that the representative not be invited to either dine or share any information with us. Neither Ethel nor I knew all there was to know about the conflict between the two countries. We saw the opportunity to learn more about the conflict.

To balance the moment Ethel, Professor Watson, and I took on a team approach. We certainly did not wish to un-invite the representative from the Taiwan Culture Association. That would be inappropriate, undiplomatic, and unfriendly. We also could not bar our two board members from attending the luncheon, because our bylaws did not have such a provision. We decided to work through the situation. Our choice approach was to diffuse the conflict for that moment in time at the luncheon. It was our members who suggested that we invite the representative of the Taiwan Cultural Association. We designed a seating arrangement at the head table where each one of us would be seated between the conflicting parties.

On the day of the luncheon I headed to Miami where the event was being held. I have never met the representative, but I heard he was a fine person. I received his biographical information a few days before the luncheon, and I was told he would be accompanied by an assistant. The name of the assistant was not given but I wondered if it will be Ms. Endo. I took the Florida Turnpike because it was much more scenic than I-95. I arrived at my destination more relaxed and prepared when I take the Florida Turnpike as oppose to I-95 that lets me arrive totally decomposed of preparedness and relaxation. I figure it was probably because of the number of tractor trailers on the I-95 route. It is a very noisy and busy highway.

On my way to the luncheon I listened to the radio. John Forgery's song "*Bad Moon Rising*" was the first song that I heard when the radio came on. It takes about twenty to thirty minutes from my place to Miami, depending on the traffic. It was Saturday; there was virtually no traffic on my way. I had lots of time to listen to the radio while I was driving to Miami.

I arrived at the restaurant and many of our members were already inside; there were a lot of cars in the parking lot. I recognized some of the cars as belonging to members of our chapter. Ethel, Professor Watson and I took our seating positions and waited for our guests to arrive. Name tags were pre-placed at the head table with designated seating positions. Ethel had taken care of those arrangements the night before. We were truly living up to our creed—*people at work laying the foundation of a lasting peace.*

Everyone arrived and after a brief mingling session we sat down to have our meal. While we were eating we had small discussions. Ethel, Professor Watson and I made use of every opportunity to involve the parties on our right and on our left in the conversation. Sometimes we strategically opted out by not responding thus providing the opportunity for the conflicting parties to communicate with each other. It worked like a gem.

Neither Professor Watson nor Ethel nor I touched on the issues that created the differences of opinion between the conflicting parties. We simply provide a buffer to assist in the communication process. By the time I introduced the representative to share information about Taiwan's culture with our members, both parties had moved beyond their differences and were openly communicating; they even managed to share a bit of laughter between them at times. More interestingly however was the opportunity to address the issues that created the differences of opinions in the questions and answers session. Both parties were able to present their facts and points of views openly and freely which enabled our members to participate in the discussion. There were no hostility but a friendly environment. Our members were able to learn about the issues and weigh both sides as the questions and answers session progressed.

At some point in time each of us one way or another will encounter differences in opinions. Some of those experiences may last a short time while others may go on for generations. Maintaining open communications and exercising tolerance and respect is one way of getting over the hump. I have encountered numerous rounds of differences of opinions. Perhaps the one that I have learned from the most is the one I termed my east west issue. This experience occurred during my undergraduate studies.

One of my professors wrote on one of my papers "east is east and west is west and who knows where the sun shines best". I had a project to do in one of my upper levels physical geography courses. I completed the project and turned it in to my professor on time. Before I handed it in I read it several times to ensure it was being submitted according to the assignment requirements. i also read it for proper editing.

I was looking forward to getting a good grade for the paper. My assignment required a large amount of cartographic work, but no problem, I did those too. That particular course required a lot of illustrations and diagrams. When my professor returned my paper to me, it had no grade and on the cover page only the words *"East is east, and west is west, and who knows where the sun shines best"* were written on the paper. I consulted my professor and asked the meaning of what he wrote, and where is my grade. He told me to read my paper again.

I did that, I must have read my paper ten times, and in my opinion, there was nothing wrong with it. There were a few misspelled words but that was all. I re-submitted my paper through our faculty office. When I picked it up again, it had the same words written but now at the back of my paper. My paper was still not graded. A strong difference of opinion was now brewing on how my paper was marked and I was not given a grade for the paper.

I asked a couple of my friends who were in the same class to read my paper. They too could not find anything wrong with the paper. My professor avoided me when I tried to get his attention between lectures. I began to think that perhaps he did not like me or something. I interrupted one of his lectures demanding to get an answer on what is wrong with my paper. He said my paper was wrong. I told him that I could not find anything wrong with it. I asked him to tell me what was wrong with the paper. He said he has already done so.

Still pondering over what was wrong with the paper; I woke up early one morning and decided to look at my paper again. It was just before sunrise. I stood at my bedroom window facing a southeasterly direction. The quiet sunrise was simple breath-taking. I switched off the bedside lamp so as not to interrupt the sight of the sunrise. The hues of pink and blue blended producing a different shade of sunrise. The color was similar to that of the northern lights. The only difference, it seemed from where I was standing, was that there was no display of lights. As the sun rose, the silhouetted trees and buildings of the Toronto skyline began to disappear.

The sun emerged in sparkling orange then it slowly turned to crisp, bright fluorescent champagne with blue outer edges. As I watched the sunrise my thoughts were on my paper. The rays of sunshine began to spread in every direction. That's when it dawned on me. Directions I said to myself, my professor must be referring to directions.

It was time to fix breakfast. The house began to buzz with activity as everyone was now awake. Jackie called for Donna. She wanted her comb. The kids continued to buzz while I fixed breakfast. We had our breakfast and the three girls left to get their bus for school. My son at the time was still a toddler. I took him to his Montessori school then went on my way to campus.

I spent some time in the library that morning revising my paper. I changed all directions in the paper; east to west, and west to east. It was a lot of changes but I corrected every one of my directions, I even corrected the southeastern, southwestern, northeastern and northwestern directions. I had mislabeled my directions. That mislabeling was carried through in my narrative. What a mess it was. Only someone like my professor who knew the topic would have known that there was something terrible wrong with my reasoning.

Well, not to stress the point further, I apologized to my professor for not recognizing the problem earlier. I lost a few points for turning in my paper late, but I learned a valuable lesson about the root cause of differences of opinion. Try these on for size *mislabeling, misunderstanding, mismanaged, miscalculate, misapply, misspoke, misconception, misconstrue, miscommunication, misfire, misclassify, mislead, misinform, misinterpret*—and so on. If you did not get our discussion on difference of opinion, you may have missed the point, but not to worry we will share more as we go on.

In one of my letters to our president in 1999, I wrote the phrase as my professor did on my paper: *"East is east and west is west, and who knows where the sun shines best."* It is good to have a sense of direction when there are differences of opinions. If we know where we are going and what is coming at us through those differences, then half the world's problems could be solved. There are just too many things riding on differences of opinions.

Grammatically, the paper was perfect, but there was a problem with the contents. It had no basis in reality because all directional indicators were transposed. The climate did not fit the locations, the people did not belong, and the topography totally did not correspond with the region. The altitudes and latitudes were incorrect, the flora and fauna were out of place. Some times it is good to reconsider our differences of opinions; we may just find that a change in direction is all that is needed to put us on the correct path.

A change of direction may offer a new perspective or a new lens through which to view the issue. In some instances, difference of opinions can be resolved by the rule of authority, some with evidentiary support, and others may need persuasive arguments or a combination of all those factors. A proactive approach engaging teamwork is a progressive alternative in resolving differences of opinions.

Sam makes use of every opportunity to speak with anyone who has the time to listen to his opinion that the United Nations should have its own military to be an effective organization. But he really prefers to share his poetry with others. We encouraged him to publish his works. Ethel's position that the United Nations cannot have its own army is supported by the fact that the U.N. is not a sovereign nation. The United Nations is made up of its Member States, and functions under its Charter. A majority of our board members support Ethel's point of view, and believe that the United Nations does not need an army and should not have one because it is not a country or sovereign state.

CHAPTER 5

AT THE END of our fiscal year for 1994, we settled all our expenses and we had $139 remaining in our chapter's bank account. We were happy that we were able to cover all our expenses for the year, but we need to raise funds for 1995 to cover the cost of U.N. 50 celebrations. Our activities were going to be increased tremendously especially with our public outreach programs. It was a "TAAL" order and we did not want our community to miss out on all the celebrations that will be taking place worldwide. We distributed a lot of information asking for donations and sponsorships but up to this point have not yet received any commitments.

We developed our UN50 programs in phases, and continue to work on the approach that each activity must be self-supporting. Our "TAAL" order was to "*think and act locally.*" All of our programs and projects were locally centered. Our intentions were to conduct our outreach program so that our community would benefit from our work. We considered numerous approaches of raising funds for the year's activities.

One consideration was to approach the Dade County Commission for a small community block grant. The County Commission chair already promised to help us at our 1994 state annual meeting. We completed the grant application stating the amount of funds that we were requesting and for what purpose. We provided a budget and all the particulars in our application and submitted it to the Commission. We were very optimistic about the grant application.

On the day that the grant process opened in the Commission Chamber, our board members and I went to make our case and point for the grant. We were quite a team. Sam Brenner arrived before all of us and secured our seating in the Chamber by placing folders on the number of that we need in the same row. The seats are taken quickly because of the large number of organizations that were seeking grants. To get a seat in the Chamber one must arrive early. There were eight of us so Sam did a very good job of securing all of our seats in the same row.

We sat and listened while other organizations made their presentations to the Commission. Finally it was our turn to do so. We stood up and approached the front of the room. I spoke on behalf of our team. I introduced our team to the Commission and headed straight into the presentation. We were only allowed a limited amount of time and I wanted to make every minute count. While I was speaking Gertrude gave a brochure to each member of the Commission. It had information about our organization. One of the Commissioners did not take time to look at the brochure but instead asked what was UNA-USA. I briefly described who we were and our purpose there.

One of the Commissioners mentioned that only elected officials can appear before the Commission. Sam Brenner said to the Commission, "Our president, Mrs. McLeod, is a publicly elected official. She was democratically elected to her post." All of our board members nodded in agreement. I continued with our presentation. Arthur Teele was sitting in the middle and I looked at him from time to time hoping that he remembered our state annual meeting and his promise. It took fifteen to twenty minutes to complete our presentation. I answered a few questions from the Commissioners and in no time we were done.

Well! Suffice to say we did not get the grant from the Dade County Commission. The decision was not immediate it took a couple of months. We were very disappointed, but we did not linger we moved right along to our next potential source of funding. It was very disappointing that all that work was put into the application process to come up with zero. But the way we figure it as the saying goes nothing try nothing done.

There was a national fund-raising campaign. All 175 chapters across the U.S. were also conducting fund-raising activities for UN50. Because of all the fund-raising activities that our organization and chapters were doing, each chapter had to provide a list of the businesses and organizations that will be be contacted for sponsorship. This was to prevent any overlapping of sponsorship or funding requests by our chapters or national office.

We used a number of creative approaches in our chapter's fund-raising activities. One method that we used is cooperating organization. In our cooperating organization program we did not request any money from the organization. We simply ask that the organization provide mailing labels of their membership so that we can mail invitations to their members.

Some cooperating organizations will agree to mail the invitations if we provide them with the printed materials. That way we do not have to pay the cost of postage. Because our cooperating organization paid the postage, even though we did not get the actual funds from them we considered this one of our fund-raising approaches. If we are given membership address labels only we consider this in-kind contribution.

But even with all that help we still had needs for funding. Our traditional sponsorship programs included offering display tables, and or luncheon tables with a specified number of seats for a specified amount of donation from our sponsors. We also include the name of our sponsor on our activity and program brochures. These are no different from what other non-profit organizations do in fund raising activities.

One of the goals of our fund raising activities was to raise sufficient funds to establish a small office for our chapter. We continued to operate from my small office. UN50 activities were on a much larger scale than our regular chapter work. We were concerned about the overhead cost of the increased activities, and the continuation of chapter work when I am no longer the president of the organization. Our chapter was growing and some board members worry that a new president may not be able to commit the same resource that I was providing. Having a small administrative office for our chapter would solve that problem. Most importantly however was raising funds to produce our UN50 programs.

We did some of our work like the stuffing of envelopes in the homes of some of our board members. We rotate homes to make it easier on our volunteer board members who offer to use his or her home. It was o.k. to do that when we have small mailings, but when it involves 1000 pieces or more we did it in my office. My office was equipped with the things we need like a fax machine, a telephone system, photocopying machine, computers, desks, and a conference room with a table that seats twelve people. As UN50 programs developed my office became the central meeting place for everyone.

We continued to search for funding. We were informed that we could approach individual Dade County Commissioners and request donations from discretionary funds. That did not work because we found out that all of the Commissioners already made commitments to other projects. It was just a tough time all around to raise funds to do anything. We were working against the clock. We had activities on the calendar but we did not have the funds produce them.

To produce an activity from start to finish requires a three months turn around time. There is a one month development phase, and another month for program finalization and execution, and the invitations need to be sent out giving a one month turn around to receive responses and registrations. It is very stressful and grueling when the funds are not on hand for program development. We were operating on a transient budget. That means we start programs with seed money that is donated by our officers or board members, and hope to raise funds as we go along. I was already covering overhead and administrative costs.

One of the problems that I experienced on a regular basis is that I was also a worker. When I do UNA-USA work it interrupts my work cycle. I tried to avoid this problem but it happens time and time again. I used my own financial resource to get things done because the clock was moving and timing was very important. I justified the situation by convincing myself that it was for a good cause, and it was. It may not have been smart, but the principles were overarching. It was a huge responsibility whichever way one cuts it.

Sometimes I would jokingly point out the number of blue folders and manila folders in my office. The blue folders were UNA-USA file folders. The manila folders were my client folders. The blue folders out number the manila folders by three to one ratio, go figure. I might add however, that the lack of volume in my work folders, the manila ones, may not be due entirely to my increased volunteer activities with UNA-USA. In the spring of 1993 while I was still very busy rebuilding and relocating after Hurricane Andrew; I was dismissed from Sun Life Insurance, the company I had worked for. I was told that my production levels were not as expected.

One would think that given that I was always a top producer with my company, at least up until the time of Hurricane Andrew, I would be given some consideration in view of the major disaster; which severely affected my family and created a displacement of my clients. The entire region was affected and suffering the effects of the disaster. That did not matter anyhow, I was still fired from the job. After I was fired I spent the rest of the day listening to some of my favorite songs. I must have played Aaron Neville's "*Don't take away my heaven* "fifteen times. I need to be consoled and music was the right antidote. I later applied for unemployment insurance. Before I knew it was I made a joint party with the State of Florida Department of Labor, in an appeal made by my former employer to reconsider a ruling that was made by the Department of Labor. As if I did not have enough on my plate already. That case continued for seven years but that is another story.

The low volume in my client files from which I earn my living were so because I was transitioning from being a captive agent with my former employer to becoming self-employed. I began signing up with other companies to become a general agent after I was fired. I was also actively developing an income tax service in the business. Given the trauma of Hurricane Andrew, our relocation, a recent divorce, displacement of clientele, being fired from my job, and increased volunteer activities, It seems like a very good idea to start anew by building my own business.

Our final board meeting for 1994 was held in November, at our usual place, the Sheraton Biscayne Bay Hotel. We reserved one of the small meeting rooms for our meeting. It was held on a Saturday. We had breakfast, and then we called our meeting to order. The main item on our agenda was UN50 fund raising. We received some pledges for donations but those had not materialized yet. We did not particularly like to speak of fund-raising especially when we were putting out a lot of work but getting no results. It was something we had to do anyhow; we must move forward.

After I called the meeting to order I asked for a moment of silence as was our tradition. There were fifteen board members present which was enough for a quorum. If we do not have a quorum we do not have a meeting. After our moment of silence ended, Jim Mullins asked" Why do we always have to observed a moment of silence, is this a religious significance?" I did not expect that type of question from Jim. He has been a board member for many years, if anyone knew what our moment of silence meant, it should have been him. I suspected there was an underlying issue, but unless it was on the meeting agenda I was not going there, at least not now and not in the manner it was presented.

Jim also knew that our normal procedure when raising a point, whether or not it is on the agenda, it should not have been thrown at us the way he did. He did not address the chair properly. The meeting was already called to order. Everyone was taken aback with his question. "Jim it has always been our tradition to take a moment of silence when the meeting is called to order to collect our thoughts and get ready for the meeting" I responded. Professor Watson jumped right in reaffirming my response to Jim. "That's right, Jim, we always try to collect our thoughts before we start our discussions" Ethel brushed me with her elbow as if to say "Good job." We were a very good team, but there are days when not everyone seems to be on the same page.

We proceeded with our meeting. A few new ideas were suggested by our members to improve our fund-raising efforts; those too need to be developed before implementation. We decided to fine-tune our current approach and hope for the best. We each chipped in donations to assist with the current programs. Sandy informed us that Jeff Laurenti, vice president of global policy studies from our national office, was in town.

Jeff wanted to meet with our executive committee before he returned to the national office. He was staying at a hotel not too far from where we were having our meeting. We asked Sandy when is Jeff planning to go back to New York. Sandy said it will be later that evening. We also asked him if he knew why Jeff wanted to meet with the executive committee. Sandy was not sure why Jeff wanted to meet with us or perhaps he was just being evasive. We decided to meet with Jeff later that day. It would have been nice if he had contacted us before he came in town. We would have invited him to our board meeting which would have saved us some time, but that would have been too easy.

Before our meeting was adjourned, Sam Brenner announced that one of our members had his twenty-three-foot statue Freeda on exhibit at the Dinner Key Auditorium in Coconut Grove. He invited all of us to go down and see it. We contacted Jeffrey Laurenti before we left the meeting and arranged to see him later that day. We adjourned our meeting, and headed for Dinner Key Auditorium.

A few of us—including Ethel, Professor Watson, Gertrude Pearl, Hyman Mally, and I—decided we would go to see Don Gilbert's exhibit. We arrived at the auditorium and entered the exhibit hall. There she was; *Freeda*, all twenty-three feet of her draped in her golden body, holding a torch in one hand high above her head. We walked over to Don Gilbert and congratulated him on his exhibit. He welcomed us and expressed how happy he was to see us. We chatted with him for a while, still admiring his work before we moved on to see other displays.

There is a story behind *Freeda*. Don Gilbert had a vision of purchasing the Freedom Tower in Miami. He planned to erect a five-hundred-foot statue of *Freeda* with a torch in her hand raised high to promote peace and freedom. He believed that the five-hundred-foot statue would inspire the citizens of the world to seek freedom. It was Don's idea of a new world order. He promoted his vision by sending out information packages to just about everyone, seeking help with his project. His press kits were decorated with poems, photographs, a picture of the statue of *Freeda* and declarations.

Don planned to construct his statue with the actress Jane Fonda as the model. He planned to have the statue displayed on a mountain-top somewhere in San Francisco. Don faced many challenges with his project. He needs to raise $6.5 million to purchase the foreclosed Freedom Tower that was owned by the Lichtenstein Bank. He had trouble raising that amount of money to purchase the building. He had spent over $20,000 of his own money in constructing the twenty-three-foot *Freeda* that was displayed at the auditorium. Some of our members thought that Don's plans were a bit off the wall but nevertheless supported him in his project.

While we walked through the auditorium looking at other exhibits, Ethel informed me that Don's statue, *Freeda*, was originally intended to be displayed in Port-au-Prince, Haiti. According to her, it was intended to mark the return of democracy to Haiti when Jean-Bertrand Aristide returned to power, but that never happen because Don was unable to make arrangements to have the statue displayed in Haiti. According to Ethel, having the statue of *Freeda* displayed at the kids' show exhibition in the auditorium was a last-ditch effort for Don. I said to Ethel it must be difficult for Don, and he is so passionate about his work.

Ethel agreed with me, and then she told me that Don also suffered from bipolar disorder. "I never knew that," I said to her.

"Yes," she said. "Haven't you noticed that sometimes when he attends our membership meetings, he sometimes acts up?"

"Yes," I replied, "I have noticed the he behaves somewhat indifferently at times, but I have always thought it had something to do with the issue that was being discussed."

"Oh no, he acts that way because of his condition," said Ethel.

"Well, I would never have guessed. Ethel, that looks like a neat exhibit," I said, pointing in the direction of a display of artworks hanging from what looked like a clothesline. "Let's go and see what that is," I said to her, steering her elbow in the direction of the exhibit.

We walked over to the exhibit with the artworks. There were numerous pieces of work hanging from a line across the exhibit booth. "This is pretty neat" I said. We introduced ourselves to the person in charge of the booth and started talking about the artworks. The person introduced himself as Carlos Provencza. He was a director at Planeta Publishing Company, whose office was located Miami.

We asked Mr. Provencza about the artworks and who did them. He told us they were done by the students in a few of our local schools. I told him that Ethel and I were impressed with his exhibit. I especially liked the way the artworks are exhibited for viewing. I asked Mr. Provencza if he would be interested in sponsoring a similar project for our UN50 celebrations. He said sure, he would not mind discussing the possibility of doing so. We exchanged business cards. He also provided us with his contact information and the times that we could reach him.

We followed through with contacting Mr. Provencza and that was how our "Friends of the Future" project came into being. Ethel and I were pleased to have discovered a potential window of opportunity to sponsor one of our youth programs. Our next stop was our meeting with Jeff. Ethel dropped me off at the Sheraton Biscayne Bay Hotel where I picked up my car.

We drove separately to the hotel where Jeff was staying. The Holiday Inn was only a couple of blocks away from the Sheraton Biscayne Bay. When we arrived it was already pass lunchtime. Our other board members were already having lunch and speaking with Jeff. They were seated in one of the private meeting rooms. Ethel and I followed suit and ordered two soups and one sandwich that we spilt between the two of us. Soup and sandwich was the lunch special for the day. We joined the others at the table and get caught up in the conversation while we wait for our lunch.

After lunch I turned the floor over to Jeff. He was responsible for the global policy program. He coordinated the program including putting the global policy book together and distribute them to all of the organizations' members. Jeff informed us that UNA-USA was in the process of releasing a new book entitled *How to Do Business with the United Nations*.

The book was due to be released in January 1995. It is intended to serve as a guide for anyone who wishes to do business with the United Nations. He needs our help with the introduction of the new publication. I asked him what was it he would like for us to do. The way I figured he would not have visited us without having an intention in mind. Sandy suggested that because it will be a business guide, we could perhaps have a small meeting to introduce the guide to our local businesses. I had figured at our board meeting that Sandy knew more than he was telling us about Jeff's visit. Any way we continued to listen to Jeff and what he was saying about the new publication.

The idea of having a business conference was a great idea but it was something that we need to look into further. Ethel commented that it sounded like a great idea. We agreed in principle that we would look further into the idea, and whether or not we would host such a conference. *"How to Do Business with the United Nations"*.

Jeff pointed out that the clock was ticking for this event. By telling us that the clock was ticking it appears that there was more to it than he was disclosing. I asked him for the hidden agenda. He said that there was none; only that it would be great if the conference was held when the book is released. He told us not to take too long in making our decision. He provided me with information and who to contact at our national office. Some of our members lingered to chat with Jeff. I had a very long day and was eager to be on my way home so I left as soon as our discussion was finished.

I left the room, got in my car, and headed for the ramp to I-95 north. I kept my eyes on the road. With my left hand holding the steering wheel, I let my fingers do the walking through my console. I was searching for a cassette. I brought one up, but oops! I did not want to listen to *Hooked on Classics*. My daughter gave me that for a birthday present. I kept my eyes on the road and placed the cassette back into the console using my fingers to create a space for it. Then yes, I found the Eagles cassette. The year was 1973. That cassette had one of my favorite songs by the Eagles, "Take It to the Limit." I inserted the cassette in the tape player. I listened to the songs as I drove home. I must have listened to the song ten times. Each time the song ends I rewound it to the beginning and hit play again.

The chance meeting with Carlos Provencza at the auditorium added a new dimension to our sponsorship programs for UN50 activities. I contacted Planeta's office and spoke with Carlos the following Monday. We arranged a meeting at my office. He arrived on Wednesday accompanied by John, his assistant. Ethel was at the meeting. They gave us brochures on their company.

The headquarters of the Planeta was in Madrid, Spain. Carlos originally worked in the Argentina office, and is a native of Argentina. Carlos appeared to be a fine person with good table manners. He sported a pigtail and a full short cropped beard. He also appeared to be a very savvy businessperson, but had difficulty with speaking English. His assistant, John, was from New Jersey but lived in Miami, spoke Portuguese fluently. John assisted Carlos with English translation.

Carlos asked me if his pigtail was acceptable in the United States for a business executive look. John, Ethel, and I smiled at his question. I told Carlos that if his intentions are to climb the corporate ladder in the United States, a pigtail may not take him all the way. I also told him that he needs to have good business ethics and be able to make good business decisions. He laughed and said, "Thank you, Sylvia, I am learning." He showed Ethel and me a photograph of his wife and their two lovely daughters.

We discussed the possibility of his company's sponsorship of our UN50 program. He described how they developed the program that led to the artwork that was displayed at the auditorium. In a nutshell, he explained that what they did was invite a few schools to participate in an art contest. The artworks by the students were then collected and displayed for parents and others to see. The students were presented with gifts for their participation.

. He told us that his company may consider a sponsorship of a similar program if we could work at getting all the approvals and program in place. We asked him about underwriting all the cost of the project; provided we could get it off the ground. He told us that the company would be willing to underwrite the cost providing that the project was manageable. We asked what the company would be looking for in return if such an event were to be developed. He said quite possibly the opportunity to display their products in a separate location from the artwork. The company published encyclopedias and educational materials in different languages.

Ethel and I decided that what they would ask in return did not sound unreasonable. Our meeting lasted for one hour. We agreed in principle that this would be both beneficial to our organizations. Ethel and I told Carlos that we need to discuss the opportunity with our board, and then we would contact him for further developments.

We provided Carlos with information about UN50 celebrations. We also gave him brochures of UNA-USA and our local chapter. He promised to discuss the matter with his executive team. He was quite pleased and believed that the leadership of his company would welcome the opportunity to participate. We agreed to meet again in three weeks, at which time, pending the outcome of our discussion with our board, we would take it to the next level.

The Organizations were structured with different mandates, objectives, and missions. UNA-USA Greater Miami is a nonprofit, nonpartisans organization while Planeta is a for-profit corporation. A project with school children will bring a government organization into the picture. A very careful navigation will be necessary for a successful cooperative engagement, but where there is a will there is a way. Our activity should be beneficial to all stakeholders, and we will also be able to achieve our objective of public outreach thereby increasing awareness of the UN with the activity. At the same time it would be a way of encouraging our young people to participate in UN50 celebrations.

Ethel and I were ecstatic that our corporate sponsorship program might come to fruition. This was exactly what we were hoping to achieve. At our last board meeting, we dealt with a lot of frustrations because we were not realizing the funds from all our fund-raising activities. Thank goodness for Don Gilbert's Freeda exhibit. Had it not be for us visiting Don's exhibit we never would have met Carlos. Carlos and Planeta were placed on the agenda for our next board meeting. We were gaining grounds with corporate sponsorship for UN50.

I called Ralph Cwerman, the contact person in the national office according to the information that was given to me by Jeff Laurenti. I could not reach him, so I left a message asking him to call me back. He returned my call the next morning. We talked a little about the potential business conference. It was my first time speaking with Ralph. I knew most of the staff members and leadership at the national office. Ralph was new; he was in charge of corporate affairs. He spoke about the new book that was to be released in January. A copy was not yet available, he said, but he promised to send me one as soon as it was available.

I asked him what he had in mind for the conference. He suggested that the target audience be corporate executives and professionals who would like to do business with the United Nations. He also suggested that those who had an interest in finding out how the United Nations conducted its business may also like to attend. We discussed the time frame for the activity. Ralph suggested that it would be good if the event could take place sometime in the spring of 1995.

The conference, he explained, will be designed to provide information on how to secure U.N. contracts. The book will serve as a guide to the UN system, and its agencies' procurement process. There was no central procurement process with the U.N. Each agency has a different procurement process. Therefore because the book is well researched and will have information on the U.N. and all of its agencies procurement process, it will serve as a unique guide centrally navigating the procurement process of the UN and its agencies.

I understood Ralph's point on the procurement process of the United Nations system. I thought it was a great idea that the guide would serve as an important reference point to anyone who wants to do business with the U.N. I also thought that the information in the book, according to what Ralph explained to me, may improve the way in which the U.N. conducts its business by streamlining the procurement process thus improving the effectiveness and management of U.N. procurement.

He suggested that having such a conference would be doing a world of good by providing education and information to those who need it. At the conference business executives learn how the United Nations does business, and how companies and individuals may participate in the procurement process. I asked what kind of time frame he was looking at for the conference to take place. He told me that the book was expected out the first or second week of January 1995, and it would be very good to have the conference when it is released.

I asked him to send me a copy of the book as soon as it was out. I agreed to consider the possibility of having the conference pending the approval of our board members. He promised to fax some information, and ask me to respond as soon as possible to let him know if we are going to host the conference. Before we ended our conversation he said he hoped that our yes; we will host the conference.

Ethel and I discussed having the conference over the telephone. We loved the idea, but we were concerned about the cost. A business conference was nothing like planning a luncheon for regular UNA-USA activity. For one thing that type of conference could be an all day event, and catering to a business audience is a whole new set of attributes. Granted I am a business person and I am very familiar and know what it takes to put a business conference together. It would be the first business conference for UNA-USA. It was looking more like a project that needs to be coordinated by our executive team and the national office. We placed the business conference on the agenda for our next board meeting.

Linda Horkitz edited our final newsletter. She was an editor by profession. We mailed out the out the final newsletter for 1994 before the next board meeting was held. The uniqueness of our board and committee members was that each person had specialized skills in different areas. The resourceful pool of talent when combined was a wealth of resource for our leadership team.

We had our final board meeting in mid-December. Ethel and I were pleased to report the new developments to our board. A motion was made and seconded for the corporate partnership with Planeta Publishing. A second motion was introduced and seconded for the business conference on how to do business with the United Nations. After discussing and debating the issues of the corporate partnership with Planeta Publishing for the artwork contest, the board unanimously approved the project. The proposed conference on *How to Do Business with the United Nations*; was also unanimously approved by the board. We were more optimistic about UN50 in our final board meeting.

Ethel was very excited about all the things we had accomplished for the year. Janice Darbeau, Hyman Mally, Ethel, and I are the four members of our executive committee. We were very pleased with our accomplishments for the year. Janice was the secretary of our chapter, and she worked very hard at keeping our records especially now that we were doing so many things. The four of us kept in close contact at all times. Ethel said to me, "Sylvia, it begins to look like our hard work is paying off. I am delighted to review all we did for the year."

"We are a very good team. We ought to be very proud of all of our accomplishments for the year." I replied. Professor Watson had the honor of reading our end of year report for 1994. He reported those things that we did well and those that we did not do so well. He began by saying, "Honorable board members, it is my role to report what we did for 1994. Before I begin I want to be the first to congratulate Ms. Sylvia, our president, and her executive team for the hard work that they have done. I am proud that I was the one who invited our president to her first meeting at our chapter. I am proud of her and our team." He was Mr. Congeniality of our board. Whenever he speaks, it brings to mind a garden of roses. He had a wonderful way of saying his words. He was Mr. Diplomat in every sense of the word.

Professor Watson was one of our past presidents. He and his wife, Dr. Rose Watson, had a permanent position on our board. He began to name our accomplishments for 1994. First to be mentioned was our successful participation in the national convention in New York in January. He took time to suggest that it was quite likely that the presentation I delivered in New York led to the development of what was now to be the first conference on how to do business with the United Nations.

He spoke of our role in the South African election in Miami and the role that was played by Ethel and me representing our chapter. He spoke about the state annual meeting that was held at the Marco Polo Hotel Resort at great lengths. His words were "we simply outdid ourselves." He spoke about our UN Day and Mr. Picco's visit as keynote speaker. Professor Watson stood up and started a round of applause. We all joined him in cheering our 1994 accomplishments. We were happy that we survived the year on such a successful note.

We adjourned our meeting with the executive committee entrusted with the work of developing the new opportunities with Planeta Publishing for the artwork program, and with Ralph Cwerman for development of the business conference. I contacted Carlos Provencza and informed him that our board has given its approval for the artwork contest. He was very pleased that our board approved the project. He informed me that he too received approval from the executives of his company. We scheduled a meeting to begin charting our course of actions. In the meantime, we agreed to exchange formal correspondence of the approvals. I also contacted Ralph at the national office and told him that we were approved for the business conference.

He was pleased and very happy that I got back in touch with him so soon, and with such good news. He was very happy that the board approved the hosting of the business conference. We chatted a while about the exploratory stages of getting interest in the conference. I told him that I will begin speaking with our local trade groups and chambers of commerce leaders to field out and scout for potential interest in the conference.

He promised to send me a copy of the book as soon as it was off the press. We set a date in early January to speak with each other. In the meantime, he will begin looking at a potential dates for the event. He believe that we could work towards sometime in the spring, but he had to see what other events were on the calendar for that time of the year. We ended our conversation with great anticipation, looking forward to the opportunity of working together on the project.

Carlos and I exchanged our approval letters and scheduled our first developmental meeting for the last week in December. It was a tight fit to schedule a meeting during the holiday season but we managed to do so. Anne Della Camera one of our board members hosted our Christmas party. Her home was totally remodeled since being damaged by Hurricane Andrew. I was looking forward to see her new look.

At the Christmas party we exchanged gifts and well wishes. It was a good opportunity for everyone to meet my grandmother Lolita who was visiting us for Christmas 1994. Miami was her last stop on her worldwide tour. What can I say; she was one of the greatest persons ever. She was the lady that raised me and my siblings. Our mom passed away in 1962. She had eight children the youngest of whom was only ten months old. My older brother was twelve years old. Mama, our grandmother, did not think twice about moving all of my brothers and sisters into her home after the death of our mother. My older sister Gloria, our cousin Larry, and I were already living with our grandmother.

When my mom became ill, my older sister went to Roland's Field to help care for our brothers and sisters while my mom was hospitalized. She was not ill for a long time. She passed away within seven days of being hospitalized. The Friday before my mom passed away, I had an urgent need to see her. The last I saw her was during the summer holidays when I visited for two weeks. Everyone thought my mom was doing fine, and that quite possibly she would be discharged from the hospital by the weekend. That never happened.

I was sitting on a large rock at the foot of the hill looking south on the lowlands. There was a ship sailing into the harbor. The sun was rising in the east. The ball of light in bright orange radiated over the horizon, changing the color of the harbor and the skyline to a crystal blue with pink hues over the coastline. It was very early in the morning. There was the occasional crowing of roosters, some nearby and some in the distance. First one crows then the other respond in the distance. It must have been their way of talking. I sat on the rock, looking at the miniature figures of automobiles on the road in the lowlands. The vehicles looked like ladybugs hurrying along in opposite directions.

The Plantain Garden River meanders through the green cane fields that looked like a perfectly cut lawn. I was sitting on the rock on top of the ridge. That was the name of the property, The Ridge. Picture if you will a peak with valleys to the right and left. From the incline, the land rose again into mountainous regions that were lush with tropical flora and forest. I wondered how the trees stood on the hillside without falling into the streams in the valleys. So there I sat on a rock on the ridge, looking out on the lowlands. It was a picture-perfect Saturday morning, but there was a certain stillness of the morning.

The dampness of the morning dew was still visible on the rocks and leaves. There was a patch of morning glory just beneath the foot of the rock on which I was sitting. I will close the shame mockers when it gets dry, I did not want the dew to touch me feet, I thought to myself. I do not know how long I was sitting on the rock. At ten years old time did not matter. I heard the sound of the horns. It was odd that the horns were sounding constantly without pausing. I knew something was wrong. The sound of the auto got louder as it drew closer to our home. I was still on the ridge. I stood on the rock, turned around and began peering through the tall branches of the trees that rose out of the valley. I shifted my position to get a better view, peering through the opening among the tree limbs. I saw a white car. It was my dad's car. I knew that something was wrong; I could feel it in the pit of my stomach.

I jumped off the rock and began running up the hill. I reached the top of the hill and was in the front yard before my dad's car could turn the corner. The car pulled up in the driveway. My dad opened the car door and stepped out. He did not have to say anything; I looked at him and said, "My mom died." The tears rolled down his cheeks. My grandmother rushed out of the house in total confusion. She rushed to my dad and said to him, "Son, Jane left us?" She embraced my dad. The whole world stood still. All I heard was silence. It was September 1, 1962.

I picked rosebuds from the garden and placed them in my frock pocket. Then I heard the *knock, knock, knock.* The silence was broken. "I don't know why the peckers are so noisy," I said as my uncle Bob, who came in the car with my dad. Uncle Bob was my mother's brother. He came over and took my hand and led me out of the flower bed. He opened both arms and lifted me up. One of my rosebuds fell to the ground. "Uncle Bob, I don't know why the peckers are so noisy," I said to him as the tears began to roll down my face. He embraced me as he too began to cry.

People in our community began to slowly gather at our house. My cousin Larry and I were left in the care of Aunt Jean our grandaunt and Uncle Bob. Mama and my dad got in the car and drove to Roland's Field to get my brothers and sisters. My grandmother took everyone in her home. She raised all of us, and a fine job she did caring for my siblings and me.

My grandmother was visiting us for the Christmas holidays. Ethel called to remind me that my grandmother was invited as a special guest to our Christmas party. Ethel wanted to meet her, and she was not going to give up the chance to have a fireside chat over eggnog with my grandmother.

It was a very good party. Friends and relatives met, exchanged gifts, and shared in the festive season and Christmas spirit. There was something about the flickering lights on the Christmas tree that put a smile on everyone's face. There was plenty to eat and plenty to talk about. Hors d'oeuvres, cookies, and good food were in abundance. My grandmother and Ethel sat in the Florida room. The two ladies hit it off, I saw they were enjoying their conversations and having fun.

Bill Miller joined them occasionally to talk about UN50. Bill could not put aside UN50 for one moment. Every chance he got he spoke about UN50 celebrations. Bill was a national board member. He also worked with the Kentucky legislature. He was also a leader in the Council of Chapter and Division Presidents. My grandmother enjoyed the party, but she especially enjoyed meeting some of the people with whom I worked in the organization. We tried to stay away from talking about UNA-USA activities as much as we could. We concentrated on family and friends and what our plans were for the holiday season and the New Year.

CHAPTER 6

F RIENDS OF THE *Future* was the name of our UN50 program that was designed for middle and elementary schools in our community. It is a unique program that allows students to communicate messages to the United Nations by drawing pictures or writing poems for the fiftieth anniversary celebrations. The objectives were to encourage the participation of students in an event that was being observed and celebrated world wide; and to increase public awareness of the works of the United Nations through public outreach.

Over sixteen thousand students and over four thousand parents and teachers participated in that event. We collected twenty thousand pieces of artwork from our students. The participation levels far exceeded our expectations. We expected at the most about three hundred participants and were astounded by the results. It was a great showing for our students, and a worthwhile effort for all of our team members bringing UN50 to our community.

The project involved teamwork on all levels among teachers, principals, parents, the UNA-USA school committee, members of the school board, Planeta Publishing, and a whole host of volunteers. Our program for elementary and middle schools was centered in Dade County the home base of our chapter. After the events were completed the schools were ranked by the percentage of enrolled students who participated.

The district finalists were Kenwood Elementary that won first place, Gratigny was placed second, and Broadmoor placed third. We were amazed and very pleased with the levels of participation. We kept a flow of the activities in each phase as they were executed, but it was not until everything was over that we realized the full magnitude and the significance of the participation levels. The following list shows the participating schools and their placements in the program.

Friends of the Future Dade County School Placements

Region	1st Place	2nd Place	3rd Place
I	North Dade Center for Modern Languages	North Twin Lakes Elementary	Lake Stevens Elementary
II	Gratigny Elementary	Biscayne Gardens Elementary	Bay Harbor Elementary
III	Broadmoor Elementary	Lillie C. Evans Elementary	Melrose Elementary
IV	Kensington Elementary	Auburndale Elementary	Sunset Elementary
V	Kenwood	Devonaire	Gloria Floyd
VI	Claude Pepper	Emerson	Caribbean

Our team worked very hard to develop the program for the schools. The unique array of team members representing different organizational structures and cultures posed great challenges. We overcame those challenges with team spirit and the great desire for our students to participate in UN50

The program was founded when we visited the auditorium to see Don Gilberts' exhibit of *Freeda*, a twenty-three-foot statue. The statue was Don's expression of the representation of freedom. While at the exhibit, we met Carlos Provencza, a representative of Planeta Publishing Company. After several meetings and discussions, the company agreed to sponsor and underwrite the cost of our Friends of the Future project. Planeta Publishing Company was one of our local businesses in Miami Dade County. Planeta's corporate headquarters is located in Madrid, Spain. Our board of directors unanimously approved the event and likewise the executive members of Planeta also gave their approval of the program.

Before the program could be finalized and executed, we had to clear all the hurdles with the Dade County School Board. We did not have much time to do this because it was now January, and the school year ends in June. We worked with the clock to get the approval of the school board; design and develop the program; get material and worksheets printed; and execute the program. It was one of our "TAAL" order for UN50 celebrations. We were thinking and acting locally. We had to complete our program within the current school year if it was ever going to be a part of our UN50 celebrations. UN50 celebrations will end October 24, 1995.

Our school committee was led by Dr. Michael Kesselman, Carlos Provencza, Ethel, Hyman Mally, Janice Darbeau, and I met with Dr. Barbara Carey, who was the chair of the Alternate Education Program for the school board. It was important that Carlos Provencza, who represented Planeta Publishing the sponsoring company, also be a member of our school committee. We met at Dr. Carey's office where we outlined the program and its purpose. We solicited input on how the program may be presented to the school board from Dr. Carey. With the information we gathered at the meeting, and through intense coordination efforts, we made the first draft of the programs' content.

Dr. Kesselman was very instrumental in this effort. His knowledge of the school system made it easier to navigate our way by reducing the leg work. He also worked with Dr. Carey on the Alternative Education Program. The Dade County public school population was comprised of over 120 different ethnic cultures. We expected students from all backgrounds to participate in the program.

The fact that the program was provided at no cost to the schools was very appealing. The cost of our program was underwritten by our corporate partner. UNA-USA Greater Miami continue to contribute our efforts through volunteerism. Dr. Carey was motivated by the opportunity for the students to participate in a UN50 activity. UN50 was being observed across the globe.

Our foremost challenge in developing and executing the program was logistics. We wanted a program design that encouraged maximum participation, but at the same time would have minimum impact on the schools curriculum, if any at all. We did not wish to interrupt the current emphasis of school work. We realized that both students and teachers already had a lot of work to do from the preplanned curricula for the school year.

Our Friends of the Future team got down to business and worked at designing a fun program for the students. The program required precision execution and implementation. Each team member's role was clearly defined. We drafted all of the program materials that will be used. All of our designs and logos were laid out. We made sure all of our teams were well represented on our program materials. The next area of consideration was how were we going to distribute the worksheets for the students artworks to the schools.

Miami Dade County Public Schools is the nations fourth largest school district. It is comprised of over 350 schools with a student population of over 325,000 students. The student population are diverse representing over 150 countries. Our Friends of the Future Program was designed for Miami—Dade County Elementary and Middle Schools. Because of the size of the school district over geographical area and the large student population; logistics and distribution was formidable challenge. We could not have taken on this project without our corporate partner.

The Alternative Education department furnished us with the school calendars. We worked around the preplanned activities to ensure there were no conflicts of the program with school activities. Our program activities were limited to the current school year with no carry over. We were told to expect a participation level of approximately three hundred students. That expectation was based on past experiences of similar programs within the schools.

There were no pre-requisite for participation in the program and neither were there any minimum or maximum threshold in participation levels. It was an open participation fun program for the students. In drafting the plans for the program we included all six regions in the school district, and program materials were to be distributed to each school in each region. We went to the drawing board and created a flow chart of the entire program. We mapped the location of each school in each region. As difficult as it was to create a distribution and collection plan for the worksheets, we did a fine job that we thought would work perfectly.

This was our approach in distributing the worksheets to all the middle and elementary schools in Dade County. The plan was, in the first week of the program we distribute worksheets to all of the schools. In the second week collect all the finished worksheets following the same order in which they were distributed in the first week. In the third week distributed the invitations to view the exhibits in the same order beginning with the first school that received the first set of worksheets in the first week of distribution; and continue in that order until all invitations are distributed.

The first exhibit was scheduled for Saturday, April 29, 1995. The final exhibit was for June 3, 1995. All of our exhibits were scheduled to take place on Saturdays only. This way it was convenient for parents, students and teachers to attend. We conducted numerous team meetings to revamp, re-construct and back to the draft board scenarios before finalizing the program. Our executive committee revisited the corporate executives to finalize all arrangements for the project. This time we asked for a donation to be made to the chapter to cover our escalating costs in producing the program.

We met with the school board representatives for our final presentation and approval. We took our program blueprints and made complete disclosure about every aspect of the program. We took copies of all materials that were to be used in the program; we also include copies of agreements for disclosure purposes. The program description and outline including timeline, execution dates, implementation, backup plans, and flowcharts were presented with our proposal to the board. The meeting for the final presentation was held in the first week of February. It took us one month to develop the entire program but we could not have done it without teamwork. Our Friends of the Future project for middle and elementary schools was ready for execution and implementation.

Our team met at the office of the Alternate Education Program. We explained the entire process of distribution and collection of worksheets for each school and the distribution of invitations for the exhibits. Planeta's staff will distribute all of the worksheets and invitations. The completed artworks are to be delivered to Dr. Kesselman at the office of the Alternate Education Program. Dr. Kesselman then tabulate the results for participation levels by schools and region, then report those results to Planeta; who then distributes the invitations to each school for the exhibits.

The invitations were distributed to the principal of each participating school; and then given to the students who participated to take home to their parents. If the parents choose to visit the exhibits with their child or children, they were provided with refreshments, and the students received gifts for participating, and certificates in honor of UN50 celebrations.

The exhibits were hosted by UNA-USA volunteers. In the exhibit halls and rooms information and videos about the United Nations and US leadership in the world organization, and information on UNA-USA. Planeta's display of encyclopedia were at another location in the same hotel, but close enough so that those parents who choose to attend could have done so without difficulty. Parents had the option of either choosing to visit those displays or not. After we finished explaining the entire program and processes we left copies of the blueprints and all pertinent information for approval. We were all satisfied that it was a productive meeting, we ended our meeting and waited for approval.

Our business conference was developed concurrently with the Friends of the Future project. It is difficult to discuss both projects at the same time because they were separate venues and different sets of developments. All of UNA-USA workers are volunteers. I only had a small paid staff in my office. We could not have done what we were doing without teamwork. Our programs are "TAAL" orders which is to *think and act locally.* The development of the business conference will be discussed in the next chapter.

The word came from Dr. Kesselman that the *Friends of the Future* program was approved. Shortly after he called my office to tell us the good news, we received the letter of approval. We communicated the information to Carlos who was ready with his distribution team. The team immediately shifted into execution mode. First, the printers were contacted and given the go ahead to produce the worksheets. All worksheets for the artworks were now in print. Before the worksheets were off the press a letter was sent to each principal in the schools announcing the event and the dates when worksheets will be distributed to his or her school.

Shortly before the program worksheets were to be distributed I received a call from Dr. Carey's office. She informed me that the telephone was on the speaker. She also informed me that she had one of our school's principal on the line. I asked her to hold while I move to the conference room to take the call. I asked my assistant to join us and I too placed the call on the speaker phone. I informed Dr. Carey that I have placed the phone on the speaker and that my assistant Andrea was with me in the room.

Our discussion began with the principal stating that the program was a ponzi scheme. She also stated that we had no connections to fiftieth anniversary of the United Nations or the U.N. for that matter. She was very upset and angry. She suggested that Dr. Carey was totally misled by us. She wanted to have nothing to do with the program or us.

We listened to her and I understood her concerns. She continued to speak and we allowed her to vent her feelings. When she paused and I had a chance to speak, I told her that I understood her concerns and I am willing to provide her with additional information on the program. The principal was not satisfied with the information that I provided to her. She became more resistant to the program. She made remarks that could be considered abusive. It was apparent that there was nothing we could do or say to change her opinion of us or the program.

I informed her that there was no mandate of participation. If she elected not to participate that would be fine. The choice was entirely up to her. The principal's hostility continued and nothing could have been done to change her mind about the way she perceived our team. She turned her anger on Dr. Carey accusing her of succumbing to scammers. I informed the principal that Dr. Carey has been very helpful by assisting us with the program. She was very receptive and holds the interest of her peers and students at heart with the highest integrity. I informed her that Dr.Carey has been very helpful by assisting us with the program. She has been very receptive and holds the interest of her peers and students at heart with the highest of integrity.

We did everything that we could to persuade the principal to participate in our program. We were unable to convince her to change her perception and to participate in the program. We were more saddened that the students would not be able to participate in UN50. It was her school and she ruled. I finally told Dr. Carey that I had to end the call to tend to other matters, she did the same too and our conversation ended.

We encountered other challenges in our program, but this time it was with one of our own board members. She developed a very antagonistic attitude about the program. I do not know how that attitude came about because she was one of the board members who voted on the approval of the program. She contacted one a member of the executive team of our corporate partner and made not too pleasant remarks.

I have been working closely with our sponsors. I wondered why anyone would pick up the telephone to do such a thing. Did she think the corporate executive had no judgment of character? Because we operated under a team structure in our project, and the fact that we had a transparency policy, there was no fear of dismantling the project. It was to the vested interest of the team that we successfully completed the program abiding by or defined parameters. Because the remarks that were made by the board member were personal interjections there was no need to validate the point. To do so would have quite possible take up more of our time. That board member was not a member of the immediate team who were working on the project. We continued with our program.

The first set of worksheets were distributed to the schools in the first week of April. From that time onward the work cycle of distributing worksheets, and collecting the students' artworks continued. In the second week of the program Dr. Kesselman called us to report the level of participation. We were absolutely pleased with the report. The participation level was higher than 90 percent from the first school whose artworks were collected. The numbers kept increasing each day as worksheets were turned in.

We had a big problem however, but it was problem that our team welcomed. Planeta ordered just enough invitations based on the expected participation levels. We expected a total of 300 participants in the program so we did not have all the invitations that were needed to meet the new participation levels. There was not enough even for the first school's level of participation. That problem was quickly resolved when Planeta ordered more invitations from the printers to meet the new levels of expected participation. Our new expected levels of participation was over 80 percent for all schools who participate in the program.

Each student participated only once. Over sixteen thousand students participated. Because of the high levels of participation Carlos rearranged the venues by increasing the capacity of spaces for more people. The exhibits were arranged to be held at a local hotel in each region where the schools that participated were located. This way there was easy access, and convenience for parents who accepted invitations and attended the display of the students artworks.

A thank you letter was sent each principal, and invitations were distributed to each school for each student who participated in the program. The exhibits were held on each Saturday from from April 29 to June 3, 1995. The official

official presentations to schools culminate at the UN50 celebrations in October. I was unable to attend the first exhibit due to an auto accident that occurred two days before the event.

On April 27, 1995 I went to pick up the lunch at a nearby Chinese restaurant for everyone in our office. While I was backing out of the parking space another motorist ran into the backside of my vehicle. I was taken to the hospital and later released to the care of my physician. Because of my injuries from the accident I was laid up for a few days. Ethel filled in for me and signed the UN50 certificates for the students who attended the exhibit that day. I was told that the exhibit went very well. A large number of students and parents turned out to view the students' artworks.

The second exhibit was scheduled for Saturday May 6, 1995. The day before the event I left my home and was heading to my office. As I approached the intersection, which was in close proximity to where the first auto accident occurred a week earlier, another motorist ran into the back of my car. I had not yet taken the car into the shop for repairs. My car looked like a crumpled piece of paper.

The same police officer who took the report for the first accident a week earlier, showed for the reporting of second accident. I told him it must have something to do with the color of my car. It was a silver Taurus. He shook his head and said he doubted it had anything to do with the color of my car. It was back to the hospital again. I was released the same day with an increase of my pain medication. I was feeling banged up with pain all over but thank goodness the doctors did not waste any time in getting me into physical therapy. It was very difficult to differentiate what was caused by which of the accidents. Fortunately I had before and after pictures of damages to my automobile from the first accident to the second one.

While all the events and scenarios surrounding the auto accidents were going on we had to bring in more volunteers to assist with the exhibits. The turn out was much more than what was expected. We increased the breaks and lunches for our volunteers. We also made sure that we had enough volunteers for the entire day because the flow of people in an out of the exhibits was constant.

It was quite an experience to observe the interaction of students and parents as they walked among the displays of artworks. There were more than three schools in each region. The dates of the exhibits were scheduled by regions, but each school's student artworks were exhibited in a separate hall. If there were six schools in one region for example, there were six rooms of exhibits. One room displayed the students artworks from one school.

Our Friends of the Future project achieved our objectives of public outreach while encouraging our students to participate in UN50. At the same time in line with our "thinking and acting locally" motto our activities were stimulants to our local economy. It was a win win situation for everyone. Our local printers, trophy shops, and hotels went through a whirl wind of activities because of our project. Our students, their parents and their teachers had the wonderful opportunity of viewing their artworks, as well as those of their friends from the same school, and also the artworks of other students from other schools in the same region. That was a once in a life time opportunity that was made possible because of the celebration of the fiftieth anniversary of the United Nations.

Planeta's display of their products were in another location at the other end of the hotel. It was planned this way because we knew that the exhibit would have have a higher flow of traffic. So we limit the activities in close proximity of the exhibits to UN and UNA-USA activities. One could easily observe the parents pleasure and pride in viewing the students' artworks. It was a fun activity for all, the students were overjoyed, and so were our team; we were very pleased with the success of our UN50 program. The student's theme "My Message to the United Nations" were welcome and befitting the celebrations of the fiftieth anniversary of the United Nations.

The invitations were prepared for delayed time sequences with an hour-and-a-half delay between schools in the same region. This way the number of people in the exhibit at given hours was limited to one school at a time. The exhibits were open from 10:00 a.m. until 5:00 p.m. If a parent was late for the hour that was printed on the invitation, they could still see their child or children's work anytime during those hours.

Ethel, Hyman, and I took turns in signing UN50 certificates for the students. Once the parent and student viewed the exhibits, they were ushered to the UNA-USA table to receive a certificate that was presented to the student for participating in the event. The pride and joy was visible in the demeanor of each student as they shook hands and received his or her certificate. I would not have missed this interaction for the world. It was a wonderful experience.

There was one student who I remembered very well because of the composure with which he entered the line to receive his certificate. It was a grade one student. He was accompanied by his father. Before he entered the line, he took time to place his shirt in his pants and pulled them up. He kept on tucking his shirt in his pants as he walked in the line. He did it again just before I shook his hand and gave him his certificate. Without anyone prompting him to do what he did, He stood with his shoulders back, standing up straight. His smile was from one cheek to the other, he tucked in his shirt them came to receive his certificate. His dad stood beside him, I looked at the young man and smiled while I shook his hand. I knew his dad was very proud of him.

The theme that was suggested on the students worksheets was "My message to the United Nations". This was done to keep it uniform with the theme of the national essay contest for the same year. Although this theme was suggested students were not compelled to follow that format or theme. Students through their teachers were encouraged to use their own creativity. Our intent was simply to provide an opportunity for our students to participate in UN50. Some of the students artworks included included messages such as : *stop world hunger; save our planet; save our children; end all wars; get rid of drugs; protect children from sweat shops; save the trees; I want to work at the UN when I grow up,* and whole host of variety of messages. That was over sixteen years ago and by now all of those students are adults. Given all the changes that took place in our world since that time, it is interesting to know what there messages to the United Nations would be today.

Some of the artworks brought tears to the eyes of parents who visited the exhibition. The students expressions in their artworks were very moving. Some of the parents were not aware that the students were capable of communicating such profound messages as were depicted in their works. It was difficult to say if it was the artworks, the messages, or the realization that the students were in touch with global issues that caused the stirring experiences. I am more apt to believe that it was a combination of all of the above. While some pieces of their artwork brought tears, others brought laughter and smiles. Some even raised a few eyebrows. A feedback from the volunteers in the exhibits thematically suggested that the parents would like the works to be preserved. Their artworks increased public awareness of the United Nations and U.S. leadership in the world organization.

The final exhibit for the students' artworks was scheduled for Saturday, June 3, 1995. My plans were to drive to Miami and stay overnight, this way I would not have to drive too far to get to the exhibit location. I had some equipment that I need to set up before the exhibit open. I was on my way not too far from where I lived, and while waiting for a traffic light to change, someone plowed into the back of my car. I was taken to the hospital by an ambulance.

My car sat in the parking lot of a nearby shopping mall while I was taken to the hospital. The police officers who came to the scene of the accident had the car moved off the road and placed there until I was able to retrieve it. I was discharged from the hospital in the wee hours of the morning. I took a cab to where the car was parked. I did not call home to alert anyone of the accident. I did not want my son to worry; the auto accidents were occurring too frequently. The rental car that was given to me temporarily while my vehicle was in repair was totally smashed in the back. There was no damage to the front end and it was drivable. It was a hit-and-run accident. The other motorist left the scene of the accident before the police and ambulance arrived.

I drove to Miami. My friend wondered where I was. He wondered what had happened to me. I had contacted him before I left home to let him know that I was on my way. He called my son when I did not arrive within the time it would have taken to get to his place. Neither of them knew where I was.

When I got to his place I told him there was an accident and I was taken to the hospital. I later called my son and told him what happened and assure him that I would be O.K. They were both worried when they did not hear from me. Hugh helped me with the cold packs for my bruises and pain.

He left the house before I did to set up the equipment and displays at the hotel. He removed the monitor and other supplies from my vehicle and placed them in his. He told me to get some rest and not to worry because he would take care of getting everything ready for the exhibit. He informed my team members about the accident. My son came and got me and we drove to the exhibit later that day.

The students exhibit on June 3, 1995 were from the region where the schools had the highest student population. We expected a high flow of traffic at the exhibit. When I arrived at the location there was a big problem. The number of people who turned out to view the artworks exceeded the capacity based on fire regulations for the hotel. We held an emergency meeting with the facility management. It was held at the Sheraton Hotel at Dadeland Mall. We closed off the lines because we could not allow more people to enter the exhibits.

The names of the schools from which students did not get to see the exhibits were recorded. We did not plan for the program to go beyond the school year.

However, we redistributed invitations to those schools because the parents and students wanted to see their artworks in exhibit. We were disappointed but we had no choice but to consider the safety of everyone first. For those schools and students who did not get a chance to see their exhibits, Carlos arranged an exhibit for the following Saturday, June 10. It was the final week of the school year.

Parents and students showed up to view their exhibits. The students received their gifts and UN50 certificates. The smiles and laughter returned to our team. We were very happy that all schools, students, and parents were able to view the artworks. The only difference in the final exhibit was that the artworks displayed were only for those schools in the region that could not enter the exhibit the previous Saturday.

The Friends of the Future program that was designed for middle and elementary schools was intended to be a one-time program in honor of the fiftieth anniversary of the United Nations. The objective was to have the local students participate in a UN50 event. The logistics for the program were intricate and required precision planning due to time constraints. The theme of the program was "My Message to the United Nations." It was a local event in line with our "TAAL" order approach. That is, we "think and act locally."

The success of our program was due to the great teamwork and team spirit of everyone involved. Our corporate sponsors, our school committee, our volunteers, our teachers, our parents, and students gave one hundred percent effort within as short window of time to produce the levels of participation in UN50. We expected a participation level of three hundred students. Over sixteen thousand students and over four thousand parents and teachers participated. The results shattered any stereotypical images of inner city students and parents with respect to willingness to participate.

Most importantly, the participation levels in relationship to the theme of the program demonstrate interests in not only what happens locally and nationally but also on the global scale. Our volunteers and corporate partner worked very hard and diligently to deliver the program and its contents. We were simply people working to educate our community on the work of the United Nations and U.S. leadership in the world organization. As the local chapter of UNA-USA we would have failed our community had we not sought to involve our students in UN50 activities and to increase public awareness of the same. Our association believed we accomplished our objectives of conducting public outreach and by encouraging participation.

At the end of June, 1995, Planeta delivered to my office twenty large boxes with the artworks of the students. The final awards and recognition for participation would culminate in the UN50 celebration, which was held in October. We lived up to our commitments in the Friends of the Future. It was a demonstration of what can be accomplished with teamwork, planning, and dedicated team members.

As for the three automobile accidents that occurred at critical times during the program; they are almost too true to believe. Chances are they were not program related but are due to external forces. It is only after the dust settles when everyone can see clearly. We were motivated and inspired by the enthusiasm, desire, and willingness of each student who participated in UN50. They are truly our *Friends of the Future*.

CHAPTER 7

THE FIRST BUSINESS conference *"How to do business with the United Nations"* was held on March 31, 1995, at the Eden Roc Hotel in Miami Beach. The conference was developed concurrently with the *Friends of the Future* program. The conference focused on providing business owners, professionals, and business executives with information on how the United Nations and its agencies conduct business and how to be a part of that process. That conference, similarly to our *Friends of the Future* program, was conduct as a part of our UN50 activities increasing public awareness on the U.S. Leadership in the world organization.

The business conference featured the newly released 370-page procurement business manual that was published by UNA-USA. The book's title was *How to Do Business with the United Nations: the Complete Guide to U.N. Procurement*. Over eighty companies attended the conference, which brought several high-level UN officials from New York and from Haiti to Miami to discuss how the United Nations does business.

Organizing and hosting the conference was another of our "TAAL" order thinking *and acting locally*. On the day of the conference President Bill Clinton transferred operations in Haiti to the United Nations. The event generated wide publicity which was largely responsible for the level of attendance. It was the first time that our chapter undertook such an event, but it was done in the spirit of UN50. The conference was UN related and it was just another opportunity to increase public awareness of the work of the United Nations and U.S. Leadership in that organization.

In early January 1995, I received four copies of the new publication from Ralph Cwerman, the director of corporate affairs at our national office. In late 1994 when Ralph and I had last spoken, which was the time we explored having the conference, he promised to send me a few copies of the publication as soon as they were available. The conference was approved unanimously by our board.

As of mid-January, we were not sure on what date the conference was going to be held. We knew we were working with a tight time line, and if we were ever going to get the business conference off the ground we had to get busy. Our UN50 activities must be completed within the scope of UN50. The fiftieth anniversary was October 25, 1995. Our activities were a series of year long programs that began in October 1994 through October 1995. While I work at developing funding and program designs, I often wondered why UN50 was not placed on the calendar before now. Everything for that celebration was on a tight timeline.

So I received copies of the book as Ralph had promised. I gave one copy to one of our board members to share among themselves. I needed to get their opinion of the book. I sent one copy to the *Miami Herald* business editor. Ethel and I had one copy each as members of the executive committee. We were on the frontline of the business conference, and we need to have the feature publication on hand at all times for reference.

Ethel and I began working on a list of those whom we thought may have an interest in attending the conference. Ralph worked on his list from the national area. Ethel and I contacted the president of the Beacon Council. We arranged to meet with him to enlist his support for the conference. We had zero funds for the activity. It required a lot of innovation and creativity if we were going to bring the business conference to fruition.

We already have the board's approval for the activity; the development of the conference was delegated to the executive committee, as was the case with any new business or program developments in our chapter. Thus most of our discussion on the business conference development was kept in our executive portfolio.

Although the board approved the business conference there was some dissentions among our chapter members about the whole thing of a business conference. It was the first time ever that our chapter was hosting a business conference; it was the first time that UNA-USA was having a business conference of that nature, and perhaps the first too for the United Nations.

Because it was the first time conducting such an event on all levels it represented a change, so we encountered resistance to change. The problem, however, was that there were no status quo against which to base an evaluation at any level of our organizations. It was just something new. Our only approach therefore was to engage creativity and innovation. We could only learn from

our experience, improve where needed and move forward. Our problems were not unsolvable, the key was to find a way to solve them. This is the reason why creativity and innovation played such a key role in our moving forward.

We discussed the problems among ourselves in the executive committee. Our pressing problem was garnering the support for the conference in the business community as well as how we were going to finance the activity. We resolved that quite possibly what we were dealing with was perhaps a question of "cannot see the forest for the trees" or "what comes first, chicken or egg" situation. Another consideration to the problems we encountered was the question "if a tree falls in the forest and there was no one or animal around, would there be a sound of the falling tree?"

The activity was approved at the national and local levels; therefore, the executive committee figured that the dissentions could not have been a policy issue. It must have been something else. Suffice to say, because approvals were given on all levels, had we not moved ahead with the program, any blames for failure to execute would have been placed squarely on our heads; speaking of damned if you do and damned if you don't.

We were working within a short time frame to develop and execute the project; as the host of the event, we had the lion's share of the work. For sure we had a strong team with resourceful team members, but like everything else in life we also had the let's wait and see situations in our team too. Ethel and I were the Mickey squared complex. If we tried it and liked it then everyone else goes along with it.

Ethel suggested that we make our first contact with the Beacon Council. She knew the president of the Beacon Council. They both were members of the same church. We contacted John Hall, the vice president of the Beacon Council. I told him why I was calling, what we are planning to do and when it will be, and we would like to have the support of the Beacon Council. Ethel offered to send him her copy of the procurement guide. He promised he would get back to us in a couple of days after he made rounds with his executive team, to see what they think of the idea.

The Beacon Council is Miami-Dade County's primary and official economic development partnership. It is charged with bringing new job-generating investments to the community. Since its creation in 1985, it has assisted over eight hundred companies, which have created jobs in the community. UNA-USA Greater Miami was not in the business of economic development, but we figured that having the support of the Beacon Council was a good way to start the development of our business conference; one may lead to another and so on.

The copy of the procurement guide was delivered to the office of John Hall. A few days later, he called us with the time and date of our first meeting with the Beacon Council. He told us that we would be meeting with John

Anderson, the president of the Beacon Council, and himself. Ethel and I were very pleased of that development. Of course we never led on or informed John Hall that Ethel and John Anderson were members of the same church. While we were working on the conference development, we were also working on the Friends of the Future program concurrently.

The day came for our meeting. I assembled a presentation package with brochures on UNA-USA, our UN50 committees, and other useful information that will provide the Beacon Council with as much information as possible about our organization and the work we do. I was in the north and Ethel was only minutes away from the Beacon Council; I headed south to meet her at 80 SW Eight Street.

We took the elevator to the twenty-fourth floor. At the reception area, we announced our arrival. As we usually do when we attend official chapter business meetings, Ethel was dressed in red and white, and I wore a blue suit with a white blouse. We do this all the time; we dress in the colors of the United States and the United Nations flags. We always try to make a good impression by coordinating our colors. It works some of the time, and at other times, it simply does not work. We hope to make a good impression in the meeting with the executive members of the Beacon Council.

After a brief getting-acquainted session, I began the presentation. I told the gentlemen who we were and what we were doing and I also explained the type of support that we were looking for from the Beacon Council. It was a good meeting. The fact that Ethel and John Anderson knew each other created an easier flow of our discussion. John has been the president of the council since 1991. John asked who is the backbone of all our local chapter operations. I turned the question over to Ethel to provide the answer. Ethel responded by pointing in my direction and saying, "We are operating out of her office." We informed John that the business conference was a one-time thing as a part of our UN50 celebrations.

Before we left the meeting, he offered his support for the business conference. He provided us with our contact person at the Beacon Council and pledged any support that we needed. We were ecstatic and thrilled by his offer of support. Our meeting lasted for about an hour. We discussed the work of the Beacon Council and its latest developments. This was our first meeting with the council. We were not sure of all that we would need from them except that we would need to have invitations distributed to its membership. We left the meeting feeling satisfied and with a great sense of accomplishment.

We continued to build interest in the conference by contacting the local chambers of commerce, including those in Miami-Dade, Broward, Palm Beach, and other surrounding areas. For the most part, our request of those organizations was that we provide the invitations to their offices, and they in turn were to mail the invitations to their members.

We received agreements in principle. In return, the organization would be listed as a cooperating organization on our programs and brochures for the event. We began to build a strong momentum for the conference. We made progress reports to Ralph at the national office, and he did the same. We made several attempts to get sponsorship for the conference. We approached some of our local professional associations and a few businesses. Several promised us some kind of financial assistance. But those promises never materialized.

It was late January and we still had no commitments of funding. Without the funds there was no way we could underwrite the cost of that program. In the interim Ralph informed me that the tentative date for the event was March 31, 1995. He also suggested that the place where the conference would be held is the Eden Roc Hotel in Miami Beach. All that was good and fine but we still had no funds to underwrite the event.

He faxed me a preliminary draft of the program and the list of speakers. I almost flipped out. I showed the program to Ethel; she too almost flipped out. There were too many speakers. I called Ralph and asked him where am I to get the money from to pay the cost for so many speakers to travel to the event. Who was going to pay the cost of accommodation for so many people? I told him that the conference is off. We have no money and there would be too many speakers and who knows what else he had in mind. It appears that we had different ideas of what the program would be. He realized that I was upset and suggested I take some time out.

I called again later that day and I left him a message on his voice mail. The message I left was to the effect that we had no money, we cannot afford to underwrite the conference, and therefore we are cancelling or backing out of the deal. As far as I am concerned the conference is off, at least it will not be hosted by our chapter. I really did not see the need to pussy foot around with Ralph at that point. I had enough on my plate.

Ethel thought that I should not have left him such a direct message, but I told her that we had to cut to the chase and lay it out to him. The next morning, Ralph returned my call. He had an unusually softer tone in his voice. He paid special attention of saying my name nicely. I knew that I was being pacified or coaxed. I went along with him. We spoke about different things for a long time. He gradually channeled the conversation to the direction of the business conference.

I told him that I knew where he was headed in the conversation, but it isn't happening because we had no funds to do the conference. I had hoped by now that we would have some sponsorship but there was none. He told me he received my message. He convinced me that there was a lot riding on the conference and they would not leave me holding the bag. The business conference was not like other programs. I really did not enjoy being placed in the position where the conference now depends on me.

I told him we would need to shorten the speakers list. There were too many speakers. He agreed in principle. After our very long conversation I told him that I will reconsider my position on the issue. Ethel and I discussed the issue. I told her what Ralph and I discussed. She too agreed that perhaps I should reconsider my decision of cancelling the business conference.

My personal funds were nearly exhausted from having to fund so many of our chapter's activities and operations. The overhead costs were increasing. I was already paying too much. It was good that Planeta was underwriting the program costs of the students' project. Our arrangement with Planeta was that all bills would go to them and they were to settle them. I did not have the staff to handle all that additional paperwork. That was I relief I thought to myself.

Airfare for speakers alone at the conference is estimated to cost almost five thousand dollars, not to mention additional accommodation costs. I could not understand why we need all those speakers when we have a procurement guide anyway. I thought about the matter some more. I did not want to be the party pooper. I did not want to be the one who was responsible for the event not taking place, but regardless the cost was still too much. We needed to cut some of the things that are not needed. I approached a very good friend and asked him for a short-term loan.

Hugh was an American Maritime Officer (AMO). American Maritime Officers is a national labor union affiliated with the Seafarers International Union of North America. Its active membership of approximately 4,000 is the largest union of merchant marine officers in the U.S., and primarily represents licensed mariners who work in the United States Merchant Marine on U.S. flagged merchant and military sealift vessels. Captain Hastings has been in the U.S. Merchant Marines for many years. We knew each other from childhood. He has always been one of my trusted friends since our youth. I called him and asked for a time to meet with him. He said, "No problem" and gave me a time to meet with him.

We met at his house, and over a cup of green tea, I discussed with him the development of the business conference. I also explained to him that we did not have all the funds that were needed to cover the cost of the event. I asked Hugh for a loan of ten thousand dollars. He asked how the loan would be repaid. I told him that the procurement guide would be sold to business executives for $373 per copy. We expected an attendance of over two hundred business executives. I would repay him after the conference.

He did not think twice about giving the short-term loan. Furthermore, he knew that I would not have asked him for the loan had it not been for a good and pressing need. He agreed to give me the loan. I had arrived with promissory note in my folder. I called Ralph from Hugh's house and told him that I had the funding for the project. But we must repay the short term loan. Ralph was ecstatic. I heard him saying "Yes, yes, yes!"

Hugh and I drove to his bank to have the promissory note signed, witnessed, and notarized. He wrote a check for ten thousand dollars and gave it to me. With those funds and my personal resources, we were able to go full force in producing the business conference. At the time, I had no intentions of that loan becoming a long term instrument. It was only suppose to be a short term thing.

As mentioned earlier the conference was set to take place at the Eden Roc Renaissance Resort located at 4525 Collins Avenue in Miami Beach, Florida. Ralph faxed us the information on the venue for the conference and we thought it a neat idea to have it in Miami Beach. Our guests loved our choice of Miami Beach for the 1994 state annual meeting. The Eden Roc has the same proximity to downtown Miami, the Miami International airport and other attractions in the area.

With the brown paper bag in which he carries the check book, Hyman Mally, Ethel, and I headed to the Eden Roc to secure the venue. From that point onward the conference production shifted into high gear. Ralph contacted me to find out if there were any areas that may constitute a conflict of interest. I asked him how could there be a conflict of interest when no one pays me a salary for the work that I am doing, furthermore the organization does not have the fund to produce the program. However, I understand the point that was raised and the need to have a scandal free production. The conference was a totally new and an unchartered course type of event.

The conference was being hosted by our local chapter, but it really was a national program. There were concerns of appropriateness because the program was targeted to business executives. The program was directly related to the United Nations. We were acting in line with our mission of UNA-USA. The program was tailored for business executives, how do we justify having volunteers work their fingers off to produce a program that offered opportunity to businesses?

Whether it is peacekeeping operations or regular procurement, the United Nations purchases millions of dollars of supplies, services, and products each year, and providing education and information on how the world organization conducts its business was seen as a way of helping the world organization become more efficient in its operation. But the lingering question would not go away; the tree was in the way of forest.

To resolve the issue I agreed to have my small business become the producer of the event. The name of my company was Pennywise International Trade Services. Well, before the need to be the producer of the business conference, the name was Pennywise Investors Group. To fit the conference, the name was changed to Pennywise International Trade Services.

The next step was to provide a letter to Ralph at the national office with disclosure, accountability and an outline of the terms. In that letter I outlined to Ralph that the fact that my company was producing the event does not mean that I am standing the cost of the event. All expenses and costs for the business conference were expected to be reimbursed. There was no conflict of interest, the letter declared. I was not paid a salary by the association or by the United Nations or by anyone associated with the program. I did not conduct any form of business to produce any personal and or business income or earnings from any of the organizations that were involved in the project. We discussed it among our executive committee and I was simply the needle in the haystack.

By the middle of February, our cooperating organizations and trade groups began to send labels to our office. We made sure that each organization or group replied to our letter of invitation either accepting or declining our proposal. If our proposal was declined then the company's or organization's name was not listed on our program. By the third week of February, our list of invitees exceeded three thousand names. Ralph and the author of the procurement guide Sandrine were working on the press releases.

The invitations were scheduled to be mailed during the first week of March. This allow roughly a thirty-days turn around for response and registrations. We received the final draft of the program and registration forms from the national office. We took them to the printers and ordered four thousand copies including four thousand envelopes. It was our largest mailing ever for any one activity.

I booked the reservations for all of our speakers with the airlines. Next I made arrangements for their hotel accommodations; then I confirmed all travel and hotel arrangements with each of our speakers. Hyman Mally coordinated ground transportation from the airport to the hotel for all of our guests. Again, we worked on the business conference concurrently with our Friends of the Future project.

Ethel worked at coordinating volunteers to stuff envelopes. Janice stacked groups of invitations and envelopes to be distributed to our cooperating organizations. These were the organizations that agreed to do the mailing to their members. We had boxes everywhere in our office. I said our office and not my office because it had become our operating center. We used the conference room for our makeshift lunch area. It has a large table and chairs. That too was filled with pizza boxes, pop bottles, cups and plates. We were getting ready to stuff envelopes but first we took the time to energize by eating our pizzas and drinking our pop.

Gertrude Pearl complimented World Printing for an excellent job with the printing of the invitations. They looked "very official and professional," she said to the first round of team members who met at my office to stuff envelopes. Gertrude was a retired school teacher. A very petite woman she is but has large aspirations. The Hosangs owned and operated World Printing, one of our local businesses. They gave us an admirable and huge discount on the printing job. We accepted the discounts in return for printing the name of their company on our program brochures.

There were tons of boxes everywhere in the office. Thirteen of us met at my office. We shared the cost of the pizzas and soft drinks. We organized smaller work teams. Some of us separated the programs, some folded them to fit the envelopes, and some stuffed the envelopes, which were then passed along to those who were affixing the address labels to stuffed envelopes. We formed an assembly line and with synchronicity moved the process along. We created a very pleasant work atmosphere.

We engaged funny conversations and jokes as we worked. We just finished stuffing and labeling about eight hundred envelopes when Burnell mumbled something to herself. All of our team members were tuned in to what each other was saying and doing, so mumbling would hardly have gone unnoticed. Carlos sat next to her and repeated what she said. Professor Watson our president emeritus first name is Carlos. He is the one I am referring to here and not our other team member Carlos of Planeta Publishing. Professor Watson repeated Burnell's comment, he said "For those of us who did not hear Ms. Charles's comment, she said she knows why people who work in the post office do not like each other". It did not take too much guessing to understand what she meant. We were all stuffed out even though the atmosphere was pleasant.

We were doing repetitive movements for over five hours. Andrea, our receptionist, overheard the discussion. She came into the conference room and asked, "Tea and cookies anyone?" At that point, we decided to call it a day's work. I announced the end of our work day, thanked our volunteers and told them that we will pick up from where we left off the next day. It was a very long day. All of us just wanted to get into our vehicles and go home. We closed shop for the day and went home. The materials that we were mailing contained four pages; an announcement of the conference; an invitation letter; an outline of the program; and a clip off registration form. We also provided a self-addressed envelopes for the return registration forms. The program in our mailings was not the final program for the conference. The final program was printed at a later time and included in each folder that was presented to the attendees.

It took us three and a half days to get the entire lot done. All envelopes were stuffed and labeled, and ready to be taken to the post office. We had one box of invitations left over, but that was intentional. The way we figured, we may have more requests for invitations and registration forms from those who did not receive one. It is always good to have a reserve on hand just in case we need them.

We carted off tons of crates with the mailings to the post office. We were on target; it was two days before the end of the month. We had planned to do our mailing the first week in March. Volunteer work was not unique. Thousands of volunteer organizations across the United States have done and will continue to do what we have done. But we were a unique team of volunteers. We were dedicated and committed. With our mailings done we now waited to see what kind of response we would get for the business conference.

We shifted gears to focus on the printing and development of the *Friends of the Future* project for the middle and elementary school students. The national essay contest was also taking place at the same time, but that program was ongoing each year and did not require much development. All we had to do was to contact the high schools and colleges through our Campus Network to find out who was interested in participating in the activity.

As soon as an interest was expressed, we mailed the packages with instructions to the teacher who was the contact person at the school or college for the activity. The winner of the essay contest would receive an all-expense-paid trip for teacher and student or students to our national convention. Locally, we recognized the winners in our UN50 celebrations.

A week after the business conference invitations and registration forms were mailed out, Ralph called to see if there were any responses. He kept calling at the end of each day, and always the answer was the same no, there were no registrations, but we were getting inquiries about the conference. For two weeks the response was the same whenever he called. He informed us that they were working on the press releases at the national office. We were hoping that by this time, we would have heard something from the *Miami Herald*, but we did not hear from them.

I wondered if the Business Editor read the procurement guide that I sent him earlier in January. It was now the third week in March and a week away from the date of the conference; still there was no response. We were beginning to feel a sense of failure because we mailed out thousands of invitations and we have not receive any registrations to date.

We were organized and ready. Andrea created a database for registration, everything was set up, but there were no registrations. We even had name tags ready for printing of the names of those who were registered, but still nothing was happening. Ralph shipped us stacks of procurement guides. Those were to be sold to the business-people who wanted them at the conference, but I wondered if we would have to return them to him. It will cost a lot to ship the books back to New York because there were so many of them, and one of those books weighed quite a bit.

About five days before the conference I called the Business Editor at the *Miami Herald*. When the Editor came on the telephone, I greeted him and politely asked him to return my procurement guide. I told Mr. Satterfield that he could send it any way he chooses just as long as it came back to me. I was not upset with him at all—I was angry that he did nothing about our conference but I was not upset with him. I was very cordial to him on the telephone.

As an afterthought before I hung up the telephone, I mentioned to him that the conference will coincide with the UN mission in Haiti. I also told him that we expected to have tons of registrations from other regions across the United States as well as from international companies who would be doing business with the United Nations, and especially in view of the mission in Haiti; which meant that those companies will secure UN contracts to provide supplies for the mission. My final words to him were "I am disappointed that you could have helped us by publicizing the event, and bring it to the attention of our local businesses so that they would at least have an opportunity to participate by supplying the mission with goods, services, and supplies. Regardless if the company is local or not, the mission will be making purchases.". I thanked him for the opportunity to share our thoughts and projects. I reminded him to return the procurement guide and that I will be looking out for it. I said good bye and hung up the telephone.

The next day I received a telephone call from a business reporter. She identified herself and told me that the business editor asked her to call me to cover the event. She wanted a few lines from me regarding the event. She said that it would be reported in the morning edition of the next day's paper. "Yes!" I said to the staff in the office. "We have made a breakthrough."

I contacted Ralph at the national office to tell him the news. Then I called Ethel and also told her the good news. The next morning, there it was in the *Miami Herald*. Right next to the article on the debut of Sesame Street in the Spanish-language version in bold print was "U.N. solicits business from S. Fla. Firms"; that was the headline. Susana Barciela, a *Miami Herald* business writer, wrote,

> *South Florida firms put on your running shoes. The United Nations wants to do business with you. This Friday, as President Clinton visits Haiti to transfer peacekeeping duties to the United Nations, U N representatives will visit Miami Beach to explain how firms could sell to U. N. operations. A one day conference at the Eden Roc hotel aims to explain what the U.N. buys and how it conducts its bidding process. It will cover opportunities not only in Haiti but with U.N. agencies around the world, said Sylvia McLeod; president of the Greater Miami chapter of the United Nations Association of the U.S.A. McLeod is the president of Pennywise International Trade Services, an Oakland Park firm organizing the event. She said that in 1993, the UN spent 3.5 billion on goods and services, but only four Florida-based firms got a share.*

Ms. Barciela also listed the cost of attendance, which was $175 per person, the location of the event, and where to call to register for the conference. Well, there is absolutely no question to the power of the media. It was only days from the event.

On the same day that the article appeared in the *Miami Herald*, by ten o'clock we received twenty registrations by telephone and fax. By the end of the day, other newspapers called the office because they too wanted to do articles on the conference. Charles Lunan, a business writer, headlined the next day "Talk topic: supplies for U.N. conference to address alliance's business side." From that point onward, we were not short of registrations for the conference because they kept coming in.

Everyone who called in to register had a manner of urgency. It reminded me of how I felt when I heard about Hurricane Andrew and thought I was behind the eighth ball, thinking I was the last one to find out about it. Business-people were acting as if they were about to miss the boat, and needed to be registered right away to get on board. We were only too happy to assist them in getting on board.

Some of our volunteers and assistants in the office chanted: "All aboard, step right up, the event is only hours away." We were extremely pleased with the turn of events. Ralph reported to us that he too was busy doing press releases for other areas. Our fax machine and telephones were now constantly ringing off the hook. It was good that our fax machine used the rolls of papers instead of sheet paper. Registrations were coming in night and day. With the paper roll we were not concern with the fax machine running our of paper while we were away.

The more we got busy, the more people wanted to become involved. A day before the conference, we received a visit from the publisher of the *Miami Business Review*. He was accompanied by one of their board members. It was a first time meeting. The representatives of the *Miami Business Review* proposed to us that they cover the conference by collecting and documenting data. We informed them that any business arrangements regarding the conference were conducted out of the national office. We provided them with the information and Ralph's contact number. The author of the procurement guide was also at the national office. All we were doing was hosting the event.

We received a letter from the president of the Broward Development Council. He was very upset that he did not receive an invitation to participate in the conference. We apologized for his organization not receiving the letters we sent to them and invited their participation. Our intention was to include as many organizations as possible. We asked any organization that did not receive their materials to contact us so that we may send out a new batch of invitations. We sent conference material to the Broward Development Council via express delivery. This was an above and beyond measure because our budget did not support the cost of express mailings.

We received the shipment of official folders and conference materials from the national office a day before the event. Speakers began to arrive a day before the event. Our ground transportation team which was coordinated by Hyman moved into action. Hyman and our other drivers met our speakers at the Miami International Airport and took them to their hotels. By now we were in an overdrive mode but we moved along smoothly with all the final details for the conference.

On the early afternoon of March 30 the day before the business conference, Andrea tried to print the registrants' names for the name tags from the computer. She made several attempts but nothing happened. She looked mesmerized and confused. I went over and stood by her desk to see if I could be of assistance. She told me that the data was missing. "What data?" I asked her.

"Sylvia, all the registration data of those who have paid and registered for the conference are missing." I told her to pull over to let me see if I could find it. We searched and searched; there was nothing in the computer on the conference. Everything was going as well as could be expected, up until this point. The data was nowhere to be found in the computer.

The printing of the names to put in the name tags was the final thing we had to do before packing all the stuff to take to the Eden Roc Hotel. We searched and searched for the information in the database, but the registration list with the names of the companies and their representatives were missing. We have been experiencing some strange occurrences in the office for a few months. Things like hearing voices through the telephone speaker when all the receivers were in place and no one was using the telephone. The voices came in with one-liners, and sometimes there were more than one person in the conversation. We had no explanation for those annoyances and neither did we know who the culprits were. Perhaps they were just looking for a free ride to where ever it was they wanted to go. The west was won a long time ago and we certainly did not have bandwagons in our office. The only hopping on that was taking place were of volunteers who believed in the work that we were doing and wanted to help.

Sometimes when we answered the telephone we recognized that some of the calls were just prank phone calls. But at other times and quite frequently unidentified persons made veiled threats then hang up quickly. It was very annoying to be getting those phone calls. I sometimes used *69 and asked the person on the other end to stop calling our office. Sometimes I used the phrase "You damn terrorist, you are nothing but a coward. Don't you ever call this number again" and hung up the phone. We reported those threatening calls to the telephone company but little was done to resolve the problem. All we were doing was opening cases which was consuming our time to deal with the issues.

We had a lot of work to do and under pressing time lines. It was very important that we use our time wisely and keep focus on our work. Given all the stuff that was going on and the sinister telephone calls I considered the possibility of our computer being tampered with. If that was the case than at least it be a rational explanation of why we could not find our data in the computer.

The missing data posed a big problem but we were prepared with a backup system. It requires some time to get it done but even at this twelfth hour it will be done. All registrations paid and unpaid were first recorded in hardcopy in a book designed solely for that purpose. Reconstructing the data was not an easy job especially when it is being done under pressure. I should be at the reception but I could not be there because I have to work on the name tags. Andrea retrieved the box with the hard copies from the file cabinet and placed it on the desk. We also kept a manual register with the names and companies to track the response from the invitations that were sent out.

I should have been well on my way to the Eden Roc to greet the guests and speakers who arrived the evening before the event. Andrea and the other staff members had to leave to get ready for the event the next day. Andrea said she needed to have her hair done, and she was now late for the hairdresser. She called the hairdresser and informed her that she would arrive late but she was on the way. I had a calm sense of anger about the whole ordeal.

I began to re-enter the data into the computer. I was alone in the office. Everyone had left to get ready for the conference. Our volunteers had to do the same. Some of them were already busy coordinating and transporting guest and speakers from the airport. The telephone was very busy with last minute inquiries about the conference. The late registrations were still coming in. At that point I could no longer process payments. I advised those who were registering late to make payments when they arrive at the conference, and they should make every effort to arrive thirty minutes ahead of time.

It was now about 6:30 p.m. The telephone rang, I answered it. Ralph was on the other end of the line.

"Hi, Ralph, how are you?" I asked him.

"Sylvia, I am at the hotel, and everyone else is here, and there is no one here but us, where are you? You were supposed to be here a long time ago. How can you be hosting an event and not be here to welcome the guests?"

I took a deep breath, balancing the telephone handset between my shoulder and chin while still typing names in the database. I said to him. "Ralph, you are there, aren't you?" He said "Yes" before he could say another word I asked, "Have you ever hosted an event?" and without waiting for a response from him, I said, "This is your chance, please be the perfect host until I arrive. Some of our board members should arrive shortly to assist you, I will see you soon." I told him that I was handling a situation but that was all. I did not explain the details. It would have been pointless to do so; furthermore I did not wish to create any undo alarm over the situation. It would have only made things worse. Any long explanation over the telephone would be taking up the time I need to continue entering the data and keep my concentration so that I do not make mistakes.

I continued to enter the data in the computer. An hour and a half later I printed the labels and place them in box with the plastic holders for the name tags. I finished packing all the containers that will be going to the Eden Rock with me. I placed all the stuff in the car.

My car trunk was filled with tons of folders, brochures for the conference, programs, and copies of the procurement guide that were shipped to the office. I locked the office then drove home to get my overnight suitcase, which was already packed before I left for the office earlier in day. As I headed unto the ramp southward to Miami I inserted my *Graceland* cassette.

One must always be prepared for challenges in leadership. Cooperating forces add new dimensions to any leadership, but one must also be prepared for counter forces and challenges. There is also the constant pushing of the envelope to encourage reactive behavior. *"Great"*, I said to myself. The *Boy in the Bubble* song ended. The introduction to *"Graceland"* surrounded my silver Taurus. I pumped up the volume and sang along. I hit I-95 South toward my destination.

I began to unwind and was mentally preparing myself for the conference. The reality of reaching this point hit me as I thought to myself "What in the world was I doing hosting this conference" *What if something went wrong? Would I be the one to blame?* I quickly shifted that thought knowing fully well that the blame would be on those people from up north, it was their idea in the first place. Just at that moment, the words of the song pierce my thoughts, *"I know what I know."* I listened to the songs as I drove to the Eden Roc Hotel.

"Diamonds on the Soles of Her Shoes" was the final song as I approached the final leg to my destination. I crossed the causeway moving closer to Eden Roc. There was a certain type of serenity as the lights rose while crossing the causeway. It was a magical greeting. The bright lights rose over the bay, reflecting warm welcoming images on the surface of the ocean. The gentle evening breeze soothingly caressed the right side of my cheekbones as it circled the vehicle now touching my left ear softly with a gentle consolation that everything will be o.k.

Oh! it is such a warm splendor, I thought to myself as I settle back to enjoy the breeze as I drove across the causeway. I took in the scenery and for one moment I did not think about the conference. It was such a great feeling to think of nothing as if it was not there. But I snapped back to reality as I approached Miami Beach. I was truly looking forward to the conference and the mixing of souls sharing their knowledge. I knew what I expected, but I did not know what would be the outcome. After all it was something new. I arrived and unloaded my stuff for the conference. I was given valet parking, wow! *That's nice*, I thought. The attendant wheeled my stuff to the check-in counter. In no time I was checked in. I separated the items that were to be taken to my room from those for the meeting hall.

I was whisked upstairs. I tipped the attendant and entered my room. After I freshened up, I went downstairs to where the reception was supposed to be. The reception hall looked like everything after the party; empty trays, beverage bottles, used coffee cups, and everything used were sitting to the side. I missed the reception but I hoped that everyone had fun. I saw Ralph in the lobby. I just knew it was him even though I have never met him personally before. He had the look of someone who I have been working with for years.

I walked up to him "Sylvia?" he said reaching out to shake my hand. "Ralph, it is such a pleasure to meet you" I responded accepting his outstretched hand. He had a very warming smile. He was a very charming, gentle mannered person. There was a very petite lady standing beside him. I figured she must have been Sandrine, the author of the procurement guide. We shook hands that turned into hugs as we all greeted each other. No one would believe that we were all meeting each other for the first time; we simply picked up from where we left off with our last telephone conversation.

We decided to go to Joe's Stone Crab to have dinner. It was located only a few blocks from the hotel and I heard that they serve up delightful seafood. The legend goes that anyone who goes to Miami Beach from anywhere in the world stopped in at Joe's. I took Ralph to a side-bar discussion and asked him and asked him who will cover the cost of the dinner. He said that we will be doing so. I did not want to wait until after our dinner to find that out. I had a slight issue with escalating costs. I had to put a lid on it. About ten of us including some of our speakers went to Joe's Stone Crab for dinner.

It was usually through these informal dining where everyone get to exchange notes on what to expect during the conference. I provided a brief snapshot of who would be attending the conference, and the companies that would be represented. It was a very diverse group of registrants. By knowing who the audience will be speakers and presenters can prepare accordingly. Among our expected attendees were representatives from multi-national corporations, large companies, small and mid-sized companies, non-profit organizations, professionals from all sectors such as legal firms, medical providers, and people from all walks of life who had an interest in the topic of the conference.

I had a chance to ask some questions and listened to everyone sharing a bit about their background and work. In our discussion no one person was in control of anything. We all had a sense of anticipation. We did not know quite what to expect of the conference the next day, but we were all looking forward to the experience. Sandrine was well informed but that was to be expected because she wrote the procurement guide. The speakers were very knowledgeable because of their expertise in their specific areas of work.

For now, we settled in to having a good meal and sharing good company. We all were dressed casually in jeans and all on the same level. We did not hang out at Joe's Stone Crab for long because we had a long day ahead of us tomorrow. We did get a chance, however, to become more acquainted and comfortable with each other. Soon after our meal, we headed back to our hotel.

I was up at dawn checking all final preparations. In a couple of hours based on the list of attendees I expected that there would be a flood of people who for the first time in public would be hearing *"How to do business with the United Nations."* The attaché from the national office, Ralph, Sandrine, Liz, Heather, and Kamra—were busy setting up their stations. One of their stations had a display of procurement guides. There were ample supplies for anyone attending the conference, and who would like to purchase a copy. The cost per guide was $295.

Our local team members were out in full force. Andrea, my daughter Michelle, Gertrude Pearl, and Janice Darbeau were at the registration table. Linda, Ethel, and Burnell were manning the brochure tables. A quick check at each station showed that everything was in order and ready. The conference room was set up classroom-style.

There was a folder, a notepad, pens, and pencils on the tables at each seat. In the back of the room were tables with ample supply of different types of iced juices, beverages, and water. The Overhead-viewing equipment was set up and in place. All the flags of the United States, the United Nations, the State of Florida, Miami Beach, and Dade County were in place. The podium and platform tables were draped as directed with the logos of UNA-USA splashed across the front. All mikes and name-plates were in place for the first set of speakers and panelists.

I checked to see if the room where breakfast will be served was ready. It was ready for breakfast to be served. The grand ballroom was not yet ready for lunch but that was o.k. because lunch was hours away. At about seven o'clock attendees began to check in at registration. Our volunteer ushers arrived on time and were busy providing directions to our guests. Bennett Darbeau, Hyman Mally, Professor Carlos Watson, Sam Brenner, Hugh Hastings, Sandy Leon, and Jim Mullins, were ready, willing and able to assist our guests.

By 8:00 a.m., breakfast was over, and everyone began to move into the conference room. A large number of people who had not registered showed up for the conference. Some seats were still available. The ushers placed additional seating in the back of the conference room without interrupting the meeting. We promised an 8:30 a.m. sharp start time for the conference, and that was just what we did.

Ralph sat next to me at the table on the raised platform. He had a curious calmness to his demeanor. Perhaps it was his form of moment of silence to get his thoughts together but then again it could have been a form of apprehension of the outcome of the conference. But he looked very sharp in his stunning pinstripe suit. Sandrine was seated to his right. Sandrine is a very petite woman. She wore a beautifully tapered pink dress and black patent leather shoes with square toes and thick heels. Her dress and shoes were unique to European designs similarly to those of Paris, France. I wore a blue and white outfit as I normally do at UNA-USA activities. Our speakers wore regular suits and ties but looked the part that they were playing. Their demeanors were American professionals. Our first session featured four speakers. By their posture way they carried themselves one could discern that they were knowledgeable, they walked with confidence.

Throughout the conference, we had U.N. peacekeeping officials, procurement officers, humanitarian officers, U.S. Department of Commerce officials, and U.S. mission to the U.N. representatives. The number of people in the room, their alertness, and the nature of the conference created an atmosphere of inquiry. The attendees were eager to learn about the U.N. procurement process.

Our audience and speakers were ready and waiting so without further scrutiny I went to the podium to give the opening remarks for the conference. I introduced myself to the audience, and gave a brief statement of what UNA-USA does, and about our cooperating organizations, and the reasons for having the conference. I introduced Ralph by reading his short biography. I welcomed him to the podium, and turned over the microphone to him. Ralph provided an overview of the conference to our audience than proceeded to introduce our first speaker.

The conference was truly a class act. Our attendees were a diverse group of men and women representing companies, organizations, professionals, associations, and self. Attendees checked to make sure there were note pads, and that pens and pencils worked. A few people inquired about tape recording the conference. Unfortunately that was not allowed. The only video taping of the conference was done by the person who was hired by our chapter to do so.

The media and their cameras were outside the conference room in the halls. Some of the media personnel were allowed in the conference. Corporate executives and laypersons, everyone waited for the delivery of our first speaker. The sessions were very informative. Attendees not only received first hand information of the process that was required to conduct business with the world organization, but they also learned more about the nature of the organization, and why they did things the way they did.

One of the better take away was the understanding that in situations where there are refugees, disasters, or political instability, the procurement officers function in extreme environments. Under those circumstances, a service provider or supplier needs to observe what I refer to as the "sundown rule". The sundown rule is simply where products or services are needed in extreme situations, suppliers respond quickly even outside of their operating hours to meet those needs.

At lunchtime, everyone met in the great ballroom that seated over five hundred people. The catering staff were busy filling beverage glasses at the tables. A tall gentleman approached me just as I was about to take my seat at the table. I glanced at his name tag to see his name and the organization that he represented. He introduced himself as the president of the Arab American Association. With a program in one hand, and the other stretched towards me, he smiled at me and said "Sylvia, you arranged the program brochure printing from left to right." He opened the program and pointed to show me what he meant. I saw it but did not know exactly what he was referring to, but not wanting to immediately reveal my ignorance of what he was talking about, I smiled and nodded my head in acknowledgement.

He explained that in his culture, one reads from the left to right. He told me that it was very good that I was sensitive to all who may attend the conference by being so responsive to cultural considerations. I acknowledged his compliments with a thank-you. In all of our programs and chapter work we embraced an "inclusive" policy. We encourage diverse participation on all levels. But the fact was I had no idea how the program turned out to be the way it did.

This is what I believed happened to explain the situation. On the day I visited the printers to give them the layout of the programs for printing; I sat in the waiting area for a while because the printer was busy with another customer in his office. From where I sat, we overheard the conversation that was taking place behind the closed doors. There were other customers in the waiting area. We heard the words "Shoot this one, and blow up that one." The conversation continued in the same manner for quite some time.

Some of the more senior customers in the waiting area began to project facial expressions that were not very pleasant. It could have been reflections from their sense of humor or something else. I got up from my seat and knocked at the door of the office in an attempt to interrupt the conversation and perhaps create a distraction. I figured the conversation was in relationship to the exposures of photographs that were to be printed.

The owner came out and began tending to the customers in the waiting area. I was the last one to be served because of my position of arrival. The owner and I shared a few laughs about the scenario. Perhaps in the jovial nature of our conversation, I may have overlooked explaining to him the layout of our program, or he may have misunderstood my communication, which perhaps explained why the programs came out the way they did. But no problem; that someone was happy about the way the program was laid out, we are happy too.

I was very happy and relieved that it was not a country flag issue. We decorated the luncheon room with miniature flags set containing the flag of each Member State of the United Nations. Sometimes attendees simply remove the flags for souvenirs or memorabilia. When that happens we wound up in deep you know what. People do not like to see a display of flags for member states where the flag for his or her home country is missing.

Sometimes member-state flags are missing because attendees mistakenly take them for souvenirs. I do not know whether or not attendees scanned each table looking for their countries or home country's flags. We have ran into situations where individuals have ties to more than one country. I am not sure if attendees walk up to the miniature flag set and conduct a close scrutiny. But even though the hall may be packed with hundreds of people, missing miniature flags are spotted quite easily, people are very serious about home country flags.

When flags are missing, which occur quite often, the individual will approach one of our members and accused the organization of conspiracy against their homeland. We try to explain that unknown to us one of their countryman or countrywoman may have mistakenly took the flag for souvenir. We walked a thin line with that explanation because we are taking the risk of being accused of labelling the countryman a thief which would only reinforce the conspiracy theory.

That explanation worked many times but sometimes it doesn't work at all, especially if there are any issues on the United Nations or United States agenda with respect to the particular country whose flag is missing. For that reason, it was quite common for small groups of people to break out discussing pressing issues that relates to their country at our events. Almost certainly at every event the issue of missing flag comes up. And you can bet your bottom dollar that we will be accused of conspiracy. The thing with accusing others of conspiracy in my opinion can go a bit far at times.

I am sure that conspiracy theory does have merit in some instances, but in our case it certainly had no merit what so ever. I sometimes think perhaps it is a default accusation to anything that begs for a rational explanation. We considered the possibility of having a miniature flag set guard but our budget could not support such an activity.

Our keynote speaker at the luncheon had a no-holds-barred approach in describing some of the conditions under which operations are conducted, especially where there is political unrest and population destabilization. According to the speaker, whether the call to duty is to an area or region where the circumstances are natural disaster or political unrest, the conditions are usually very harsh and extreme. Under those conditions resource are very limited or does not exist at all.

Therefore, for anyone or any company doing business with the UN and especially during those difficult times where harsh and extreme conditions exist, it may require going above and beyond to deliver supplies, which is different from the regular channels of purchase and delivery as it would be with everyday business operations in stable environments.

After lunch, the guides on how to do business with the United Nations were going like hotcakes. Everyone wanted a copy of the procurement guide but some people who had an interest in the publication could not afford to buy one at that moment. Those people who had an interest in doing business with the UN purchased the guide. This was not surprising knowing that a new UN mission in Haiti had begun. There were opportunities to supply the mission with goods and services for peacekeeping efforts through UN procurement.

The second half of the seminar was as robust and energetic as the first half. The luncheon speaker spoke about the conditions under which UN officers in the field must endure. Workers need to adapt to an environment that is constantly changing. Our second set of speakers spoke of what suppliers need to do to gain access to the procurement process. Our speakers also spoke about the conditions that suppliers will face when doing business with the UN. The environment will be the same as those in which UN officers function in the field. Suppliers too must adapt to those changes. This information was very important to those who were considering the new mission in Haiti which was one of the reasons for the high attendance to the conference.

The first conference on how to do business with the United Nations ended. Many of the attendees took advantage of the good weather and stayed for the weekend in Miami. The weeks after the conference brought many people to our office seeking assistance with their registration process to become U.N. suppliers. We did not anticipate this type of contact. Our office did what we could to assist those companies and people who contacted us for assistance.

We referred the calls to our national office where Ralph or Sandrine assisted them. After the conference our attention became more centered on our Friends of the Future project for middle and elementary schools. We just were not prepared for the after effects of the conference. I received a call from Broward County resident who at the time worked with the Department of Children and Family Service He asked for a meeting to discuss the possibility of having a briefing about the conference. Apparently, not everyone who wanted to attend the conference was able to do so. It was well publicized, but some people only found out about it after it took place.

Louis Toussaint was a native of Haiti but has been in the United States for many years. He met with me and discussed the possibility of having a briefing of the conference in Ft. Lauderdale. I contacted Ralph and discussed the idea with him. Ralph agreed to give that briefing provided that Louis was able to make all the necessary arrangements. The original conference was videotaped, so the information that was delivered at the conference was available for use in the briefing.

Louis made the necessary arrangements and invited the people who wanted to attend that session. We were also joined by Hubert Wray, who also resided in Broward County. Hubert worked for the UN for many years in the administrative section. Hubert Wray and Kofi Annan worked in the same department at the U.N. before Kofi Annan became the secretary-general. Hubert Wray played an important role in the planning of the briefing in Broward County. He later became a member of our chapter.

On Saturday May 13, Ralph made the summary presentation of our March 31 business conference in Broward County. The videos of the taped conference were shown. The attendants were satisfied with the presentation. Ralph did an excellent job of filling in the gaps. The videos also had taped questions and answers so our attendees were able to view the responses as given by the original speakers and presenters. This briefing was just as informative as the original conference. A lot of activities were spun off the conference of doing business with the United Nations.

The registration department of the UN procurement office informed us that they have never been as busy as they were after the conference. The corporate affairs of our national office was also busy signing up companies who were seeking to become corporate members. The national office was also receiving requests from organizations who were interested in hosting a similar business conference. Several of our UNA-USA chapters from across the nation contacted us for information on the conference development. They too were interested in hosting a UN business conference too.

From our perspective having the conference was only suppose to be a one time event as part of our UN50 program. By popular demand we hosted a second annual business conference on May 26, 1996. It was held at the Sheraton Biscayne Bay Hotel on Brickell Avenue in Miami. The second annual UN business conference had a variety of themes and topics related to the United Nations and its operations. The new 1996 update to the procurement guide was featured in the business conference.

Sandrine was now the director of the UNA-USA Corporate Affairs. Ralph was promoted to vice president of Corporate Affairs. The speakers at the second annual conference included Alexander Waldrum, chief of Logistics and Communication Services in the Department of Peacekeeping Operations. He spoke about supporting the peacekeepers in UN field operations.

Sanjay Baher, chief of Commodity Procurement Section in the Department of Administration and Management, spoke about the procurement of transportation. Thomas Mottley, an international trade specialist from the

United States Department of Commerce, talked about American companies that were doing business with the United Nations. Imran Rizza, a senior external relations officer with the United Nations High Commissioner for Refugees from Geneva Headquarters, spoke and discussed the process of resettling refugees, including helping refugees to go back home. Dominique Michel, a special assistant to the executive director for UNOPS, spoke about procurement opportunities for economic development program. Our keynote speaker at the conference was Florida State Senator Daryl L. Jones.

Unlike the first conference, the attendance at the second annual conference was much smaller. There were several reasons for that. Firstly, that was due to lessons learned from having the first conference. Our mailing list was scaled back to one fifth of the volume of our first mailing. Our mailings for the first business conference in 1995 was much to large. That mailing created a much bigger. Secondly, the UN procurement guide was readily available. Companies who want to do business with the United Nations could do it themselves. The guide provided information on the entire process in securing U.N. contracts.

Companies who need help with the process were able to contact our newly established corporate affairs division at our national office. Ralph and Sandrine were rapporteurs on visits to UN peacekeeping operations in Rwanda, Haiti, and Angola. More business conferences were held in places like Australia, Israel, Thailand, Cyprus, and throughout the United States.

The latest edition of the updated procurement guide was published in 1997. Of course by that time my favorite pastime was walking on the shores of Miami Beach watching the gentle waves lap and roll onto the sand, caressing my feet with the warm waters from the Atlantic Ocean. A dried fruit from the coconut palm floated on the wave and rest at my feet. I picked it up and tossed it high in the air, then I caught it and bounced it in my palm.

It was soaked with saltwater, but it could not have weighed more that six or seven ounces. I tossed the fruit back into the third wave giving a jump start on its journey across the ocean. I put on my headset, turned up the volume to drown the sounds of the waves. "Homeless, homeless. Many dead, tonight it could be you." Those words were very real to me and they had significant meaning. Paul Simon's Graceland is one of my favorite albums but I also love Frank Sinatra's song "That's Life". It is one of those songs that motivates me to pick my self up when I come across bumps or monkey wrenches. I will tell you about the monkey wrenches later. For now I will continue with UN50.

CHAPTER 8

T HERE WERE STILL lots of grounds to cover before the grand celebration on UN50 at our chapter. Ethel and I were delegates to our national annual meeting. It was held at the Fairmont Hotel in San Francisco, California, June 24 through June 28, 1995. There was not much of a break between our programs and activities. My injuries from the three auto accidents that occurred on April 27, May 5, and June 2, 1995 were unexpected and they put a dent on my ability to function at peak performance.

My busyness was not the cause of all those accidents. I have been a busy person all of my life, and never experienced such occurrences anytime since I became a licensed driver. It was so obvious that my insurance adjuster, physical therapist, and doctors raised the question of why were these strange things happening so frequently. It was definitely more than what meets the eye they suggested. If it looks like a duck, walks like a duck, and quacks like a duck then it must be a duck. The question was whose duck was it. Some people who knew of the accidents suggested that perhaps somebody or persons were trying to either stop us from doing what we were doing, or they wanted to create chaos. I could not imagine who could be against anyone doing volunteer work for a good cause and especially where it benefits our community.

I was receiving physical therapy including having to undergo surgical procedures for my injuries. Apart from the time it required to tend to my medical conditions, I had some physical limitations as well. I still managed to do what I could because my team was relying on me. Nothing could be done without our team spirit the driving force of our team work. I consulted with my medical care provider, and I was given the green light to attend the annual meeting, provided I observed my physical limitations and take my medications.

UNA-USA's national convention was held in San Francisco. This was not the regular or usual national convention. It was held at the same location where the United Nations Charter was signed fifty years ago. This was truly a historic event for our organization with the meeting being held at the birthplace of the United Nations. The Fairmont Hotel is located on Nob Hill.

Ethel and I arrived in San Francisco on the eve of June 24. We arrived just in time to complete our registration process at the Fairmont Hotel before loosing out on the blocked room rates for our convention. We checked into the hotel and then went straight to the convention registration desk. We picked up our convention packet which was stuffed with all sorts of convention goodies. We sat in the lounge browsing through the brochures and all the stuff in our bags. We organized all the goodies by incorporating local events with our convention program. That was our way of creating a system so that we won't miss anything.

The bag that held our convention goodies was a blue canvas tote bag with a bright white UN50 logo on it. Ethel said it would be neat to get some of those bags to take back to our board members. I agreed with her and told her that I would check with our national staff after our convention to see if there are any left over. If there are, we may as well use them up because they have the UN50 logo, and it would be pointless to let them go to waste when we could find good use for them.

We finished looking through and organizing our goodies in our convention packet and decided it was time to get some rest after our long flight. I did not want to over exert myself with my limited physical mobility. After we rested, we looked in on the first pre-convention plenary session. The place was already buzzing with activities. Each chapter was asked to create a miniature display showing some of the chapter's activities for UN50.

Ethel and I decided that before we attended the first planning session, it would be better to take a few minutes and set up our Greater Miami chapter display. Our chapter members created a collage of photographs with brief narratives of our activities. Our display featured our Friends of the Future project for middle and elementary schools. We brought with us some of the video tapes that were recorded at the exhibits of the artworks.

We selected some of the frames from the video tapes and created a continuous looped video that was used in our display. We had the studio who did the video taping made a special looped video for our display at the national convention. We also had still photographs of our members working on different activities such as stuffing envelopes, and working at some of our events. Some of our members were exceptional at cutting and pasting. The photographs were placed on a blue Bristol board and were highlighted with white picture frames.

It is amazing what raw talent and creativity can accomplish. By looking at the display one would think that our members were graphic designers. It was done beautifully.

We were late going to the plenary session, but so were many other representatives who took the time to set up their chapter's display before attending the session. It did not take us very long to get caught up. We did not miss much in the meeting and in no time we were on the same page with the others who were there before us. There were a lot of people at the first session; everything was buzzing.

The attendance at this convention reminds me of Christmas and Easter Sundays. Many people only attend church or mass twice yearly which are usually on those two days. UN50 is celebrated only once, and with a part of this celebration taking place in the same hotel where the Charter was signed fifty years ago, just like on Easter Sundays, a lot of people are in attendance. Perhaps there should be a special event or occasion for every Sunday in each year; more people would attend church.

There were several issues and resolutions for the annual meeting. Our Bylaws, Resolution, and Substantive issues Committee led by chair persons Leo Nevas, Lilialyce Akers, and Ambassador Herbert S. Okum had a lot of work to do. Leo Nevas was a member of the board of governors of UNA-USA. He also worked with the International League for Human Rights. Lilialyce Akers of the Louisville chapter of UNA-USA was also with the National Federation of Business and Professional Women's Club. Ambassador Herbert Okum was the former U.S. representative to the U.N. Economic and Social Council.

There were many people in the meeting whom we had not seen in a long time. It was a good time to say hello and become re-acquainted. We recognized some of our representatives from the Florida Division, as well as from other chapters in Florida. There were so many people in the session that a smile and a wink, or even a scribbled note saying "Hi, see you later" was a good way to reach out to each other. In our organization titles are tags but teamwork is testimony.

Sunday, June 25, was our first full day of activities. Our annual meeting was designed to accommodate events that were being held in San Francisco for UN50. We started our day at 9:00 a.m. with a meeting of the Council of Chapter and Division Presidents. The meeting lasted for one and a half hours. Next was an open plenary which took place at noon. Our guest speaker was Hon. Dianne Feinstein, U.S. Senator from California. She was introduced by our president, Thomas B. Morgan.

After Senator Feinstein spoke it was my turn to do my bit for the Credentials Committee. I was the chair of that committee. My role was to assure our membership at large that all those who were elected for offices were properly credentialed. I did that beautifully but with one omission. I forgot to invite the membership's acceptance of the slate of officers. I was reminded to do so but by that time it was already late and I would have cut into the time of the next speaker. That was funny but it lightened the moment. Everyone laughed and we just kept going with the program. My grandmother had a famous saying about weddings and things going wrong on the wedding day. She said that it will not be a wedding if there is not a hitch somewhere on the wedding day. Well ! forgetting to ask the membership to accept the slate of officers was the hitch that day.

Tom Morgan was a fun person although I must admit he must have been tired of hearing me talk about our Friends of the Future success. Each encounter with him I ran up to him and said "Sixteen thousand students," which was the number of participants in the program. I figured if I kept on repeating it he would mention it when he gets a chance to speak about the work of our chapters. I wanted our chapter to shine at the national meeting just like our other chapters across the nation. My jingle was "Over Sixteen thousand students". Tom Morgan hears me because he did mention our success when he spoke about chapter work for UN50.

Ethel and I tried to get tickets to the Royal Philharmonic concert, which was held at Davies Symphony Hall. The tickets only cost $10.00 but they were sold out. The interfaith service was held at 3:00 p.m. at the Grace Cathedral. That was a closed event. UNA-USA was offered a small block of seats but only members of the national council were able to attend on a first-come-first-serve basis. The way we figured, we were too far down on the list to even make an attempt to get any of those special tickets. We settled for an off-site viewing of the service.

UN50 events were being held at numerous places in the city. Along with the celebrations were several marchers protesting different things at those sites. The television stations camera men were not far away either. They were covering the events and those who were protesting. There was so much noise I could not hear what issues they were protesting. I needed to slow down a bit because I did not want to overdo it by my moving from place to place. I had to heed the doctor's advice due to my injuries and physical mobility. But getting caught up in the spirit of the celebration, I sometimes forget until my body sends out a warning. It was a case of the heart being willing but the flesh was weak. When I felt stiffness accompanied by a jolt of pain, I knew it was it was my body saying time out. I tried to not let it get that far where my body has to speak to me because I was aware of my limitations, and I was in the driver's seat. I knew what my limits were and how far I could go.

I went back to our hotel room. I lie down and listen to a couple of songs from my 70's Gold cassette that I took with me. I first selected Manfred Mann's Earthband *Blinded by the Light*. Whenever I listed to that song I get carried away on the strings of the guitar. Besides, I find the lyrics are very funny and entertaining. The keyboard player does wonder too, they are pretty good at what they do. I selected the next song, Cat Stevens Peace Train. I must have slept for a while because I can't remember making any other selection or hearing any of the other songs on the cassette.

Later that evening Ethel and I decided to walk around and check out our surroundings. The hotel was located at the top of Nob Hill. On exiting the hotel entrance we went a few yards to the left. The hill had an incline so steep it looked like a ninety-degree angle. Ethel suggested we walk down the hill. I told her that I didn't think I could because of my physical limitations. It was not the going down but the getting back would be a problem. Ethel laughed, nodding in agreement and saying it would be the same for her. We were quite a pair, I do not believe that either of us could have done anything without the other.

We walked slowly outside of the hotel. We were discussing hills and how many there were in San Francisco. While we were doing that a passerby stopped to join in our conversation. "Nob Hill is also known as Snob Hill," he said. "Most of the residences in this area are for wealthy people, and you go figure." He told us that there were Forty-nine hills in San Francisco. The number 49 and San Francisco rang a bell, and I said, "Oh, the 49ers, so that is how the name came about." Ethel tugged at my blouse, "Not so fast young lady, I would double-check that if I were you" She said lowering her tone of voice. Ethel pulls me back if I go out of a limb. She was always wary of our source of information. It is not so much that she did not believe what the guy was telling us as much as it was based on President Ronald Reagan's famous use of the Russian proverb in the 1980's "*trust but verify*". It was only common sense to check out the information for ourselves before we accept it or begin passing it along.

The hotel is located at the intersections of California and Powell Street. The Fairmont was so named for a famous San Francisco tycoon, James G. Fair. We also found out the most expensive hotels in San Francisco were the Fairmont, the InterContinental Mark Hopkins hotel, the Stanford, and the Huntington. The Grace Cathedral was also located in the neighborhood opposite the Fairmont and Pacific Union Club.

The Grace Cathedral is one of the city's' largest structures. A large Masonic temple is located across from the church. Another passerby had joined in our discussion. We had a full mystical explanation of how everything came into being at Nob Hill. Ethel gave a word of caution after they left that before we go passing on what we heard, we better check out all that information for ourselves first.

We were delighted to learn some of the history of our surroundings. Ethel and I thought the Fairmont was only significant because of the signing of the

UN Charter at that location in 1945, but we were filled in with more information by the locals. We went one quarter of the way down the hill. We met some of the staff from our national headquarters who went down the hill to have dinner at one of the steak house restaurant. We joined them on the way back to the top of the hill. A volunteer's life is never boring. When we travel to different places for our meetings we learn some neat stuff from meeting and striking up conversations with members of the local community. The stuff that we learn from speaking with them aren't stuff that are written in books and magazines for tourists. I mean we learn neat stuff about the true grit of the community and its culture. Before we pass on what we have heard we make every attempt to verify the information thus separating the facts from the hearsay.

We reached the top of the hill. It was a lovely evening; red tulips were everywhere. We continued our walk to the opposite side of the hotel. Ethel pointed to the figures moving about on top of the hotel in the distance. At first look they resembled ninjas dressed in black. "Who are those men?" I asked her.

"I don't know, your guess is as good as mine," she replied. We wondered and speculated that there must be something happening in the hotel to have those men on the roof. We figured they were law enforcement officers. A closer look shows that some of the men were armed. We figured they are members of a SWAT team. We looked in the other direction and saw SWAT teams on top of other buildings too. We became more curious and intrigued by what we were seeing.

We inquired about the law enforcement officers and found out they were there because a number of heads of states were staying in the hotel. They were visiting for the UN Charter Ceremony. We were told President Clinton was staying at the Fairmont, which accounted for the secret service and SWAT team that we saw on the premises. We knew that Secretary-General Boutros-Ghali would be in town for the ceremony, as well as representatives from other member states.

The Charter ceremony was held on Monday, June 26, 1995 at the War Memorial Opera House in San Francisco. We had a chance to participate in that event. The ceremony began at 10:30 a.m. Early that morning we joined the crowd in the streets and slowly wound our way in the direction of where the ceremony was being held. Ethel and I were joined by two members of the Louisville, Kentucky, chapter.

We reached the location and secured a position close to the head of the line. The opera house was not yet open to the public. While waiting for the doors of the opera house to open for the Charter ceremony, the four of us talked about everything we have seen so far at the annual meeting. We had a neat time talking about our chapters and the work we do. It was a moment away from the formal discussions in our plenary sessions. One of the members commented that we are really the foot soldiers. While we spoke about our chapters and shared our work experiences, we told jokes and laughed about our similar experiences.

While we stood in line one of the ushers came and stood beside us. We were at the head of the line. We asked him how much longer before the doors are open for the ceremony. He told us the doors will be open soon but volunteers are allowed to enter. One of our members from the Louisville chapter immediately declared—pointing to Ethel, myself, and the other member—"we are volunteers" The usher lowered the guard chain and let us through. We entered the War Memorial Opera House, It was a great relief to sit down; I don't believe I could have stood in the line any longer. My injuries were beginning to feel aggravated.

We had a clear view of the stage from where we were sitting. The place was decorated exquisitely for the ceremonial event. The nations flags graced the stage; there was an oversized screen in the back of the stage. It had a clear sky background with a picture of the U.N. headquarters building and flags blowing in the wind. The picture was smack center of the screen. A lonely podium, looking shrunken against the screen in the background, stood in the middle of the stage.

We were given commemorative program handbooks. "Nice work," I said to the members of our "volunteer group." We had good seats but we were too far away from the stage. People began to fill the opera house. There were several empty seats closer to the stage. We asked the usher to allow us to move closer to the stage to fill the empty seats. He told us those seats were reserved.

Halfway through the ceremony the seats were still empty. We asked again if we could move to the empty seats to be closer to the stage, this time we reminded the usher that the doors were now closed for security purposes, no one else would be allowed to enter the theatre. It seemed pointless to let good seats go to waste by remaining empty. He told us we could have the seats if no one shows up within thirty minutes. No one showed up to claim those seats so the four of us moved to take occupation of our four reserved seats which was much closer to the stage. We now had a magnified view of all the proceedings, and settled to enjoy the remainder of the Charter ceremony.

President Bill Clinton, Secretary-General Boutros Boutros-Ghali, and heads of U.N. member states were present. Also at the Charter Ceremony were Bishop Tutu, Ambassador Albright, the President of Poland, and Mayor Shorenstein of San Francisco. Speaking of the United Nations Charter and the hope of the future that it represents, President Clinton stated that it is proof that nations like men, can state their differences, can face them, and "can find common ground on which to stand". The Presidents speech ended with a call to commitment by the citizens of the world to say no to isolation, yes to reform;

yes to a brave and ambitious agenda and most of all yes to the United Nations. Wow! those words are profound.

It is a very good to have a world organization such as the United Nations because it provides a forum where nations can meet and multi-laterally work at solving world issues. The problem is that not all of its Member States behave responsibly. We know that it is a human institution and is prone to errors, but there is a a distinction between errors and irresponsible behavior. Some of its Member States representatives just mickey mouse around by not representing their nations issues the way they should. Our chapter's napping problem is no where comparable to what some member states representatives do on their job. I observed our students in their model UN programs. During those activities students adopt the roles of representatives to the United Nations. Each student represents one member state and must present an issue that is unique to his or her adopted nation. While some students may have a problem representing an issue for their adopted country when that issue has something to do with the United States—a blessed be the ties that bind question—for the most part our model UN students present their issues with passion, caucusing their way, thus gaining consensus on their issue. It would be neat if Member States recognize the value of the UN Charter the way President Bill Clinton explained it in his speech at the UN Charter ceremony.

Maya Angelou recited one of her poems. It was a very fine ceremony and certainly one to be remembered. The general theme and focus of the ceremony was the next generation. The leaders spoke about the state of world affairs. Their voices resoundingly circled the War Memorial Opera House, but there were disconnects.

The world issues proportionately were as huge as the giant screen in the back of the podium. As each of our speakers deliver his or her message in the Charter ceremony the disconnect was visible proportionately to the size of the screen in the background. No one leader can solve all of the world issues. It requires teamwork. It is good that the UN is a democratic organization. Teamwork is based on democratic principles and is common ground on which to stand.

None of us had any idea that the ceremony was a closed event. We found that out when we were leaving the opera house. We had no tickets for the event. Our volunteer work paid off. On our way out we each collected a few of the commemorative program books to take back to our chapters for board members. The program books were nicely done. It had historic photographs and documents of the founding of the United Nations and the signing of the U.N. Charter.

After the Charter ceremony we went back to the Fairmon hotel. The streets were congested with protesters and traffic. We were on foot, so we did not have to worry about the traffic. We had enough time for lunch before our next plenary session. The plenary was scheduled for 2:30 p.m. The final event for the day was an Intergenerational Model Security Council. That lasted for two and a half hours. Ethel and I stayed for the first half of the Model Security Council. We had a very long day and needed to retire to our room early.

On Tuesday we had an early breakfast. Our daily activities began at 9:00 a.m., we were ready for our first plenary of the day. The reports from our Substantive Issues Committee were distributed. There were several issues to be debated before arriving at the final resolutions. Some of those issues were resolved in that meeting and some were tabled or routed through other processes like re-drafting and to be continued. The session lasted for over two hours. It was lunchtime when we finished.

Hon Madeleine K. Albright, Permanent Representative of the United States to the U.N. and Hon Harold Stassen, who was a member of the U.S. delegation in 1945 were speakers at our luncheon. We honored those who were present for the signing of the U.N. Charter in 1945, and we also honored our youths of 1995. The awards for our national essay contest were presented during this luncheon. We were inspired by the presentations to our young people, our next generation.

We had a round-robin jammed session of skills seminar after lunch. The two hours of skill seminars had different workshops on various topics including: securing U.S. financial support for the UN; keeping and enforcing the peace; arming or disarming—a "billion dollars going to waste" issue; promises to keep in advancing human rights; from Rio, Cairo, Copenhagen, and Beijing to where else; promoting the culture of peace: UNESCO and other cultural and international linkages; and more.

Tuesday's activities were wrapped up with a reception in honor of the Council of Organizations and NGOs that were present in 1945 for the signing of the UN Charter. Hon. Elliot L. Richardson, co-chair of UNA-USA National Council, was our speaker. That was another one of our packed-to-capacity event at the annual meeting. History and humor filled the air. Perhaps this was because our convention was winding down and everyone was either more relaxed or was looking forward to going home. History and humor filled the air.

Wednesday June 28 was our final day at the convention. We had a final luncheon that was sponsored by The World Federation of United Nations Association (WFUNA). UNA-USA is a member of WFUNA. The Arnold Goodman Award and the Eleanor Roosevelt Leadership Award were presented during the luncheon. Geoffrey Greenville-Wood, chair of WFUNA Executive Committee, and the Honorable William J. van den Heuvel, chair of UNA-USA Board of Governors were the speakers at this final luncheon.

WFUNA activities continued until June 30. Any UNA-USA members were welcomed to stay on as observers, but Ethel and I did not plan to stay over. Our chapter business and delegate duties were finished. We were looking forward to going home. Ethel had plans to visit her son, who lived in California, before returning home. We packed all the items we collected to share with our board members. Ethel and I parted ways until we see each other again in Miami. She planned on returning to Miami sometime in August. I went off to the airport for my flight back to Miami on the same day.

And so it was, as described in our brochure for the annual meeting commemorating the fiftieth anniversary of the world organization:

> At the conclusion of the 1945 U.N. Conference on International Organization in San Francisco, U.S. President Harry Truman described the Charter of the newly created United Nations as a "solid structure upon which to build a better world" Americans at the conference, including the bipartisan official delegation and 42 non-governmental organization consultants, shared the President's commitment to constructive U.S. leadership in the new world body.
>
> Fifty years later, the need for such U.S. leadership is urgent. Despite many successes, the future of the world body is clouded. The U.N. is over-extended and under-funded; it lacks both the mandate and the resources its needs. Voices are heard in Washington and across the nation calling for reduced U.S. participation in the U.N.
>
> At this moment of profound challenge, UNA-USA's National Convention will meet in San Francisco to mark the fiftieth anniversary of the United Nations, to reaffirm the importance of the U.S. / U.N. relationship, and to chart the Association's future course. The Convention will adopt a "Priorities Agenda" to guide UNA-USA into the 21st Century. Plenary and workshops will provide information and skills.
>
> Members of the Association's Chapters and Divisions, Council of Organizations, National Council, and Board of Governors will be joined by at least forty presidents of non-governmental organizations, as well as students participating the Model United Nations Summit and Youth Leadership Conference to be held in conjunction with the Convention. Convention guests will include the leaders of 80 United Nations Association from around the world, attending the Plenary Assembly of the World Federation of United Nations Associations from June 25-28.

So it was written, and so it was done. We the members of UNA-USA representing our respective chapters and divisions across the United States descended upon San Francisco, ascending on Nob Hill at the Fairmont Hotel. It was there in 1945 that the United Nations was first established. Fifty years ago that was.

In the spirit of the occasion we mixed and mingled, huddled and muddled, emerging with a new sense of direction. Charged light brigades, we ascended to the heavens with eagle's wings. Forward we go humming and toiling upward in the night. "From the halls of Montezuma, to the shores of Tripoli, we fight our country's battles in the air, on land, and sea. We had lots of fun at our national convention that marks the fiftieth anniversary of the UN. We debated issues, shared giggles, humor, and resources in the hope of building a better and more peaceful world. San Francisco is a beautiful city. Ethel and I had fun riding on the street cars, especially going down one of the hills. It was really cool.

CHAPTER 9

OUR YEAR-LONG CELEBRATIONS of the fiftieth anniversary of the United Nations culminated to a grand finale on October 27, 1995, at the Intercontinental Hotel in downtown Miami. The road to the grand finale began with us contacting the hotel to make arrangements to hang a large twenty-foot U.N. flag in front of the hotel. Ethel, Hyman Mally, and I contacted the event scheduler and arranged the meeting to make that request. We intended to persuade the hotel management to have the U.N. flag flown for a month leading up to our celebration.

With our flag neatly packed, we met with the management and event scheduler. We secured the venue for the date of the event. We were given the Bayside Room which had a full view of the ocean. U.N. 50 already had its own momentum which has been driven by nationally televised events, as well as our own high profile activities that were conducted locally. Our business conference, Friends of the Future program, and our activities with other organizations for their UN50 celebrations saturated our community with information on UN50.

Because of the momentous driven U.N. 50 events across the nation and the world, it did not take much to convince the hotel to hang the U.N. flag for a month. Everyone was riding the wave of publicity. We were surfing and it was a lot of fun. That's how Ethel and I felt, it was certainly a lot of work but we were having fun. We gave the U.N. flag to the hotel management. It would be hung one month before the event and flown for the entire month.

We visited the hotel numerous times before the event took place. Our visits were routine to make and finalize different aspects of the venue for our

UN Day. As we worked on coordinating our U.N. Day plans with the hotel we noticed that the U.N. flag was hung in the entrance of the hotel. It was mid-August when we first notice it. We did not expect it to be hung before the end of September. When we saw the huge U.N. flag draped in the entrance we thought we must have found favors to have the flag flown almost three months leading up to the event.

We were proud to see the flag, and extremely pleased that we were working with an establishment that was willing to give us much more than what we asked for. We were proud to be working with people who knew what we were about. I am sure the management noticed our warm disposition each time we interacted with them. We adopted them as our team members. Well, that was good while it lasted. We found out in early October, and to our surprise, it was an error, it should have been the U.S. flag instead of the U.N. flag that should have been hung in the entrance in August.

Hon. Carrie P. Meek, our Congressional Representative for Florida 17th congressional district, had an event at the hotel before we had ours. The U.S. flag should have been hung for her event. It didn't happen that way. The management hung the U.N. flag in error. It was a big mistake. We did not know quite what to say. We told the hotel management that we were sorry for the confusion, but they told us it was their error. We were sorry that Hon. Carrie Meek had her event under the banner of the UN flag instead of the U.S. flag. But all is well that ends well.

Another great thing occurred from late August to early September. You may recall the discussion in a previous chapter of our efforts to raise some seed capital from the Dade County Commission for UN50 activities. Well, we saw no funding from them, but the City of Miami came through for us. Ethel suggested that I contact Mayor Stephen Clark and put in a request for support. I met with Mr. Clark at his office and made a brief presentation of what we were doing. Ethel and I were at that meeting.

Mayor Clark advised us to make a formal presentation at the next council meeting. We requested that our presentation be placed as a pocket item. We showed up at the meeting at city hall on the date we were supposed to. I thought it would be another one of those meetings like the one at the Dade County Commission Chamber. A meeting in the Miami City council was entirely different from Dade County Commission Chamber. I stood up and was ready to plea my case; we were told that our request was already approved. That statement must have not registered right away, because I continued to say that it was very important. I heard the words again that our request was approved.

Ethel and I were beside ourselves when we heard the news of our good fortune. We arrived ready to fight for whatever it was that we were fighting for only to discover that we won without a fight. We were simply blown away because we could not believe it. We were delighted that Mayor Stephen Clark came through for us. We left the council chambers still finding it difficult to believe that we were approved for the small grant. I started singing the chorus to John Parr's *St. Elmo's fire*"

Our plans for the fiftieth celebration shifted into full gear. Our UN Day committee coordinated our program for our celebrations. We did not incorporate any long speeches in the program. All we wanted to do was to celebrate UN50 locally. It was a culmination of all the work we did since October 1994. It was time to recognized everyone and all of our team members for their had work over the past year. The celebration was forecasted to be one of awards and recognition. We designed a special fiftieth anniversary commemorative program booklet for the occasion. Our theme for UN50 was dubbed "A Salute to the United Nations Fifty Years and beyond". In keeping with our TAAL order, we reached out to all of South Florida for UN50 Day as we have done with all of our other activities. We continued to "think and act locally".

On October 27, 1995, at the Intercontinental Hotel in Miami Florida, we opened our celebrations with a warm welcome to everyone. We proceeded with the acceptance of UN Day proclamations. Mayor Stephen P. Clark was on the program to give welcome remarks but he was unable to attend due to his illness. Commissioner Willie Gort attended and filled in for him. Invocation was given by the Right Reverend Calvin O. Schofield Jr. of the Diocese of Southeast Florida. We had over five hundred people in attendance. It was one of our most well attended events ever.

The New World School of the Arts singers entertained us with a rendition of the United Nations song. It was an excellent performance. Many of our guests were not aware that there was a United Nations song. It was the first time they heard that song. We live and learn something new everyday was the general comment of those who were hearing the song for the first time. In the back of this book I have displayed some photographs that were taken at some of our events. It is said that a picture tells a thousand words. For each of those events, the faces of our audience tell a unique story. We are people from all walks of life.

Mr. Nat Turnbull Jr. was the UN50 chairperson for the state of Florida. He was appointed by Governor Lawton Chiles. He was invited, and he accepted to speak at our event. Unfortunately, Mr. Turnbull could not join us in our celebrations. He had a family emergency. Like a true team player, he sent us a representative from his office to speak in his place. His representative brought a UN50 proclamation from the state of Florida. He did not expect to see so many people at the event. In his speech he told us that being at the event was quite an awakening. He too jumped into the spirit of the occasion. Another soul was won in support of planetary citizenship.

Professor Jeanne Kates, one of our board members and also our director of the Model UN program at Florida International University, spoke about Model

UN and global classrooms. She captivated the audience. She really knew her stuff. Many of our attendees were seeing the big picture for the first time. Some members of our audience were able to begin connecting the dots in the dawn of globalization.

Globalization, which as described by some of our audience as a conundrum of morass, was lurking out there on the horizon. Like a giant storm building strength, it was out there ready to flood us like a giant tsunami. To be forewarned was to be forearmed. We were very proud that our organization was providing this education to our community. Professor Kates addressed the issue and she broke it down in simple form. One way in which she explained the big enchilada was with a small object like a bicycle, for example, the spokes are manufactured in one country, the tires in another country, and more parts in another, and so on and so on. The time did not allow for an in-depth discussion on the topic. It was a follow-up to her previous presentation at our state annual meeting which took place in the 1994. Suffice to say our audience got the drift on globalization.

Ms. Betsy Kaplan, chairperson of Dade County School Board, spoke about the impact of the Friends of the Future project. There were principals, teachers, students, and parents among our audiences. Many of them attended to receive awards and recognition for participating in that project. It was a UN50 program with a historic level of participation. Over sixteen thousand students, and four thousand parents and teachers participated in the program.

Dr. Barbara Carey was very instrumental in our cooperative effort with the Friends of the Future project. She was a solid team member. Dr. Carey, like Ms. Kaplan, approached the podium with pride to speak about the project and the students who participated. It was indeed a pleasure and honor to present Dr. Carey with a plaque in appreciation of the work she did in helping us to bring UN50 to our elementary and middle school students and their parents. As I handed her the award and shook her hand, we looked at each other, our thoughts collided, and the grip of both of our hands was a reassurance and acknowledgement of yes! we did it. We hugged each other and patted each other on the back before she left the stage.

None of our UN50 programs had an impact on me as did our Friends of the Future program. Before we executed the program we were told time and time again to expect only about three hundred students to participate. When we asked the naysayers why only that amount, we were told that inner city students and parents do normally show interest in such things. That was what we expected, but look at what happened. It was a supercalifragilisticexpialidocious, jaw-dropping, shattering to smithereens destruction of the bombastic stereotypical views of the potentials of our students. The results reaffirmed my faith and my conviction in the potentials of our youth. I say to our naysayers bug-off, and *let our garden grow*.

Our celebration continued with our youth speakers in our "Circle of Excellence." The students of Palmetto, Coral Gables, and Southwood Senior high schools addressed the audience. Ramya Morali spoke on the rights of children. It was a splendid thought-provoking, critical view of the perspective of children and their place in society. Ramya explained that although children do not have any authority in decision making, nevertheless, children are people too. That statement was very profound. Our Circle of Excellence segment concluded with the New World School of the Arts singers performing "Make Our Garden Grow" by Leonard Bernstein from *Candide*.

Dr. Demetrious Argyriades of the United Nations Department for Development Support and Management Service (UNDDSMS) was our keynote speaker. Dr. Argyriades told me that he delivered only a part of his pre-prepared speech. He was so captured by the synergistic energy of our celebration; he deviated from his prepared speech to join the energy of interaction that was present in our celebration. It was a live interaction of peoples from all walks of life. The dynamics, he commented, was his observance of ultimate cooperation through diversity, which was no ordinary interaction.

Everyone in that ballroom was present, and there were no boundaries or boxes. The atmosphere in our celebration gave permission to speak freely. There was a seamless boundary among different age groups, the lines between different races and ethnic groups vanished; carved spaces between genders disappeared, and the different structures of entities were shredded. Our event was one of kaleidoscopic cultural symmetry with admiration of wisdom and knowledge, respective of young, old and those in between. It was that one moment in time, a brotherhood and sisterhood of man and woman.

Everyone was simply enjoying the event; imagine that. As customary, Dr. Argyriades allowed fifteen minutes of questions, answers, and discussion. The audience participated with high energy. After the question-and-answer session, I presented Dr Argyriades with a small honorarium as was our tradition and custom, to show our gratitude for sharing his time with us. It was certainly the least we could do to show our appreciation of him being with us for UN50.

While I shook his hand to make the presentation, Dr. Argyriades pulled me close and whispered in my ear, "I do not know how you have accomplished this herculean feat" I whispered in response "I do not know what you mean". He looked at Dr. Xanthopolous, one of our UN50 committee members, who was standing on the stage to my right and said, "Ask him, he will tell you what I knew what he meant but the place and time did not permit to explain to him the power of team work and team dynamics."

Kathy was our master of ceremonies. She was a graduate student, and also Dr. Lu's granddaughter. Her mother Lilly Lu was also one of our board members. Our presenters for the awards and recognition segment of our program were Dr. Michael Kesselman and Farrokh Jhabvala. Both of these men were members of our board as well as committee chairpersons. Our stage was nicely decorated for the occasion. It represented the spirit of a world united. By the term world united I am not referring to a utopian state of being but the outcomes of our year long set of activities resulting from our teamwork.

The large flags of the United States, the United Nations, State of Florida, Dade County, and the City of Miami graced both sides of our stage. In front of the stage were miniature flags of each member state of the United Nations. One tier down from the miniature flags was a beautiful display of floral arrangements. To the far right was a shining grand piano that was provided for our entertainers. To the far left of the stage was a long table lined with trophies, certificates, proclamations, and plaques glistening blindingly under the overhead lights.

The moment arrived to say thank you and to recognize everyone for participating, for teamwork and for supporting our year long UN50 programs. Kathy called me to the podium to assist with the presentations. It was a moment of mixed emotions for me. I was thrilled that I was now having the opportunity to say thank you in a big way. I can't remember how I got to the podium but I did. I must have walked on air. I cleared my throat to speak and let the moment take control.

Filled with mixed emotions I felt tears welling up in my eyes but I was smiling through it all. The audience rode the experience with me. There was a great hush, a silence like I had never heard before. I adjusted the microphone and looked at the audience. I scanned the ballroom, then I saw the lights; a kaleidoscopic display of gems in concentric circles radiantly glowing in bright colors. True colors and *common ground*, I thought.

You may choose to believe it or not, but it is true. I saw the choir—which sounded like an orchestra. It was a profound and resounding chorus, and a waving jeweled flag of the United States emerged in the forefront. Amid the musical chorus were the words "Well done, we are glad you came." The imprint was of the founding fathers and the heavenly hosts.

I said thank you to Kathy for inviting me to assist with the presentations. I then called on all our presenters and those who will be assisting in making the presentations to step forward. The entire team of presenters stood up and took their places. I gave the signal to our video technician to start rolling the looped video that will quietly show segments of all our work for the entire year. The video was shown on a large overhead screen in the back of the stage. I asked our audiences to hold all applause until the end of our presentation. How does one say thank you to everyone for all the volunteer work they did all year, and how do you recognize those who have participated so willingly?.

The video showing all our programs and participants for the year long set of activities began to roll. The technician lowered some of the lights so that there would be a better view of the screen. Kathy began reading the names and categories of our awards. One by one the recipients and honorees walked to the podium to accept their awards. It was a climactic moment and the grand finale to our celebration for UN50.

Dr. Kesselman and Farrokh Jhabvala joined me on the stage, and we started the proceedings. First to receive their awards were the five students from Atlantic High School in Palm Beach County; these were the winning and placing students in the national high school essay contest. Their school was recognized for participating in the contest. A plaque was presented and accepted by the students' teacher. The winning student and her teacher were given a few minutes to share their experiences.

The audience held the applause but acknowledgement and accolades were communicated in the sounds of approval. There were plenty of smiles with the bowing and nodding of heads from the audience. The quality, aspirations, sincerity, commitment, and reach for excellence were easily observed in the demeanor of our awards recipients. One by one each recipient walked to the platform to receive an award. Their participation was a one time effort in honor of UN50. They willingly took that one moment in time to let their voices be heard, and in their own way contributed to the success of our celebrations recognizing the world organization and U.S. leadership in that world body.

Since 1986, thousands of secondary school students have been introduced to the UN system, and encouraged to think about America's role in the world body through UNA-USA's annual nationwide essay contest. This program was initiated and funded by the 1985 National UN Day chair, Ambassador Peter H. Dailey, and the Dailey Family Foundation. The year 1995's contest theme, "My Message to the United Nations," elicited essays from schools around the country. Annie Nosieux, Eric Hartman, Stephanie Lyew, Jordana Jarjeura, and Fariu Chowdburg of Atlantic High School in Palm Beach County, Florida, emerged as the top five winners in our region.

Dade County elementary schools were presented with awards based on participation in the Friends of the Future art and literary contest. During the spring of 1995, UNA-USA Greater Miami chapter conducted UN50 activities in the Dade County public schools. The event was sponsored by the Greater Miami chapter of UNA-USA, Planeta Publishing Company, and the Dade County Public Schools Multicultural/Alternative Education Department. Over ninety schools, sixteen thousand students, and four thousand families participated. Schools were ranked by the percentage of enrolled students who participated.

The schools that received awards and recognitions were Kenwood, Gratigny, and Broadmoor elementary schools recognized with highest participation levels in the district. North Dade Center for Modern Languages, North Twin Lakes, and Lake Stevens were ranked the highest based on participation levels in Region I, and were recognized as first, second and third respectively. Gratigny, Biscayne Gardens, and Bay Harbor were awarded and recognized in the same fashion of first, second, and third in Region II. Broadmoor, Lillie C. Evans, and Melrose elementary schools were recognized and received awards for first, second, and third ranking in Region III. Kensington, Auburndale, and Sunset in the same order were recognized for first, second, and third in Region IV. Kenwood, Devon Aire, and Gloria Floyd were first, second, and third in Region V. Claude Pepper, Emerson, and Caribbean were recognized for first, second, and third in Region VI. Colonial Drive and Palmetto were recognized for exceptionally high participation levels.

The participation spirit was illuminated with a scorching flame that undoubtedly incinerated the myths of the naysayers who foretold far less than minuscule participations levels. To end that segment of our awards and presentation ceremony it was befitting and appropriate to make the statement" Ladies and gentlemen, our next generation". The audience could not hold the applause any longer. They let it poured for our students. I too joined in, never mind that at the beginning of our presentation I asked them to hold all applause until we were finished making all presentations. It was a situation that called for on the spot applause.

The sounds of congratulations, joy, and pride rang out for our students and the team members. It was a foot-stomping, hand-clapping, glass-tapping, whistle-blowing, yeah-saying, joyous moment of celebration and recognition. It was a moment befitting what my grandmother would say, allemande, left, and do-sa-do—the figures of eight in the quadrille, polka if you can, or simply dance to the disco beat. It was the taking off of hats, a bow and courtesy, if you please. The young people did us proud.

The applauses hushed for a moment. We thanked our corporate sponsors. Without their assistance we could not have done the programs we did. Our UN50 activities in South Florida covered the area from Palm Beach to Key West. It was a "TAAL" order in *thinking and acting locally* in our public outreach and awareness programs. We actively sought the sponsorship of our corporate community and invited their participation in support of our programs. Planeta Publishing one of our local businesses was a major contributor in underwriting the cost of our Friends of the Future program. We recognized their significant contributions in helping to promote public awareness of the world organization. Carlos Provencza and his wife, Carmen, accepted the award for their team spirit and on the behalf of their company.

A seamless interaction and cross functionality of teamwork as demonstrated by Carlos and his company was the foundation of the success of our Friends of the Future project. Ethel was presented with our "sustainable peace" award. Ms. Felts has been a member of UNA-USA since the 1960s. She twice served as president of the Greater Miami chapter and as a vice president for five years. She is a dedicated and active volunteer on the local, state, and national levels. Ethel served on the steering committee of the Council and Chapter and

Division Presidents (CCDP) and was the secretary of the Florida division of UNA-USA.

Mayor Stephen P. Clark of the city of Miami was presented with an award for his role in strengthening the relationship between the United States and the United Nations. Mayor Clark was ill and unable to attend the ceremonies, but Commissioner Willy Gort accepted the award on behalf of Mayor Stephen P. Clark. After receiving the award he spoke and received our well-wishes for the speedy recovery of our Mayor. We took photographs of Commissioner Gort accepting the award for Mayor Clark so that we could show it to the Mayor when he recovered from his illness.

Our thank-you list to everyone who participated was lengthy—a demonstration of the many people from different cultures and walks of life who participated, contributed, and celebrated with us. It was truly a world-class act in every sense of the word. I invited all of our board members to join me on the stage. We were applauded by the audiences which we gracefully accepted. I was crowned with some of our floral arrangements. I did the same to other board members. I then gave the final remarks bestowing a "world of thanks" to everyone for a successful outcome and a grand finale to our UN50 celebrations.

The United Nations stands as the world's foremost testament to the spirit of international cooperation, bringing together 190 nations in a multinational forum to discuss and debate issues that affect our lives globally. It has worked to maintain peace and security for all the peoples of the world and to address such extraordinary challenges as famine and disease, natural disasters and man-made disasters, endemic poverty, and human rights abuse. In every hemisphere and on every continent, UN efforts have contributed to a safer and more livable world.

The fiftieth anniversary provided a unique opportunity to recognize its achievements and appreciate the tremendous contributions that the United States has made to the United Nations, beginning with its founding in 1945 and continuing to this day, as the world body moves toward even greater responsibilities and greater maturity. Our celebrations for UN50 were brought to a close with a round of applause.

So it was charted and so it was done. We the members of Greater Miami UNA-USA undertook the TAAL order to increase public awareness of the works of the world organization, and to celebrate its fiftieth anniversary in our community. We "think and act locally." Our success was powered by our all-inclusive dynamic teamwork. Creativity and innovation were our natural resources. We sprung into action, building teams along each and every step of the way. We huddled and muddled through our maze of cultural diversity taping knowledge and skills as we moved forward.

Our journey was not without challenges. We had plenty of those, and they were as diverse as there were many cultures and organizations who interacted and participated in our programs. We encountered resistance at every crossroads of organizational, people, physical and cultural intersection. We built bridges, took detours, negotiated our way, created trade-offs, offered compromises, huddled and muddled, engaged strategic alliances, drafted agreements, charted working relationships, adopted new team members, and we kept moving forward. We avoided personal conflicts and head on collisions. Any of those types of conflicts or situations would only drain our limited resources and consume time which we did not have a lot of. Whenever personal conflicts begin to sprout the larger body of team members engage quiet diplomacy. In any event we never take the bull by the horn when it comes to personal conflicts. It was not unusual for one of our team members to become a self appointed goodwill matador. That may involve taking our conflicting team member to lunch or becoming a bosom buddy until the conflict subsides. And even in such a case it was done with utmost team spirit.

Our South Florida engagement for UN50 under the leadership of UNA-USA Greater Miami chapter demonstrated the progress in interactive cultural engagement for that one moment in time. Our motto for our celebrations was "A salute to the United Nations fifty years and beyond." Our celebrations were not intended to focus only on that one moment in time, but to project a progressive engagement and interaction of cultures beyond the milestone of those fifty years.

CHAPTER 10

AT THE END of UN50 celebrations we expected to settle down to regular chapter activities and going back to doing business as usual. We were looking forward to returning to our low-keyed quiet existence. We valued our state of being which was quiet diplomacy. Our pens ruled the day. Where there were issues affecting our lives that need to be addressed, we exercised our penmanship. We write our issues on post cards and mailed them to our congressional representatives and our senators. When one of us write to one of our congressional representative it is an alert; when five members send post cards on an issue it is considered serious problem; but when ten or more post cards are mailed on the same issue to our congressional representative, it is considered a crisis. Our chapter's average membership was two hundred people. We walked softly and the big stick was our membership strength in numbers. We engaged team work, and we put our issue and our expected resolution in writing. We alerted our congressional representative to the seriousness of any issue that is a developing crisis. We continue to send in post cards until action is taken by our representative.

If no action is taken on our issue by our congressional representative, it is not unlikely for our chapter to arrange a candlelight vigil or to become a participant of a larger candlelight vigil for the cause or issue that is taking place nationally or internationally. A candlelight vigil is another form of our quiet diplomacy. It was our way of quietly meeting and supporting each other while at the same time getting our message out to a larger audience.

However, going back to our normal existence was not to be, at least not yet. More things were coming our way. In the spring of 1996, we facilitated and hosted the second conference on how to do business with the United Nations. It was a much smaller-scale event compared to the first conference that was held in March 1995. The second conference on doing business with the United Nations was held on May 21, 1996.

A month after the conference, we were invited to a town hall meeting in New York by our national headquarters. Those who attended would have an opportunity to visit the offices of U.S. Mission to the U.N. Our national office took care of all our security clearances. I represented our chapter. It was another opportunity to learn more about the organizations and how they function.

While at that meeting I received information that US foreign policy town hall meetings were being conducted across our nation. I also found out that there was none scheduled, as of yet, for our region. We were always on the lookout for opportunities that would help us in our public outreach and education programs. I spotted an opportunity to bring one of those town hall meetings to Miami. I gathered as much information that I could and upon returning to Miami shared the information with our board members.

Our board members liked the idea of a US foreign policy town hall meeting. One of our members introduced the motion that we host one of those meetings. It was seconded by another member, and the floor was opened for discussion on the topic. In our discussion several of our board members suggested the importance of having such a town hall meeting in our community. It was decided unanimously that we would host one of the foreign policy town meetings. We believed that it was a good opportunity for members of our community to participate and have first hand discussion with foreign policy decision makers and administrators.

We contacted the US Department of State, Public Affairs section and spoke with the person who was coordinating the town hall meetings. We informed her of our decision and agreed to put the event together. We cosponsored the event which was scheduled to take place on September 17, 1996.

We immediately developed our team approach. We discussed our resources and defined what role each of us would undertake in the development of the event. We developed and planned our town hall meeting just like we did all previous events. But there was one slight difference in the planning of this event. We considered and incorporated a higher grade of security. We were told that at other town hall meetings across the U.S. some protesters and hecklers showed up at those meetings. We wanted to be prepared just in case we had similar experiences. Our board decided that it would be best to incorporate security with our planning.

The security issue became more pressing when we realized that our town hall meeting will be dealing with current and controversial issues. The objective of our town hall meetings was to create public awareness by providing a forum for the public to hear and engage dialogue through questions and answers from policy makers. The meeting was held in the Graham Center at Florida International University in Miami. The theme for the meeting was the "Four Pillars of US Foreign Policy". It was expected that this theme will present a global perspective of the topics that were to be discussed at the meeting. One of the topics of the meeting was the Helm-Burton Act. That was a hot and divisive topic in our community as it was elsewhere in the nation. Another hot topic for the meeting was China and its WTO membership.

We did not expect to have any unruliness or disorderly conduct at the event, but we expected that the issues were going to be discussed with a great deal of passion. We did not overlook the sensitivity aspects that may arise during the meeting. We were aware of the depth of the strains of those issues and the impact on the lives of our fellow citizens, which for many were profound real life experiences. We considered the possibility that some people will perhaps be more concerned with ideological ramifications. Because of those factors in all instances sensitivity was a guiding light in the planning and development of the town hall meeting. At the same time we did not wish to use sensitivity as a filtering tool. We wanted to have an open, fair and free discussions of the issues and topics. Therefore to balance the equation, it was very important to have adequate and proper security measures to ensure a favorable environment for all participants and attendees.

Florida International University has excellent security on all of their campuses. Because of that one would think that we did not need to have additional security, but that was not the case. I contacted the chief of security at the main campus. I told him about the event and asked if the thought we needed additional security. He took the information and told me he would consult with his team then he would get back to us with more information.

A few days later he called us and told us that we need to have additional security. I asked him about the cost and he gave an estimate of what the cost would be for the additional security. The cost of the service for additional security seemed reasonable. The problem was we had no money to pay the cost of security. The chief insisted that we needed additional security for the event. I knew that, it was the very reason why I called him in the first place. Our board wanted us to have additional security for the event. The issue wasn't a question of needing security it was the daunting problem of how were we going to pay for the service. We did not have the kind of money it would take to secure the services in our skeletal budget. Our cosponsors did not provide us with any type of funding.

We had very limited resources and depended highly on innovation and creativity. I told the chief of security some of the names of people who were expected to attend the meeting. I also told him the name of some of our speakers. I sounded off Ambassador Hattie Babbitt, our US representative to the Organization of American States, as well as other names of speakers. I was getting ready to negotiate with him.

As I pleaded my case, I continued to tell the chief of security about the long line of ambassadors and guests who were expected to attend the event. "We cannot afford to pay for security, so I guess we will just have to do without it," I told him apologetically. "We will have to pray on the matter and hope for the best outcome," I said to him over the telephone. I was hinting that our conversation was reaching a terminal point. I told him that I thanked him for providing us with the information and the estimate, but the cost for security was totally out of our reach. I was about to say good bye;

The chief of security cleared his throat and said, "Now wait a minute, let's not rush this."

"I am sorry, but we do not have that kind of money, and I do not know where we would find that kind of money either," I repeated to him.

Before our conversation ended the chief of security impresses upon me that we need additional security and could not take the risk of not doing so for the event. I agreed with him because he was right. He agreed to provide us with full-scale security for the event. He told me that he would work our the security details for inside the town hall meeting as well as for on the premises. The additional security will be provided at no cost to us. He told me not to worry about the cost because he would take care of that. The burden was literally lifted from my shoulders. I forgot how many times I thanked him for his kindness and professionalism in handling the situation. The chief of security at Florida International University was now one of our team members.

In the huddle and muddle of things quite often we emerged with innovative and creative approaches. I leveled with the chief and he responded to our plight. I am more apt to believe that the chief saw the importance of the event and the value it would be to our community. He also saw the need to have security at the event, and he came through for us.

The negotiation with the chief of security brings to mind another similar situation that wound up in a win-win situation for everyone. Ambassador Alvin Adams was due in town to discuss human rights issues. He was to be accompanied by a speaker from the United Nations. We need a venue at a short moment's notice for the event. One of our board members suggests that we contact the University of Miami North-South Center and ask for help.

I contacted Ambassador Ambler Moss's office and explained what it is we wanted to do and what we need from them. The protocol was that the matter would be looked into and some one would get back with me and or I could do a follow up call. I made my follow-up call and spoke with someone in that office. Our discussion led me to believe that we had the green light for the event to be held at the North South Center's faculty lounge. I thought it was great that the approval came so quickly, not that I mind because we needed the approval like yesterday.

I was so delighted with the outcome I contacted Ambassador Moss right away to personally say thank you for the approval and the expediency with which the matter was handled. He was very pleased that I contacted him to personally thank him for the outcome. He told me that it was his pleasure and that if there was anything else that we need I should not hesitate to call him. We had a wonderful conversation over the telephone filling in tidbits of what and how we were doing.

Well ! as it turned out, telephone calls were crisscrossing back and forth from staff members at the North South Center and my office, and also to Ethel. One message that was left for me was to the effect that the staff member will discuss the matter with Ambassador Moss, and he or she will let me know the next day whether or not approval was given for the event to take place at the North South Center. I was not sure what the problem was because I already expressed a personal thank you to Ambassador Moss for his approval to use faculty's lounge for the event.

Ethel was just as confused as I was about the matter. I called back the staff member at the North South Center and told him that I already had approval. I also told him that I already contacted Ambassador Moss and expressed my gratitude for him having allowed us to have the event in the faculty's lounge. It was not unusual to experience confusion in planning our activities, especially with those that are being executed in a short time frame. It is always good to know, however, that with creativity, innovation, the ability to negotiate, and with added quiet diplomacy, we managed to get the job done.

We had our meeting at the North South Center. It was at very short notice but everything went o.k. We served sandwiches for lunch. We had a good turnout. Lunch was serve with the compliments of the North South Center. It was a very informative session. After the event the members of staff at the North South Center continued to try to figure out how and when approval was given to us. To this day I do not believe that anyone has been able to nail down exactly what had transpired. The staff member followed-up with me after the event. I guess the approval process was quite intriguing to him.

According to the staff member there really was never a decision leading up to the approval. I asked him to explain to me what he thought happened. He followed-up with me with several telephone calls but never explained what he thought had transpired. I wondered why he was pressing the point with me. By this time we were in the process of formally sending our acknowledgement to the Center for their hospitality. The event had brought some positive and progressive opportunities to the North South Center. in my final conversation with the staff member I told him that all is well that ends well. He agreed with me but he was still befuddled about what transpired and how the event was approved. I told him it might have been a cart before the horse situation. He laughed and so did I.

We had several new volunteers who came to us very eager to work. Joy Murphy had just graduated from the University of South Florida. She wanted to help with our local campus network program. Alexis was a native of the Dominican Republic. She attended college in Boston but was also eager to work with our local chapter. Joy and Alexis became members of our chapter and they both helped us tremendously with our town hall meeting.

We discussed past experiences at town hall meetings elsewhere across the nation with our contact person at the Public Affairs section of the Department of State. Some of the experiences that she shared with us was the heckling at the meetings in Texas. She explained that those behaviors created many distractions from the issues that were being discussed in the meetings. We appreciated the sharing of those experiences with us. It helped us to make improvements in our town hall meeting plans. The additional security was one area of improvement. Our primary role was the facilitator and host of the meeting. The speakers were provided by the US Department of State.

Our own hall meeting did not require as much detailed planning as did some of our other events. This made our lives and work a lot easier. We did not have to select menus or make any pricing plans for meals. All we had to do for our town hall meeting was to estimate the number of attendees and arrange the seating capacity accordingly. We continue to make arrangements for transportation and accommodation for all of our speakers. This was coordinated with our cosponsor the US Department of State Public Affairs section.

The staff from Public Affairs at the US Department of State who were responsible for helping with the planning arrived two days before the meeting. Ethel and I met Sheila and her assistant on the day that they arrived in Miami. We took the two ladies to lunch and spend a good deal of the time becoming acquainted. After lunch Ethel drove us to the Graham Center to show them the venue for the town hall meeting. On our way to the Graham Center we took a few scenic routes to showcase our community.

Our team members from the US Department of State Public Affairs section loved what they saw and heard. Ethel and I were pleased that they liked our choice of location for the town hall meeting. We gave them a grand tour of the Graham Center inside and out with the help of the staff members from Florida International University. Sheila brought several boxes from Washington that contained materials for the town hall meeting. She selected one of the tables where she will set up her display. Before we left the Graham Center we reviewed our program for the town hall meeting to make certain that everything met their approval. Everything was fine. Sheila will give an overview of the mission of the US Department of State, tell the audience what

Public Affairs do at the Department of State, and why we were having the town hall meeting.

Sheila planned on speaking a bit about the number of town hall meetings in the regions in which they were conducted. She also planned to announce future town hall meetings and when and where they were scheduled to take place in the near future. I will be giving the opening remarks at our town hall meeting. In those remarks I will speak a bit about UNA-USA, our local chapter and the work we do. Joy Murphy, one of our volunteer staff, will be our moderator for the first questions and answers session. Some of our members will be ushers while other members will work at the registration area.

Special sections in the meeting hall were designated for members of the press. Members of the media must show their press pass before they are allowed to enter the town hall meeting. We reviewed our registration list. Based on the numbers and taking into consideration those who will register upon arrival, we expected over two hundred and fifty people to be in attendance. Finally, we checked our security details. We were satisfied that everything will flow according to our plans.

Our security details included uniformed parking attendants and campus police officers who will be directing the flow of traffic. There were designated areas for traffic overflow. According to the plans the town hall meeting will have security inside of the meeting as well as on the premises. We were informed that there will be plain clothes officers inside of the meeting hall as well as outside of the meeting room. We were satisfied that everything was accounted for in our security details.

We finished reviewing our check list and all of the details for the meeting. Sheila commented, "Gee, Sylvia, you guys took care of everything so well." "That is how we do business around here, Sheila. We leave no stone unturned" Ethel responded. We laughed at her response because of the way Ethel swung her hips and waved her hand in the air as she said those words.

I arrived at the Miami International Airport to meet Ambassador Babbitt and Scott. I joined the queue at the exit for arrivals. I held up the sign with the bold words *UNA-USA*, so that I can be easily spotted. We have never met before but I immediately spotted my two parties. There is something about federal officers that make them stand out in a crowd. Perhaps it is because I am used to meeting them at the airport why I spot them so quickly. The way they walk or their posture, maybe, I don't know exactly what it is, but it is never difficult for me to recognize my parties when I am meeting them at the airport.

My parties came through the exit, travelling lightly of course, and we greeted each other with formal introductions. I asked them to please follow me as we moved through the crowded airport terminal to where my vehicle was parked. I opened the car and popped open the car trunk for the items and overnight bags. Scott entered the front passenger seat, and Ambassador Babbitt sat in the back. I took my position in the driver's seat, started the ignition, and began our exit. I had done this numerous times for our guests and speakers, so the trip was routine.

On our way to the hotel, we discussed their flight on the way to Miami. Ambassador Babbitt asked about the organization. I filled her in briefly on the background of the national organization, our local chapter, and the work we did. She asked me what was in it for me. I told her nothing I am just a good citizen. We are people of goodwill and the foot soldiers of our grassroots organization. We believed that we contribute to the growth and prosperity of our community by facilitating programs like the town hall meeting. Programs like these encouraged dialogue, and increase our community awareness of the policies that affects our lives.

Scott inquired about the current community climate on some of the topics that were to be discussed in the town hall meeting. I told them the number of people who are expected to attend, and ran off some of the organizations that will also be represented. I also told them who the other speakers and panelists were. I described the general climate and and temperature in our community on the issues that are to be discussed. I also provided a cross sector pulse rate on the issues in our community. It was my job to prepare our speakers and special guests on what to expect so that they are comfortable. We had no hidden agenda or surprises. We believed in providing a favorable environment so that our speakers and guests may interact under favorable circumstances regardless of how tough and pressing the issues are. It was simply the civilize thing to do.

We arrived at the Sheraton Biscayne Bay hotel. Scott and Ambassador Babbitt exited the vehicle while an attendant took their bags from the trunk of the car. I parked the car then went to the check-in counter. The front desk was already alerted of their arrival. They almost finished checking in by the time I got there. Both parties followed the attendant to their respective rooms. Before they left, I provided them with my room number and asked them to call me if they needed anything.

Ethel and I visited for a while. She wanted to be filled in on my first impression of our guest in addition to other matters that we needed to discuss before our event the next day. I told her that Scott appears to be fitting in very well, but Ambassador Babbitt seemed to have a wait and see disposition. A wait and see demeanor was not that unusual for some of our speakers. Many of our speakers behave in the same fashion especially if they are visiting us for the first time. Ethel thought that Ambassador Babbitt may need more warming up. Ethel was die-hard grass roots worker, and she expects all our speakers to recognize those characteristics and get in the flow of things with us. We reviewed all our arrangements again to make sure that everything was going as planned.

Joy called from the office to tell us that everything that was to be taken to the event was packed in the car. She wanted to know if there was anything else she should bring with her before she leaves the office. She was super exited about the event. She had an official role. She was one of our moderators and will be moderating the first session. She told us that she had her hair done especially to look the part of her role. She also told us that her mom and dad will be most likely attending with her.

Alexis also called to tell us that her mom will be attending too. She was about to leave her home to meet Joy at the office to pick up the brochures and flags. Before she got off the telephone, she told us that she developed an exit strategy and Joy thought it was a neat idea. She promised to share the idea with us when we met at the Graham Center. She believed that Ethel and I may want to consider using the strategy ourselves.

We were not totally oblivious to the passion concerning the issues that were to be discussed in the meeting. When discussions are filled with passion it is no telling what some people will do to get their points across. We enlisted and encouraged participation from all sides of the debate. In our planning process we do not discuss the issues per se, but we provide information on the issues that will be discussed.

During the process of putting the meeting together we frequently receive feedbacks and comments about the issues. More often than not those comments and feedbacks are unsolicited, never the less we kept records of them. That is how we are able to determine the temperature and pulse rate on the issues in our community. Media reports provided us with the general overview of the climate in our community about those issues. We expected that the town hall meeting will flow smoothly, but because of what we knew, it was not so far fetched that Alexis would have come up with an exit strategy.

We try to explain to those people who have very strong opinions that we are simply the facilitators and hosts of the event; our organization and our work are nonpartisan. We encouraged dialogue and public participation, in order to increase public awareness by providing education on the issues. Sometimes we encounter friendly engagements at other times we meet with hostility. We preferred favorable engagement, but that is not always possible. It depends on the climate and temperature. With that said, it was therefore not unlikely that any member of our staff or any of our volunteers would use the term *exit strategy*.

We have learned time and time again to expect the unexpected. A Jamaican proverb states "If yuh can't ketch Quaco, yuh ketch him shut." The translation is "If you cannot catch Quaco, you catch his shirt," which means if the person that is wanted escapes, then the vengeance may be taken upon his relatives or friends. Alexis was looking out for our team and our safety.

We embraced all of our speakers, guests, co-sponsors, cooperative organizations, and volunteers as team members for each and every event. Our primary concern for the issues in the town hall meeting was the pulse rate in relationship to the Helms-Burton Act, regardless that there would be added security; our young volunteers felt better knowing that they had a backup plan.

The exit strategy was to crawl on our knees under the tables to the east wing of the hall, then crawl along the corridor to the exit door at the back of the room, then dart through the door at super-high speed. But we must not forget to take the U.S. and the U.N. flags because they cost too much. We could not replace them with our meager budget. We had a good laugh at the plan. If nothing else, it helped to ease the apprehension and tension among our volunteers. We were ready and motivated to host the town hall meeting for the benefit of our attendees.

The day arrived for our meeting. I took a stack of *Reader's Digest* to the hotel with me. I enjoyed reading the sections; *Laughter, the Best Medicine; Humor in Uniform, All in a Day's Work.* I browsed through those sections of several copies of the *Reader's Digest*. Some of copies that I was reading were old dating back three years or more. I lost most of my collection of *Reader's Digest* and also my collection of *National Geography* in Hurricane Andrew. I usually keep my copies for years. I sometimes like to go back and read those old copies for fun. I restarted my magazine collection when I relocated to Fort Lauderdale in the fall of 1992.

I loved reading those sections. They make me laugh and that was just what I need to lighten up. I remember reading the same sections before, but it did not matter, I read them again anyway. As the time grew closer for heading to the Graham Center I got ready and headed to the garage of the hotel to get the car. Scott and Ambassador Babbitt were to meet me at the hotel entrance. I was ahead of myself and had fifteen minutes to spare. I sat in the car and listened to my *Graceland* cassette before leaving the parking area. I chose the song "*You Can Call Me Al*".

After that song finished, I ejected the tape, placed it in the console, and then proceeded to meet Scott and Ambassador Babbitt at the front of the hotel. We greeted each other as they entered the car and we were off to the town hall meeting. I was given a designated area for parking. I drove up the driveway to the campus and was stopped by the uniformed parking attendant. I told him who I was, and he directed me to the designated area. We arrived at the Graham Center.

I escorted our speakers into the meeting hall and showed them where to sit. I then left them to mingle with the milieu of things while I moved along to check in with Ethel and the others. Everything was going a long beautifully. Ethel told me that Joy and Alexis had a bit of delay but they arrived OK and were now setting up their area.

Gertrude and Ethel were managing the registration table. I checked in with Sheila, she said everything was ready. I checked that all our guests had arrived, and all speakers and panelists were present. The stage was decorated with the flags of the United States, the State of Florida, Dade County, FIU, the US Department of State, and the United Nations. UNA-USA does not have a flag of our own. We used the U.S. and the United Nations flags at all of our events. A huge banner hung at the back of the stage with the crest of UNA-USA. The crest of the U.S. Department of State was in front of the podium. All equipment was operating and functional. The panelists' table on the raised stage was equipped with six microphones.

The hall began to fill with people arriving for the town hall meeting. The people represented a cross section of the community. Academia from every university in Florida, businesspeople, professionals, students, community organizations, churches, and peoples from all walks of life were in attendance at the Graham Center. We had a full house, and we were on time for the meeting. We respect our time and that of others.

One of our cardinal rules is that we must commence our activity at the time we announce it to be. It was one way of assuring that we deliver what we say we will so that people will attend our next event. Timeliness was simply protocol for us. There are times when our activity does not start at the time we say it would but that is usually due to circumstances beyond our control. But when that happens we usually have our backup plans. Every good team must have a backup plan before executing any activity, and especially those that involved pubic interaction. It is not good to keep the audience waiting.

I called the meeting to order and gave the welcome remarks. That was followed by an announcement of our distinguished guests. I also gave a short introduction of our speakers and panelists. I introduced Sheila, the staff member from U.S. Department of State, Public Affairs then turned the microphone and podium over to her. Sheila provided the audience with an overview of the mission and purpose of U.S. Department of State as well as what the Division of Public Affairs did. She introduce Joy who spoke about UNA-USA. After her brief overview of UNA-USA, Joy Introduced our first speaker.

As our town hall meeting progresses, the audience involvement was growing at a fever pitch. It was getting very hot but the meeting was being conducted in an orderly fashion. The deeper the issues were delved into, the more the pot churned. Soon steam was puffing through the sides. We moved quickly through the meeting going from isle to isle helping our audience to get to the microphone to voice their concerns. It was our way of trying to keep the lid on things. The room was filled with tough questions from our interactive audiences. Our speakers stepped up to the plate to face the questions head on. At the first sign of a head on collision between our policy makers and the audience, our team members were poised and ready for deflection. Sandy Leon, our board member was in the midst of it all. He spiced up the questions and answers session with his interrogative approach.

While Sandy was addressing his question to one of our speakers, Ethel gave me a nudge and suggested that some one must remind Sandy that he is not in a court of law, and that the speakers are not on the witness stand. Ethel smiled at me as she further commented that Sandy had a unique way of motivating others and stirring the stew in our meeting. There were many people in queue waiting their turn at the microphones that were located in the two outer isles.

We kept an eye on things as they proceeded. Scott spoke of the four pillars of U.S. foreign policy and he named each pillar by region. The temperature was rising in the town hall meeting. There were some bumps in the road and we watched as the mercury began to rise. At one point we thought it would have exploded. Scott asked for time out and the mercury level went down. He addressed some of the participants whose questions had a tone of hostility. He reminded them of the spirit of our town hall meeting. I too had to intercept a few times with the hope of lowering the temperature, but that only lasted for a brief moment before it would rise again.

Ambassador Babbitt spoke about several underlying problems and issues that hinder the progress in foreign policy especially in countries in the Western Hemisphere. One issue that she spoke of in length was corruption. According to her corruption was not only a hemispheric issue but a global one. Her speech hopefully casted much needed light on the serious concerns to U.S. foreign policy. Many people who attended the town hall meeting left feeling satisfied that their concerns with U.S. foreign policy were addressed. Others felt that the meeting only heightened their fears and anxiety. Our information was gathered through feedback from attendees at the meeting.

As the facilitators we felt we did a wonderful job in presenting the town hall meeting to our community. After the town hall meeting ended many of our speakers engaged in one and one discussion with members of the audience. Some of our speakers exchange information with those in our audience who were interested in follow-up with more detailed responses. It was the nature of our work to engage our community with getting the information that they need from first hand sources for informed decision making.

After the town hall meeting all of us, the work crew, sat in a circle to share tales of our experiences before we started collecting our materials. Joy and Alexis shared what happened to them on the way to the meeting. They were both travelling in Alexis's car. A tire blew on the highway. A passing motorist assisted them in getting the vehicle to the side of the busy highway.

The road service was unable to reach them before at least one hour. The clock was ticking and they need to reach the Graham Center as quickly as possible. They had all the programs, name tags, flags, and all the brochures in the car.

A relay of telephone calls got access to Alexis's mom who came and picked them up. While they were transferring materials from one car to the other it started to rain. The short of the story was that through all that they still made it to the Graham Center and were able to set up their stations in time for the meeting. We sat on chairs in a circle. All of our team members including staff from the US Department of State shared our experiences. We laughed some, sighed some, hugged and patted each other on the back.

We were pleased with the outcome. It was also a learning experience. The Public Affairs staff noted several points for their next town hall meeting. We collected our flags and materials and packed them in our vehicles. I had left earlier to take Scott and Ambassador Babbitt back to the hotel but I returned to help wrap things up. We all agreed it was a very long day. I slipped off my pumps and placed my feet on the carpet for a while. It was a much—needed relief on my feet. A few of our male team members loosened their ties. The town hall meeting was over. It was time to relax.

The plain clothes securities team was still in the room. I looked across the circle to see Alexis removed her shoes like I did. I smiled at Joy and Alexis, and then I started humming the tune "The Things We Do for Love." I walked across the circle and hugged Alexis before patting her on the back. I did the same with Joy. Others joined in humming the song. I thanked everyone for their hard work. They said the same for me. We did not hang around much longer. Some of our team members headed home. The staff from the State Department and I talked for a bit longer before we said farewell. They went back to their hotel and will be returning to Washington the next morning. Ethel and I talked for a while longer. We both planned on taking Ambassador Babbitt and Scott to the airport the next day for their return flight to Washington.

A participant feedback survey was distributed with our program to the audiences when they arrived. Ninety six percent of our attendees completed the questionnaire. The general response was everyone believed that it was an excellent town hall meeting. The results of the survey also suggested that our audiences would like to have more town hall meetings or conferences on U.S. foreign policy in the future. The meeting was another of our "Think and Act Locally" or TAAL order programs.

We continued our community outreach programs to increase public awareness of U.S. leadership in the United Nations. In the summer of 1996 we developed a program that was geared towards the television audience in our local cable area. We enhanced our programs with a series of Public Broadcasting System (PBS) videos, on different aspects and issues of the United Nations, that were provided to us by our national office. Our cable-tap programs *Acting and Linking Globally* were a series of topics and overviews of the U.N., the World Food Summit (which was held in the same year), and the future of the U.S.-U.N. relationship. Again, those programs were designed to increase public awareness.

All of our cable-tap programs featured local speakers who were knowledgeable about the topics and U.S.-U.N. relationship. *Acting Locally and Linking Globally* was aired on Cable Tap Community Station 36 on Mondays at 10:00 a.m., Tuesdays at 3:00 p.m., and on Wednesdays at 7:30 p.m. The Cable Tap program began in October 1996. It was scheduled to coincide with the month in which we observed UN Day.

Our U.N. Day committee, which was chaired by Ethel, coordinated our 1996 U.N. Day celebrations. Our membership increased dramatically over the past year due to the increased high-profile activities hosted by our chapter. Our organization received more exposure and so did the work we do as a chapter. We received a surge in new members increasing our membership threefold. U.N. Day observance for 1996 was held at the Sheraton Biscayne Bay Hotel. Our keynote speaker was Ambassador Alvin Adams, president of UNA-USA.

Jim Mullins and I had a discussion during our U.N. Day celebration. Jim was one of our board members. He was also one of the local leaders with the Center for International Policy. Jim suggested that our chapter should cosponsor a conference with the Center for International Policy. He said it would be a good idea to place it on the calendar. I agreed with him that it was a good idea and that we should talk about some more later before presenting it at our board meeting.

Before the year ended, Jim contacted me and provided some details about the type of conference he had in mind. After listening to idea and having more details about the conference, I suggested to Jim that he introduce the motion in our next board meeting. In our final board meeting for the year 1996, Jim introduced and made the motion for the cosponsorship of the conference. Without hesitation one of our other board members seconded the motion, and the proposed conference was open for discussion and debate. The topic and nature of the conference was U.S. Policy towards Cuba. We had an open discussion on the subject matter. After we discussed the issues and whether or not we could take on that task, our board members voted unanimously with an approval to cosponsor the conference with the Center for International Policy. Our target date for the event; which would be finalized at a later date in collaboration with the Center for International Policy, would be sometime around later summer or early fall of 1997.

CHAPTER 11

T HE YEAR 1997 began with a series of requests from our community for speakers from our chapter, and for co-sponsorship of community programs and events. Many of our chapter members including myself faced personal challenges, but in spite of those challenges, we continued with our public outreach and assisted as best as we could. We created a speakers committee and several of our members were on that committee and were ready and available to speak at events in our community when the requests came in.

One of the challenges that I personally faced was sharing my space with reptiles. You would not believe it if I were to tell you about it. There were six-to-seven-foot chameleons all over the property where I lived. They either lay in the sun or dashed at high speed into the water with their tails high in the air. I never knew the creatures could swim. I waited and watched for them to surface but the creatures never did. I could not predict what they will do next. I developed a survival strategy, but I will tell you more about it in the next chapter.

We started working on the conference "*U.S. Policy towards Cuba: Means and Ends*". It was planned for October 16-17, 1997 at the Radisson Mart Plaza Hotel in Miami, Florida. The conference was co-sponsored by the Center for International Policy and the United Nations Association of the United States of America. The Center for International Policy is headquartered in Washington D.C. and with a small office in Miami.

The Center for International Policy focuses on many issues including the promotion of peaceful opening in Cuba. The conference was nine months in planning and development. Once the venue for the event was secured, my role was to contact potential speakers, panelists, and others who were willing to participate. While we worked at developing the conference several other activities were ongoing in our chapter.

Jim Olson our national program director informed us that Mrs. Gillian Sorensen, assistant secretary-general for external affairs at the United Nations, was available for speaking engagements. Our national program director frequently informed us on new developments and any new opportunities including the availability of new speakers. We maintain a current list of available speakers from our community as well as those that are available nationally.

Our board decided it was a neat idea for Mrs. Sorensen to visit us. Instead of having her at one of our membership events, we decided to arrange for her to be on a local radio talk show. Gillian Martin Sorensen was appointed by Secretary-General Kofi Annan to be responsible for outreach to non-governmental organizations.

She was also the contact for the secretary-general with the academic world, religious leaders, parliamentarians, and other groups that were committed to peace, justice, developments, and human rights. Mrs. Sorensen was also a special advisor under Secretary-General Boutros Boutros-Ghali from 1993 to 1996. She was also responsible for directing the U.N.'s global fiftieth anniversary observance.

We successfully arranged for Mrs. Sorensen's radio talk show in the spring. We also coordinated efforts with our Campus Network at Florida Atlantic University for a luncheon meeting with Mrs. Sorensen. The luncheon was to be held before her appearance on the radio talk show. I arrived at the Miami International Airport to meet Mrs. Sorensen. I held up my UNA-USA sign. It wasn't very difficult to spot her. She had the composure of a professional diplomat. She had a neatly combed neckline haircut and a bright winning smile.

We greeted each other and navigated our way through the terminal to my car that was parked on the same level as the arrival deck. She traveled light; she was only going to be in Miami for the day. We became better acquainted as we talked while driving on the way to Florida Atlantic University. The luncheon was held in the executive boardroom. There were approximately twenty-five people at the luncheon.

The president and some of his faculty members were present, as well as members of the student body and our Campus Network group. I introduced Mrs. Sorensen to the group. She had an impressive background, one that gets attention. Between 1978 and 1990, she was appointed by Mayor Edward I. Koch as New York City Commissioner for the United Nations and Consular Corps. Her responsibilities included diplomatic security and immunity housing, education, and other cultural matters and business contact between the city of

New York and more than thirty thousand diplomats. Gillian was a graduate of Smith College. She has travelled all over the United States speaking about the United Nations and its relationship to the United States.

In the meeting, Mrs. Sorensen described the work she does at the United Nations and engaged us in a very light and informative discussion. It was an open discussion, which included questions and answers. The team at Florida Atlantic University was very pleased that she came to their college. After we left Florida Atlantic University, we drove to the location of the radio talk show in Delray Beach.

Gillian was on the air for over an hour. I later met with Mrs. Sorensen again. She was very pleased with the interaction and the volume of people who called-in to speak with her on the air. I took her to the airport for her flight home. We talked about different things as I drove to the airport but we spoke mostly about U.S. foreign policy, and how things used to be. One of our better subject of discussion was the unified approach taken in the past by our leaders on foreign policy. Those were the good old days when a sensible approach of our nations' interest takes precedence over self interest. Times weren't any easier not were issues any simpler, it was just that everyone in Washington knew who sent them there. But times have changed and it is too soon to tell if it is be for better or worse. Only time will tell.

Gillian's husband Ted was a key adviser and speechwriter for President John F. Kennedy. According to Gillian in those days our leaders had a unified approach when going beyond our national borders. That is not so these days, everyone now goes their separate way. One sure has to wonder if the lines to our congressional districts are now dispersed across the globe. We reached the Miami International Airport. Our trip was much too short and our discussion ended just as it was getting to be more interesting. It was time to exchange friendly hugs, say our farewell and go our separate ways. A final wave to each other then she disappeared in the terminal.

When I arrived home, I prepared a brief report on the meeting and faxed it to Ethel for our newsletter. A chapter's president work is never done. The Broward County School Board had sent us a letter requesting a speaker for an event that was being held at the Broward Community College in the spring. Our executive committee designated me for that role with Ethel as my back up speaker. Plans for that speaking event was in progress while Gillian visited.

I continued to work with our team coordinating the upcoming conference with the Center for International Policy. The plans were to have a two-day conference. We need sufficient speakers to fill the two day conference. I had a long list of people that I planned to contact. My primary role was to contact all potential speakers to invite and get an acceptance to participate.

Our conference was nine months away so there was time yet to work on the speakers' list When I get a non-acceptance from a potential speaker, I moved to the next person on the list. It was very time consuming because it was not always possible to reach a potential speaker when I placed my telephone call. In addition to working my list there were a lot of background noise. Managing the speakers' list was not very easy because of the potential of derailment even before I could get the letters of invitation out. I continue with the process taking it one person at a time. By the end of January a chaotic situation developed in my office.

On January 18, my daughter and I went to retrieve some materials from the office. I discovered that my office was broken into. I reported it to the building manager and called the police. A strange series of events began to take place. I was locked out of my office. Fortunately, the documents and information that I needed to continue working on our current projects were in my home.

I kept showing up at my office with the movers and trucks to remove my property numerous times, but the landlord never shows up as agreed. I kept paying the movers for their time. The Oakland Park Police Department instructed me to keep my receipts. After numerous attempts and having the same experiences, I decided to seek alternative means. I needed to conserve my time and energy for more important family matters and the current projects at hand.

A series of disturbing events developed around my home and office that were escalating. Soon after that, I had to file for Chapter 13 bankruptcy to protect my home at the advice of my attorney. She thought it was a long shot in view of the fact that my assets exceeded my liabilities. However, she suggested that it would slow down the process of whatever it was that was going on. It was a very difficult time for my family. We have never lived above our means and we practised sound conservative fiscal management. It was quite an ordeal having to consider and take the actions of filing a Chapter 13 bankruptcy protection. In the end those measures did not work. Although the process legally invoked a hold on all proceedings, it was still a full speed ahead acceleration that foreclosed my home. The fair market value of my home was approximately $70,000.00 with a mortgage balance of $19,000.00. It was not my mortgage company that foreclosed on my home but some other entity that placed a lien on my home for $300.00. I will discuss this in more detail later. WE kept moving forward. Needless to say the processes of all those developments increased my workload and costs threefold, but we pressed forward.

Ethel and I attended the Broward Community College event. I was their keynote speaker. Ethel and I received a warm reception. Ethel provided the attendees with a supply of brochures and information on our organization. She also provided the college with information on how to become a part of our Campus Network. Some of the faculty members signed up to become new members of UNA-USA.

We referred the new members to the Broward County chapter. Although we operated out of my private office which is located in Broward County, we explained to our audience that we were the Greater Miami Chapter. Ethel provided contact information for the president of our Broward County Chapter. Whenever a new member sends in his or her membership, if it is not sent directly to the national office, we relay it to them. The new member is automatically assigned a membership to the closest chapter to his or her domicile or the one closest to his or her geographical location.

There are different types of membership. Introductory membership dues were $25 per year, individual membership was $35 per year, and family membership was $40 per year. Those with limited income pay $20 and $25 respectively for individual and family memberships. Student membership was $10 annually. If a student was a Model U.N. member, then the membership was $6 annually. The benefits of membership are a one-year subscription to the *Interdependent*, the organization's quarterly publication; a 20 percent discount on UNA publications; discounts of United Nations publications, which constitutes 20 percent discount on all U.N. publications and 10 percent discount on all publications of other publishers carried in the U.N. bookstore. New members are also provided a personalized membership card; the opportunity to meet like-minded people and be active in a local chapter; access to information from UNA and the U.N.; and local benefits provided by his or her chapter and division, such as invitations, newsletters, and more.

One of the most important reasons to become a member of UNA-USA is a way to make one's voice heard. Anyone who wants the United States and other governments to conduct their affairs through cooperation rather than by confrontation finds that joining UNA-USA is a way to join with others who feel the same way, and have influence in Washington, at U.N. headquarters, and in other capitals. It is also a way to help make sure that the public receives accurate information about the United Nations.

Other reasons for joining UNA-USA include being able to receive useful information such as that which is presented in the *InterDependent* and in other UNA publications. These also include information on programs and activities at the national, division, and local chapter levels. UNA-USA members have access to information on health, environmental, and economic issues that have an impact in our pocketbook and the quality of our lives. It is also a neat way to meet new friends.

I continued to work on coordinating the speakers for the upcoming conference. In the meantime while I was doing that it was also time to go to Orlando to get my son. He had just completed his freshman year at the University of Central Florida. I arrived at his dormitory and began assisting him with packing his stuff to go home for the holidays. I lodged in one of the local hotels for two days. I had the opportunity to get a better tour of the campus. When we first visited the campus in 1996, we toured the campus, but on this my second visit I took the time to really walk the grounds and the halls, and I saw things that I missed the first time that I was there.

There is a whole other dimension and reality to a volunteer's life. Volunteers have personal lives. In our circle of volunteers, we were not doing so because we had nothing else to do. Some people may have that perception of volunteers. On the contrary all the volunteers that I worked with including myself had a full personal life. Some like myself had children in college and schools. We knew our priorities. The fact that we volunteer our time and donate resources to help to make our community a better place, and to help fellow citizens become more aware of the issues that affect their lives and our lives;it does not mean that by doing volunteer work, others have carte blanche to destroy the lives of volunteers, make us a laughing stocks, invade our privacy, perform witch hunt in our private affairs, and through all sorts of monkey wrenches in our paths to deter and prevent us from doing our volunteer work.

Those types of individuals ought to try doing volunteer work and see what it will do for their character. They may even be surprised to discover the true meaning of values like dedication, commitment and good citizenship. As JFK would say it is not so much what your country can do for you as much as what you can do for your country. A volunteer is not a free loafer. What we were experiencing by the inappropriate actions and behaviors of others was low blows, they were so low that one could hardly find an appropriate term to describe those behaviors. The only way in which I could describe those behaviors is by using a generic and default expression in JAM's lingua of expressions "ras-klaat". But for the work we were doing we had to grin and bear it. Furthermore, we are Christians. We learned and practised turning the other cheek when slapped in the face or slapped by any other means. Time is certainly longer than rope, and in due time all that has been done in the dark will surface in the light of day.

We packed my son's personal belongings and we had enough time to meet and hang with some of his friends before heading home. Afterwards we headed south to Fort Lauderdale. We were both tired when we reached home. We did not bother to unpack the car, we went straight to bed. The next morning my son went to unpack his things that were in the car. He came back into the house and told me that the car was not in the driveway. We spent the remainder of the day making police reports for the missing car. We also spent a lot of time trying to track where it could be.

By the middle of the summer, our family made the decision that it was time to relocate from the community in which we lived for the past five years. There was too much harassment; some of the methods of the harassments are beyond what anyone could have imagined. However, I will bring you up to speed on those developments later. For now it was a move forward in continuing to do our work.

We moved from our condo on or about the first week in August, 1997. We had not yet found a new home, so we decided to lodge temporarily in one of the local Days Inn, while still looking to find a more permanent place to live. We were now working and living with bare minimum resources, but I had all the stuff that I need at the moment in one carton box. Our daily activities were now reduced to contacting potential speakers, and searching the local newspapers for rental housing.

We stayed in the hotel for three weeks. We found a house for rent in Miramar. It was listed in one of our local papers. Our situation was critical. We had our reservations about renting the house. We had an awareness of channelling but we walked with faith. The critters were everywhere. We walked softly and kept moving forward.

We rented the house and moved in. My son decided that he wasn't going to return to University of Central Florida. He preferred to be close because of all the sinister things that were happening. He did not want me to be alone to deal with all those strange things. I continued to work on the upcoming conference. There were days that I seemed to get nothing accomplished but I kept working anyway. I stayed focused on what I was doing. In spite of all that was happening around us I felt a resounding calmness of spirit. It was not long after we moved into the house that I discovered that we were sharing our space with giant lizards. I will come back to this later.

I was still working on my speakers list. I was a team member and my team mates were relying on me. Never mind that I was the local chapter president and vice president of our Florida Division of UNA-USA. As a team member title did not matter,only testimony that matters, so I kept on working. I was making my telephone calls to our potential speakers. I contacted Otto Reich's office. He was on my list as a potential speaker. I spoke with his receptionist or secretary; she did not identify herself as either one. I was standing on a crate that was turned upside down in the kitchen. It was close to the kitchen sink. I positioned myself where I could keep my eyes on the lizards. The creatures were monstrous looking. I need know where they are at all times. I figured that knowing where they are will prevent me from being harmed by them. It was a question of both physical and mental well being. I introduced myself to the person on the phone and told her why I was calling.

The lady who answered the telephone told me that she did not receive the letter of invitation that was sent to Mr. Reich. She asked me to fax a copy of the invitation letter to her so that she may give it to him, and then to follow up with me later. She was laughing maniacally throughout our conversation. It was almost as if she had full knowledge of my predicament. But I thought she could not have known because I made no mention of the lizards to her. Perhaps it was a manic state of being with the lizards and all. I told her that I could not fax the copy right away but I will do so later. I moved on to the next speaker on my list. I contacted Senator Bob Menendez's office. His assistant answered the telephone. He was well mannered and very cordial in our conversation. He was like a person of my own heart. I introduced myself to him. I told him what we were doing and the reason for my call. He acknowledged receiving the invitation letter for the Senator.

I did not anticipate his next reaction. He began to yell at me over the telephone. It was as he went totally off the wall. He accused me of using the senator's name to attract an audience to the event. My response to him was in the form of a question. I asked him, "Why else would anyone invite high-profile, well-known, and knowledgeable people to be speakers at any event?" I told him that the letter that we sent to the senator was the same that was sent to everyone else.

The letters that were sent to potential speakers gave full disclosure of the type of event we were having. No where on the letter did it ever mentioned that our speakers were confirmed. We explained in our letter that we would follow up with a telephone call if we did not hear from them first. I did not get a chance to finish our conversation over the telephone. I had to switch the location of the crate on which I was standing so that I could keep an eye on the movement of the lizards in the backyard. There was a host of them on the move.

I saw one dove into the canal, and it was much bigger than the two that I had been watching. The one that dove into the water could be nothing less than seven feet. I heard the assistant saying "Hello! Hello!" His voice began to fade. It felt like my eyes were popping out of my head. I told him that I look forward to hearing from him within the next seven days, to say whether or not the Senator has accepted our invitation to speak at the event.

I did not know if Senator Menendez's assistant hung up the telephone or if I did. I stepped down from the crate and I began searching the house to see if any of the lizards found their way into the house. As I moved through the house looking for lizards, I thought to myself that we have a little over a month to go before the conference. I need to have all the speakers confirmed because time was running out.

I contacted Dr. Wayne later that day to give him an update on the speakers. I told him about the lizards but I did not get the feeling he understood what I was saying to him. We had a number of cooperating organizations for the conference. They included the Latin America Working Group in Washington, Cambio Cubano in Miami, Florida Atlantic University, Broward Economic Development Council, Cuban Committee for Democracy, and Return Peace Corps of Southern Florida among others.

The purpose of the conference was two-fold. Firstly, to provide a forum to discuss and democratically debate issues concerning U.S. policy towards Cuba. Some people held that the only way to promote change in Cuba was by maintaining pressure and a full embargo, and refusing any kind of dialogue with the Cuban government. Others believed the United States could best encourage change by beginning a dialogue, relaxing tensions, and lifting the embargo, even if it is done in slow stages. The conference provided an open forum for public discussion on those issues.

The second purpose of the conference was to focus sharply on the question of whether present policy was the best way to achieve U.S. objectives. The question that would be addressed publicly in the conference was whether or not the Helms-Burton Act, that was signed into law on March 17, 1997, served US interest, and would it make a peaceful transition more likely. That was the purpose and focus of our conference.

We coordinated and provided a wide and diverse range of speakers and panelists. They were from all sides of the debate. The conference was held for two days, October 16-17, 1997, at the Radisson Mart Plaza Hotel. It was filled to capacity in attendance for the two days. The conference was co-sponsored by the Center for International Policy and the United Nations Association of the United States—Greater Miami Chapter. It was locally, nationally, and internationally televised, and had coverage and reporting from a whole host of media.

Among our participants were Ralph Fernandez of Fernandez and Diaz in Tampa; Michael Rannenberger from the Office of Cuban Affairs at the US State Department; Nicolas Gutierrez, secretary of the National Association of Sugar Mill Owners of Cuba; Alfredo Duran from the Cuban Committee for Democracy; Wayne Smith from the Center for International Policy; Kimberly Stanton from McArthur Foundation; Jose Teruel of the Pan American Health Organization; Gillian Gunn Clissold of Georgetown University; Ana-Julia Jatar of Inter-American Dialogue; Lino Fernandez, president of Cuban Social Democratic Party; Jorge A. Sanguinetty of DevTech Systems Inc; Ernesto Betancourt from International Development and Finance Inc.; Ambassador Carl-Johan Groth, U.N. Special Rapporteur of Human Rights for Cuba; Gail DeGeorge of *Business Week*; Ambassador Cresencio Arcos, regional vice president for Caribbean/Latin America AT&T; T. Peter Blyth, president of Radisson Development Worldwide; Robert Muse, attorney of Muse and Associates; John Howard, director of International Policy and Programs, US Chamber of Commerce; Maria C. Werlau, president of Orbis International; Joseph Serota of Weiss, Serota and Helfman P.A.; Ambassador Ambler Moss from the University of Miami; David Thomas, former British undersecretary for Latin America; Wolf Grabendorff of the Institute for European-Latin American Relations; Prof. Joaquin Roy of the University of Miami, Professor Anthony

Bogues of the University of the West Indies; Frank Calzon of Freedom House; Ambassador Alvin P. Adams, president of the United Nations Association of the USA; Anthony Maingot of Florida International University; Admiral Eugene Carroll, retired director for Center for Defense Information; Admiral Norman Saunders, commandant of the US Coast Guard Seventh District; Professor Juan del Aguila of Emory University; Professor Juan Lopez of the University of Illinois, Chicago; Nita Rous Manitzas of the Center of International Policy, Miami; Walter Russell Mead of World Policy Institute; Robert Pastor of Carter Center; Raul Herrero of Cambio Cubano; Professor Irving Louis Horowitz of Rutgers University; and Ambassador Robert E. White of the Center for International Policy.

The two-day conference was delivered in six panels. Ambassador Robert E. White of the Center for International Policy and I gave the opening statements, which lasted approximately fifteen minutes starting at 8:45 a.m. From that point onward for the duration of the conference, each section ran for approximately two hours, except for the luncheon periods on each day that lasted for an hour and a half. The luncheon on day one featured Ambassador Carl-Johan Groth, U.N. Rapporteur, on human rights in Cuba. For a feel of the panel sessions and who the participants were, I will break them down into *Parts, Panels and Sessions*:

Part One-Panel One began at 9:00 a.m. and lasted until 11:00 a.m. The topic for discussion was *"What are the objectives and priorities of present US policy?"* One of our first panelists was Ralph Fernandez. Ralph was an attorney with the firm Fernandez and Diaz of Tampa, Florida. Ralph was born in Havana, Cuba, and left there in 1960 during the first exodus of the Fidel Castro years. He received his JD in 1977 at Stetson University College of Law. He was appointed chief of the drug division in Florida's Thirteenth Judicial Circuit in 1979. He began his private practice in 1980 and, since 1988, has handled dozens of cases involving charges lodged by the federal government against Cubans who were accused of engaging in neutrality act, firearms, communication, and other violations for conduct directed against the government of Fidel Castro. He successfully defended his cases pro bono. Fernandez has been general council to the World Federation of Cuban Former Political Prisoners, the Association of Ex-Political Prisoners, and the Tampa Bay Exile Council.

Our second panelist for *Part One* was Michael Rannenberger, coordinator of the Office of Cuban Affairs, US Department of State. Mr. Rannenberger was an officer of the US Senior Foreign Service who assumed his duties as coordinator for Cuban Affairs in July 1995. Michael was in Haiti to oversee the US police-assistance programs before assuming his duties in the office of Cuban Affairs. From 1992 to 1994, he served as deputy director for Central American affairs. He served as deputy chief of mission at the US embassy in

Asuncion from 1989 to 1992. His tour as deputy chief of mission at the US embassy in Maputo, Mozambique, from 1986 to 1989 included eight months in charge of affairs during a hiatus between ambassadors.

The next panelist for *Part One* was Nicolas J. Gutierrez Jr., secretary of the National Association of Sugar Mill Owners of Cuba. Mr. Gutierrez served as special counsel to the law firm of Adams, Gallimar & Iglesias, PA in Miami, Florida. He was the executive director of the International Law Practice Group at the law firm of Adorno and Zeder. He was also the property rights committee chairman of the Cuban-American Bar Association's Cuban Law Project. He was the general counsel for the National Association of Cuban Mineral and Petroleum Rights Holders. Nicolas graduated from the University of Miami in 1985 with a Bachelor of Arts degree and received his law degree (JD) in 1988 from Georgetown University Law Center. He started his own private practice in March of 1997.

Each panel session of our conference was provided with two discussants. One of our discussants in *Part One* was Mr. Alfredo Duran. He was the president of the Cuban Committee for Democracy from 1994 to 1995. He also serves on the organization's board of directors. He is an attorney by profession. He was a member of the American Bar Association, the Florida Bar Association, Dade County Bar Association, and the Cuban-American Bar Association. He also served on the Cuban Museum of Arts and Culture board of directors. He graduated from Louisiana State University, Baton Rouge, Louisiana, with a Bachelor of Science degree and received his law degree (JD) from the University of Miami Law School in Coral Gables, Florida.

The second discussant for *Part One* of the conference was Dr. Wayne Smith. He is a Senior Fellow of the Center for International Policy in Washington, DC. Dr Smith was also a visiting professor of Latin American Studies at Johns Hopkins University. During his twenty-five years of service with the US Department of State, Dr. Smith served in the Soviet Union, Argentina, Brazil, and Cuba. He served as executive secretary of President Kennedy's Latin American Task Force and received the Meritorious Honor Award for sustained excellence in political reporting from Buenos Aires. He was chief of mission at the US Interests Section in Havana, Cuba, and was recognized as the US Department of State leading expert on Cuba. Dr. Smith is a veteran of the US Marine Corps (1949-1953) who fought in the Korean War.

Each panel had a moderator. The first panel in Part One was moderated by me. Each panelist was allowed time to present his or her view on the topic. The discussants followed by expanding the topic that was presented. The discussions and expansions included a whole trail of body of knowledge, research,documented experiences and observations on the topic. After that there was an open debate among the panelists. The debate continued for an hour and fifteen minutes, after which the floor was open for questions from the audience.

The question-and-answer session continued for forty-five minutes. This way there was maximum engagement of panelists, discussants, and the audience, an excellent display of democracy in action. Built into the equation were the elements to agree to disagree, disagree to agree, agree to agree, and disagree to disagree. It was a very passionate discussion and debating of the topic, which, as mentioned previously, was focused on what were the objectives and priorities of the present U.S. policy.

For the most part the debate flowed as was expected. It was a passionate engagement of opposing and composing views. However, there were times when the moderator, performing his or her function, interjects with skills of inflection and deflection, thus maintaining the balance for a stable environment. The same format was maintained for the duration of the conference. All six parts had the same format of panelists, discussants, and moderators. The presentations were detailed and diverse. Our panelists, as shown in the brief biographies, were very knowledgeable, and were also experts in the topics and issues that were presented. Our number of panelists assured a wide and diverse coverage of the topics.

Part Two and second *Panel* started at 11:15 a.m. and continued through 1:15 p.m. A fifteen-minute break was observed between panel sessions. The topic for the second panel was *"What are the effects of US policy to date on the internal situation of Cuba?"* Moderating the second session was Kimberly Stanton. Ms. Stanton was a program officer with the Program on Peace and International Cooperation of the John D. and Catherine T. MacArthur Foundation. She was responsible for grant making related to demilitarization and democratization in Mexico, and Central America responses to economic globalization, and US-Cuban relations. Ms. Stanton at the time of the conference was in the process of receiving her doctor's degree in political science, which was to be awarded in December 1997 from the University of Chicago. Her areas of interests include democratic theory, processes of political change, international political economy, and transnational governance. Her regional expertise is Latin America.

The panelists in *Part Two* and the second session of the conference were Jose Teruel, Gillian Gunn Clissold, Ana-Julia Jatar, and Lino Fernandez. Jose Teruel was a special advisor for the director of the Pan American Health Organization (PAHO). He worked in the regional office of the World Health Organization (WHO) for the Americas, and provided services as a consultant in international health. He joined PAHO in 1973. He served as regional advisor in the training and research in public health. In 1983, he was designated chief of analysis and strategic planning and, from 1991 to 1996, was one of the technical directors of the organization. Mr. Teruel received his medical degree at the University of Sao Paulo, Brazil, in 1960. He also received his master's degree and doctor's degree at the University of Sao Paulo, Brazil.

Our second panelist was Gillian Gunn-Clissold. Ms. Gunn-Clissold was a director of the Caribbean Project of the Center for Latin American Studies at Georgetown University. In the past, she had been the senior associate at the Carnegie Endowment for International Peace, a Fellow at the African Studies Program of the Center for Strategic and International Studies, and director of the Cuba Project at Georgetown University. She has written many articles on Cuba for publications including the *Washington Post*, the *Miami Herald*, and the *Christian Science Monitor*. She has made numerous television and radio appearances, including appearances on CNN, NBC, and CBSPAN. She received her bachelor's degree in philosophy of law from Hampshire College in Amherst, Massachusetts. At the time of the conference, Ms. Gunn-Clissold was a member of the PhD program for international relations at the London School of Economics. Her thesis topic was "Coercion Versus Cooperation: Western Relations with Mozambique and Angola."

Ana-Julia Jatar was a member of the second panel. She was a Senior Fellow at the Inter-American Dialogue. She headed the Venezuelan agency for antitrust issues from 1992 to 1994 and was a member of the board of the state-owned steel company SIDOR from 1990 to 1991. She was a director of both the Venezuelan Planning Institute (IVEPLAN) and the Ministry of Planning from 1984 to 1985. Between 1986 and 1992, she was a researcher and professor at the Instituto de Estudios Superiores de Administracion (IESA). She has published on competition policy and industrial policy issues, and was currently writing a book on economic changes in Cuba. Dr. Jatar holds a PhD degree in industrial and business studies from Warwick University, Coventry, England, and an MBA degree from York University, Toronto.

Lino Fernandez is a physician in private practice in Miami. He was trained at Jackson Memorial Hospital in psychiatry. He is the founder of the Cuban Committee for Democracy. He served on the board of directors, and he was also the founder and president of the Cuban Social Democratic Party. Dr. Fernandez is a former political prisoner from 1961-1977. Dr Fernandez was a panelist in our second session: *What are the effects of US policy to date on the internal situation in Cuba.*

Our discussants for the second session were Jorge A. Sanguinetty and Ernesto Betancourt. Jorge A. Sanguinetty was a high official at the Central Planning Board in Havana in the 1960s. After migrating to the United States in 1967, he earned his PhD in economics from the City University of New York. He was a postdoctoral fellow and visiting lecturer at Yale University, and has worked as a researcher for the National Bureau of Economic Research, the Brookings Institution, and the United Nations Development Programme.

Mr. Sanguinetty was also the founder and director of the Latin American Program in Applied Economics at the American University in Washington, DC. He was then the president and CEO of DevTech Systems, a consulting firm based in Washington DC and Miami, providing technical assistance to former communist countries on transition to market economy. He wrote frequently about Cuban economic affairs and published a monthly newsletter on this topic. Dr. Sanguinetty was also the US representative of the independent economist of Cuba, whose president, Marth Beatriz Roque, was currently detained by Cuba's political police.

Ernesto Betancourt is the vice president of International Development and Finance (IDF). He is in charge of institutional development and public sector reform. He has worked in most countries in Latin America and the Caribbean as a consultant. After organizing its research operation, he became the first director of the *Radio Marti Program* of the Voice of America. He spent sixteen years at the Organization of American States, first as coordinator of the Department of Economic Affairs under the Alliance for Progress, and later on as director of budget and finance.

Mr. Betancourt was associated with the Cuban Revolution, first as a representative in Washington of the twenty-sixth of July movement during the insurrection against Batista, and afterward as member of the board of directors of the National Bank of Cuba and managing director of the Cuban Bank of External Trade. Mr. Betancourt resigned in late 1959 upon the appointment of Che Guevara to be president of the National Bank of Cuba. He is the author of many essays, articles, and reports on Cuba and Latin America, several of which have been published in the various editions of *Cuban Communism* (Transaction Books). As in the first panel session, the second panel also had an audience engagement and interaction with questions and answers. Members of the audience formed lines in the center and right aisles for question sessions.

After the presentation of our second panel in *Part Two* of the conference, it was time for our luncheon. The duration of the luncheon was one and one half hours. Our featured speaker at the luncheon was Ambassador Carl-Johan Groth. Ambassador Groth entered the Swedish Foreign Service in 1959 and first served in Madrid and Canberra. In his thirty-seven-year career, he served as charge d'affaires in Havana, Cuba, in 1969 and Santiago de Chile in 1973. In 1976, he became assistant undersecretary in the Ministry for Foreign Affairs. In 1979, he was appointed ambassador to Islamabad, Pakistan. In 1983, he became minister and DCM of the Swedish delegation to the International Organization in Geneva, Switzerland, where he headed the Swedish Observer Delegation to the Human Rights Commission.

In 1986, Ambassador Groth was appointed assistant undersecretary, head of the Multilateral Division of the Department of International Development Cooperation in the Ministry of Foreign Affairs. In 1990, he was appointed

Ambassador to Copenhagen, Denmark. In March 1991, he served as an expert in the technical mission on human rights to El Salvador (ONUSAL). In 1992, he was appointed the United Nations special rapporteur on the situation of human rights in Cuba. In 1996, Ambassador Groth retired from the Swedish Foreign Service, and at the time of the conference, a senior advisor to the Chamber of Commerce of Southern Sweden in Malmo.

The final session and *Part Three* of day one of the conference began at 3:00 p.m. and lasted until 5:00 p.m. The topic of discussion was *"How has the Helms-Burton act affected US businesses and the economic development of the Caribbean?"* Gail DeGeorge moderated that panel. Ms. DeGeorge has served as the bureau manager for *Business Week*'s Miami office since 1990. She joined the magazine in 1987 as correspondent after working for the *Miami Herald* and the *Sun Sentinel* as a business reporter. As *Business Week*'s point person in Miami, she covered business, economic, political, and international affairs stories in Florida, the Caribbean, and parts of Latin America. She has taught business reporting at the University of Miami graduate school program for journalism. Ms. DeGeorge received a BA in journalism with a minor in economics from Oakland University in Rochester, Michigan, and has completed courses and seminars in business and economics at Florida International University, Florida Institute of Technology, and the University of Missouri.

Our first panelist for the final session for day one was Ambassador Cresencio Arcos Jr. Cresencio (Cris) Arcos is the vice president for international affairs, Latin America, for AT&T Corp. He was formerly US ambassador to Honduras, senior deputy assistant secretary of state to Latin America, White House coordinator for public diplomacy, and was posted as Foreign Service officer to Brussels, Lisbon, Leningrad, and Sao Paulo. He received a BA at the University of Texas in Austin and an MA at Johns Hopkins (SAIS). Ambassador Arcos was a member of the Council on Foreign Relations in New York.

The second panelist was T. Peter Blythe. Mr Blythe was president of Radisson Hospitality Worldwide Developments, responsible for global expansion of the Radisson systems. These included growth through management contracts and franchising. His responsibilities included directing the activities of nine development vice presidents located in regions throughout the United States, and coordinating the development efforts of Radisson's worldwide alliance partners.

Robert Muse was our third panelist. Mr. Muse is a partner with Muse & Associates in Washington, DC. He specializes in international law and served as general counsel for the National Council for International Trade and Development. Mr. Muse has written extensively and has testified with respect to that law before the United States Senate and the Canadian House of Commons. Mr. Muse's private-sector clients included US corporations engaged in international trade and investments. A native of Arizona, Mr. Muse qualified in England as a barrister (Middle Temple) before attending Georgetown Law School and taking up legal practice in Washington, DC.

Our final panelist for the third session was John Howard. John was director of International Policy and Programs for the US Chamber of Commerce. In that capacity, Mr. Howard had broad responsibility for developing and implementing the chamber's international policy agenda and priorities. Mr. Howard served as the US Chamber's principal strategist and tactician for achievement of its international policy objectives. He also served as executive director for the U S Chamber's International Policy committee (IPC), a standing committee of the US Chamber Board of Directors and consists of leaders, senior officers, and representatives of member companies engaged or interested in international commerce. He served as principal deputy to the US Chamber's vice president, international. In that capacity, Mr. Howard is the second-ranking official in the US Chamber's international division, which consists of over twenty professional and administrative staff.

Mara C. Werlau was one of our discussants for the third panel. Ms. Werlau was a member of the Association for the Study of the Cuban Economy; her work for ASCE has focused on foreign investment in Cuba. An abridged version of one of her papers on the topic has been recently published in *World Affairs*. She was former second vice president of the Chase Manhattan Bank, North America. Since 1992, she was owner and president of Orbis S.A., incorporated in Chile and operating in the US as Orbis International. The firm provides diverse consulting services related to international relocation and multinational business in Latin America. Ms. Werlau has a BS degree in Foreign Service from Georgetown University. She also has a master's in international affairs from the Universidad de Chile; her thesis was titled "The Role of Commercial banks in Latin American Foreign Debt Crisis."

Joseph H. Serota was the second discussant. Mr. Serota is an attorney with the firm Weiss, Serota and Helfman and a community activist in Dade County, Florida. He was immediate past president of the Dade County Bar Association and immediate past chairperson of the Dade County Community Relations Board. He also served as chairperson of the Dade County Independent Review Panel, which reviews police conduct.

Joseph Serota has published numerous articles relating to matters on both local and the national interest in the *Miami Herald* and other Florida publications. He has appeared on local radio and television in English and Spanish with regard to topics involving ethnic tensions and conflicts in the South Florida community. He has received awards for his leadership relating to resolution of ethnic conflicts from Dade County Community Relations Board, the Simon Wiesenthal Center, and Florida Memorial College. He is a graduate of Princeton University and the University of Miami Law School.

The final session for the first day of the conference ended at 5:00 p.m. At 5:15 p.m. we had a reception that lasted until 7:00 p.m. During the reception, all participants had the opportunity to become better acquainted. Some people continued side discussions of the issues that were presented on the first day of the conference. Ethel and I had a few minutes to speak to each other during the reception.

We were approached by several of our panelists and attendees who expressed their gratitude to us for having the conference. One conversation was quite memorable because of the comments that were made by our luncheon speaker, Ambassador Carl-Johan Groth. The ambassador engaged us in a conversation with inquiries about our organization, UNA-USA. We told him about the organization and the work we did. We explained that at the chapter level, we were a grassroots organization. Ambassador Groth was impressed with our work, including the sponsorship of the conference. He commented that grassroots organizations like ours appear to be the cornerstone of our democracy and largely responsible for the success of our great democracy.

Ethel smiled at Ambassador Groth and responded, "We are the people." She gave him a couple of our brochures on UNA-USA. He said he would like to stay in touch with our organization. Ethel took one of his business cards from him. We promised to keep in touch. Others made similar comments and complimented us on our work. We accepted their comments with grace.

The second day of the conference was Friday, October 17, 1997. The topic of the fourth panel and *Part Four* discussion was *"What effect does our Cuba policy have on relations with other countries?"* The duration of this session was two hours starting at 9:00 a.m. through 11:00 a.m. Our moderator Ambassador Ambler Moss Jr. was director of the North-South Center and professor of International Studies at the University of Miami. He was counsel to the law firm of Greenberg, Traurig, Hoffman, Lipoff, and Rosen & Quental in Miami.

Ambassador Moss was a member of the board of the Espirito Santo Bank of Florida and also a member of the Florida International Banking Advisory Council. He was a member of the steering committee for the Summit of the Americas in Miami (December 1994) and was special advisor for international trade and commerce of USA and the Hemispheric Congress. Mr. Moss has been active in the Greater Miami Chamber of Commerce in the areas of international economics development and congressional relations.

He has led and has participated in various missions from Florida to Europe and Latin America. He was the founding dean of the Graduate School of International Studies at the University of Miami and held that position from 1984 to 1994. Ambassador Moss was involved with the negotiation of the US-Panama Canal treaties and their ratification and was deputy assistant secretary of state for congressional relations.

In 1978, he was appointed as ambassador to Panama and member of the US-Panama Consultative Committee where he served until 1982. He was an officer in the United States Navy (submarines) and is a life member of the American Legion and Navy League. He has received decoration from the governments of Spain, Panama, Argentina, and Catalonia. He has also received the Harold Weil Medal from New York University School of Law and the US Department of the Army Commander's Award for Public Service.

David Thomas was a member of our fourth panel on day two of the conference. Mr. Thomas is associate Fellow in the Center for Caribbean Studies at the University of Warwick. He was formerly the British ambassador to Cuba and has served as the assistant undersecretary of state for the Americas in the Foreign and Commonwealth Office. Wolf Grabendorff was also panelist on the fourth panel. Mr. Grabendorff is the founding director of the Institute for European-Latin American Relations (IREL) in Madrid. Mr. Grabendorff spent some years as a researcher in the Dominican Republic, Mexico, Venezuela, and Peru. He was visiting scholar at the Institute of Latin American Studies at Columbia University (New York). He returned to Germany in 1973 where he became research associate for Latin American Affairs at the Forschungsinstitut fur Internationale Politik of the Stiftung Wissenschaft und Politik (SWP) in Ebenhausen. Mr. Grabendorff has carried out research on Latin American foreign policy and security affairs as well as on the political development of several Latin American countries. His publications comprise more that one hundred titles, among them a number of books including *Lateinamerika wobin?* and *Brasilien, Entwicklungsmodell und Aussenpolitik.*

Professor Joaquin Roy a panelist in the fourth session on day two of the conference is a professor of international studies at the University of Miami. He holds a law degree from the University of Barcelona, Spain, and the MA and PhD from Georgetown University. His recent books are *Cuba y España: Percepciones y Relaciones, The Reconstruction of Central America: The Role of the European Community,* and *The Ibero-American Space.*

Professor Anthony Bogues is a lecturer in political theory and comparative politics in the Department of Government at the University of the West Indies, Mona, Jamaica. Between 1989 and 1992, Dr. Bogues was the chief of staff for the late prime minister of Jamaica, Michael Manley. He has participated in major political and economic negotiations on behalf of Jamaica. In 1996 he was awarded the Ralph J. Bunche Fellowship from Howard University, Washington, DC. Dr. Bogues is the author of numerous publications on Caribbean politics, and his most recent book is a political study of the seminal Caribbean intellectual, C. I. R. James.

The discussant for the fourth panel was Frank Calzon. Mr. Calzon was the director of the Free Cuba Center of Freedom House. He holds BA and MA degrees in political science from Rutgers and Georgetown universities. The

Free Cuba Center serves as a forum for policy and opinion makers to promote a peaceful transition to democracy in Cuba. Born in Cuba, he has testified before congressional committees and has appeared on numerous television and radio programs focusing on Cuba and Latin America. Among them are the following: *The NewsHour with Jim Lehrer*, Canadian Broadcasting's *Face Off*, National Public Radio, and Canal de Noticias (NHYC's Spanish language TV network). His writings have appeared in the *New York Times*, the *Washington Post*, the *Chicago Tribune*, the *Wall Street Journal*, the *Miami Herald*, and numerous other dailies in the United States and Latin America. Since 1975, he has also been the executive director of Of Human Rights, a nonprofit human rights organization dedicated to defending human rights in Cuba and the release of all political prisoners held in Castro's prisons. Mr. Calzon has led the Freedom House delegation to the annual meeting of the United Nations Commission on Human Rights in Geneva since 1992.

Panel five and *Part Five* started at 11:15 a.m. and lasted until 1:00 p.m. The topic of discussion was *"What are the potential outcomes of a continued US policy to isolate and squeeze Cuba economically?"* Ambassador Alvin P. Adams moderated this session. Mr. Adams was appointed president and CEO of the United Nations Association of the USA (UNA-USA) in October 1996 following his retirement from twenty-nine years of service as a Foreign Service officer. Ambassador Adams joined the Foreign Service in 1967.

His assignments included serving at the embassy and in the field in Vietnam, the National Security Council, and a variety of tours at the Department of State in senior management positions in counterterrorism and staff support to secretaries of state Kissinger, Haig, and Shultz. In his last official mission, Mr. Adams served as US ambassador to the Republic of Peru from 1993 to 1996 where he actively pursued American interests in counter narcotic cooperation, counterterrorism, democracy, and human rights.

Prior to his service in Peru, Ambassador Adams was ambassador in the Republic of Haiti. In this capacity, he was credited with significant contribution to human rights and the first free, democratic election in the country's history. In 1992, Mr. Adams received the state department's award for valor for his saving the life of the president of Haiti, Jean Bertrand Aristide. Mr. Adams received his BA from Yale College and received his law degree (JD) from Vanderbilt Law School. He speaks French, Spanish, Vietnamese, and Creole.

Our first panelist in the fifth session was Anthony Maingot, a professor of sociology at the Florida International University, Miami, Florida. From 1985 to 1995, he was an adjunct professor of Mexican and Caribbean studies of the US Air Force School of Special Operations. He was also adjunct senior associate of the North-South Center, the University of Miami. Born in Trinidad, he received his PhD at the University of Florida (Gainesville) in 1967. Professor Maingot has held positions at Yale University from 1966 to 1972 where he was director of the Antilles Research Program, the University of the West Indies, Trinidad (1972-1974), and since 1974 at FIU. He was president of the Caribbean Studies Association from 1982 to 1983. In 1994 he was awarded the university's Distinguished Researcher Prize, and in 1997 he received the Professional Excellence Award from the university system. Professor Maingot is also the author of six monographs and seventy-one referred articles and chapters in books.

Admiral Eugene Carroll (Ret.) was one of our three panelists for the fifth session. Rear Admiral Eugene J. Carroll Jr. was commissioned as an ensign in April 1945. His early service as a naval aviator mechanic included ten months flying AD Skyraiders from aircraft carriers in the Pacific during U.N. operations in Korea. Following a series of assignments in the Atlantic Fleet, he commanded two light-jet attack squadrons of A-4 Skyhawk aircraft. Transferred to the Pacific Fleet in 1965, he served a total of six years with units engaged in the Vietnam campaign. Promoted to the rank of rear admiral in 1972, he served as commander of Task Force 60, the carrier striking force of the US Sixth Fleet in the Mediterranean.

Admiral Carroll served on General Alexander Haig's staff in Europe from 1977 to 1979. He was the first naval officer to serve as director of US military operation for all US forces in Europe and in the Middle East. His last assignment on active duty was in the Pentagon as assistant deputy chief of naval operations for plans, policy, and operations. He holds BA and MA degrees in international relations from George Washington University. He is a graduate of both the US Navy and US Army War Colleges. He is now serving as deputy director of the private non-governmental Center for Defense Information in Washington, DC. He is actively engaged in research and analysis concerning major defense issues and is writing and speaking on the need for rational military programs, which will meet the long-term national security interests of the United States.

Admiral Norman Saunders was our third panelist for the fifth session on day two of the conference. Rear Admiral Norman T. Saunders took command of the Seventh Coast Guard District in June 1997. The Seventh District is the busiest Coast Guard district and covers 1.8 million square miles encompassing the waters around Florida, South Carolina, Georgia, and the entire Caribbean. Prior to this assignment, he was assistant commandant for operations in the US Coast Guard. His other flag assignments have included commander, military personnel command, located at US Coast Guard Headquarters.

He was the first officer to hold that position. Rear Admiral Saunders also served as the commander, Second Coast Guard District in St. Louis, Missouri. He is a 1964 graduate of the United States Coast Guard Academy. He attended the Naval Post Graduate School and earned a Master of Science degree in operations research in 1972. In 1985, he graduated from the National War College. A Vietnam veteran, Rear Admiral Saunders's military awards include the Legion of Merit with two gold stars, the Bronze Star Medal with Combat V, the Meritorious Service Medal with one gold star, the Coast Guard Commendation Medal, and other campaign and service awards.

The first discussant for the fifth session was Juan del Aguila. He is an associate professor of political science at Emory University, Atlanta, Georgia. He also served as director of the Emory Center for International Studies. He has published *Cuba: Dilemmas of a Revolution* and numerous articles, papers, and book reviews. He has also participated in many conferences focusing on Cuba and Latin America. He is on the board of directors of the Atlanta Council on International Relations. He is a member of SECOLAS, the Southeastern Council of Latin American Studies. He is also on the advisory board of Cuban Studies. He received his BA in political science from the University of Florida and his MS and PhD degrees from the University of North Carolina, Chapel Hill.

Juan J. Lopez was our second discussant. Mr. Lopez is an assistant professor of political science at the University of Illinois at Chicago. He is a comparativist who specializes in Latin America politics and political economy of development. He received his PhD in 1994 from the University of Chicago.

The fifth and sixth sessions had shorter durations by fifteen minutes each due to the fact that in each of these sessions there were only three panelists. Before the sixth session, however, there was lunch break. A buffet-style lunch was served. This provided an excellent opportunity for all speakers and audiences to interact and engage further discussions about the topics that were presented during the conference. The conference maintained a full to capacity attendance for the two days.

Our final session and *Part Six* for the conference started at 2:15 p.m. and lasted through 3:45 p.m. on October 17, 1997. Nita Rous Manitzas moderated the final session. The topic of discussion was *"What are the alternatives to present policy? Are there better ways of encouraging a peaceful transitional process?"*

Ms. Manitzas serves as Miami liaison for the Center of International Policy—Cuba Project. She was formerly a program advisor with the Ford Foundation in South America. She has coauthored a textbook on Cuba and has made multiple research trips to the island over the last twenty years. With her husband, she runs LAC News, an online information service on Cuba.

Our first panelist for the sixth and final session was Walter Russell Mead. He is president's Fellow at the World Policy Institute at the New School for Social Research, and is a political economist engaged in the study of the evolving global economic system and its implications for American policy and society. He is a senior contributing editor at *Worth* magazine, a contributing editor at the *Los Angeles Times*, and serves on the editorial board of the *World Policy Journal*, the advisory board of Mercy Corps International and *New Perspectives Quarterly*, and on the board of directors of the Arca Foundation. His books, articles, and reviews on contemporary economic and political issues are widely read in the United States and abroad. Mr. Mead is frequently asked to consult with national leaders in the White House and Congress and appears regularly on radio and television. Mr. Mead is a regular columnist at *Worth* magazine. He is an honors graduate of Groton and Yale, where he received academic prizes for history, debating, and the translation of New Testament Greek.

Robert Pastor was the second panelist for the final session. Mr. Pastor has been professor of political science at Emory University and director of the Latin American and Caribbean Program at Emory's Carter Center since 1985. Dr. Pastor is the author of ten books and over two hundred articles on US foreign policy, trade and migration issues, international political economy, and Latin American and the Caribbean.

Dr. Pastor is also the executive secretary of the Council of Freely-Elected Heads of Government, a group of twenty-nine leaders of the Americas chaired by former US president Jimmy Carter. The group has worked to reinforce democracy, and Dr. Pastor has organized the council's efforts to monitor and mediate fifteen electoral processes in ten transitional countries, mostly in the Americas but also in Africa, the Middle East, and Asia. The mediation in Nicaragua (1989-1990) and Haiti (1990) resulted in the first election in the two nations' history that were judged free and fair by all the political parties and the international community.

Dr. Pastor received his MPA from the John F. Kennedy School of Government and his PhD in political science from Harvard University. A Phi Beta Kappa graduate of Lafayette College, he served as a Peace Corps volunteer and has taught at Harvard University, the University of Maryland, and El Colegio de Mexico as a Fulbright professor.

Raul Herrero was our final panelist. Mr. Herrero is the president and CEO of Ralco International Inc. He was previously assistant director of European Food Ops of Beatrice Foods Company and chief financial officer of the luggage division at Samsonite Corporation. He is currently a Cambio Cubano member of the Political Direction. Mr. Herrero received his BS at the University of Havana, Cuba. He is fluent in Spanish, English, French, and Italian.

The discussant for the final panel was Irving Louis Horowitz. Mr. Horowitz is the Hannah-Arendt distinguished professor of political science and sociology at Rutgers, the state university of New Jersey. He is the author of a number of works on hemispheric affairs, including the *Conscience of Worms and the Cowardice of Lions: Cuban Politics and Culture in an American context*, and *Cuban Communism*, an anthology often referred to as the Bible of Cuban Studies, now going into its ninth edition.

So there it was, our conference on Cuba. Allow me to put this in a capsule: *"US Policy towards Cuba: Means and Ends"*, a conference in Miami, October 16-17, 1997. The topics that were discussed are:

Panel 1: *What are the objectives and priorities of present US policy?*
Panel 2: *What are the effects of US policy to the internal situation in Cuba?*
Panel 3: *How has the Helms-Burton Act affected US businesses and the economic development of the Caribbean?*
Panel 4: *What effect does our Cuba policy have on relations with other countries?*
Panel 5: *What are the potential outcomes of a continued US policy to isolate and squeeze Cuba economically?*
Panel 6: *What are the alternatives to present policy? Are there better ways of encouraging a peaceful transitional process?*

The closing remarks of the conference was delivered at 3:45 p.m. by Ambassador Alvin P. Adams, president of UNA-USA; Ambassador Robert E. White, president of the Center for International Policy; and Sylvia McLeod, president of UNA-USA Greater Miami chapter. The two-day conference titled *"US Policy towards Cuba: Means and Ends"* ended at 4:00 p.m. on Friday, October 17, 1997.

Our U.N. Day observance took place seven days after the conference. It was held on October 24, 1997 at the Hotel Sofitel in Miami. Ethel and our U.N. Day committee coordinated that event. Our youths were featured in our celebration. Ramya Murali, one of our chapter's student members, spoke on children's issues. The young Bhai dancers of Broward County entertained us with a presentation centered on the theme of peace and racial cooperation. Later that week I spoke at the Bhai's U.N. Day observance in Broward County.

Throughout the year 1997 we received numerous requests for speakers. Some of those requests were for speakers from our chapter as well as for speakers from the national level. We had two requests to assist with securing General Colin Powell through our network, but we were not successful with this request due to Mr. Powell's schedule. Because of the high demand for speakers our chapter formed a speakers committee. Some of our members who were appointed to the speakers committee honed their skills in public speaking by becoming active members in Toastmasters International. It is a non-profit organization where people develop their skills in public speaking and leadership. Those organizations who requested speakers from our chapter often provided suggestions of the topics they would like our speakers to talk about. To appropriately and factually deliver such topics our speakers research the facts and deliver accordingly based on the information available on the topic. The members of our speakers committee reportedly had fun and were intellectually stimulated with their new role.

All of our members are volunteers; every one of us was willing to work on behalf of others without expecting pay or other benefits. The fact that we willingly work without pay had no impact on our ability to deliver those services to the best of our ability. Our democracy has long and rich traditions in volunteerism. It was nothing new to us, we were simply doing our part by participating.

Our high-profile activities in our local chapter ran the course for four years beginning in 1994 and wounded up in 1997. It was indeed a TAAL order, *"thinking and acting locally"*. Our successes in conducting our activities were based and due to our teamwork and team spirit. Everything we did was through our network of team members. We were not always in the same place at the same time but our teamwork synchronized all of our movements and actions. It is no wonder then that five years after the fact, I decided to continue to observe and learn more about the phenomenon of teamwork. The teamwork experience was quite dynamic. The more we exercised this innovative approach,the more valuable it became.

Our teamwork provided a series of inter-connectivity and back-up system that ensures continuity to the finish line. Whenever any of our team members are faced with personal and or individual challenges the exchange of the baton drives the motion to the finish line. We did not quite set out to observe teamwork in motion. We simply had objectives and no resources. We became innovative through necessity, but it was not all hunky-dory. There was a frigging serious element of *"Looney Tunes."* It was as if I was a roadrunner with a coyote breathing down my you know what. Thank goodness for the Warner Brothers cartoon that provided me with a relatable experience. With that said, I will now take a little time to share some of my personal experiences. While doing the work of UNA-USA I had numerous first time challenges and experiences that has impacted our family severely. It was so much so that we were left homeless. We were disposed of all of our personal property, personal effects, real property and business. We were driven into hardship barely having the means for survival. It was bad, very very bad indeed. My family and I were absolutely shell shocked and stunned at the things that were being done to us.

CHAPTER 12

In THE PREVIOUS chapters I have briefly touched on some of the circumstances that led us to moved out of our home. We lived in our condo for five years. We moved to Shaker Village because of our displacement by Hurricane Andrew. We settled in the community to what we thought was a quiet existence. The turn of events that were taking place and that had continued for over two years left us no choice but to move away from there. After we moved out of the condo we wound up living among giant lizards. It began in March 1995. The condo association placed a lien for $300.00 on our home. They claimed I owed them $300.00 home owners association fees. I did not believe that I owed what they were claiming but I paid them anyway. I was paying my condo association fees three months at a time and in advance. The way I figured it at the time was that there must have been some kind of error in their records, which is not unusual because book keepers make errors from time to time. I did not pay it too much attention because during the same period I was nursing my injuries that I sustained in the three auto accidents which occurred in April, May and June of the same year. It was also the time when our organization had the first U.N. Business conference and our Friends of the Future project. So apart from nursing my injuries I was also working on the production and execution of those programs.

It began in March of 1995. I received more bill from the condo association and I continued to pay. It was as if it was a running tab. Each time that I paid the association fees it appears that the funds were going to something else. And that was not all that was taking place. Even when the records showed that I had a credit balance I would still receive notices and threatening letters of having outstanding balance. I appeared that no matter what I did, I would still receive those type of letters and still had to pay more moneys. Soon it escalated into downright harassment in the community where we lived.

For anyone who was not standing in my shoes, the number of motions that were filed in court by the condo association and their lawyers would suggest an on going conflict between the organization and myself. The number of motions that required my appearance in court were astronomical. I complied with the court request based on the numerous motions, but I did not have a conflict with the organization. The one thing that was very clear was that each time we were having a UNA-USA activity an action was taken by those individuals. To give an example of what I mean, and this I discovered many years after the fact, I found out that on the date our U.N. business conference was first published in the newspapers, it was on the said date and precisely when the courts were open to the public, that the lien for $300.00 was filed with the clerk's office. Whether or not there is a correlational is anybody's guess, but the pattern of destruction points highly in that direction.

We did not make that connection at that time; we took it at face value that the condo had a genuine issue and perhaps it had something to do with their record keeping. I was very busy working on our UNA-USA programs and taking care of my two children. My daughter was in college and my son was still in high school. Each time that I receive a letter from the association's attorneys, I responded to their demands. Through it all there was a sense or a continued aura of "who do you think you are?". The fact is we did not think we were anybody, we were just ordinary citizens who were working hard on our TAAL order. Volunteer work can be tiresome and when done with out of pocket costs it may even sometimes be burdensome, but nevertheless we were happy troopers. We believed in what we were doing and felt proud that knowing that we were contributing positively to our community which cannot be said for those who were trying to destroy us financially. We continued to move forward chalking up our experiences to organizational behavior by human actions. Those behaviors were not acts of god, it was a person or were persons who made those decisions and took the actions of filing a lien on our property frivolously.

On April 27, 1995 the first of a series of auto accidents occurred. The second auto accident occurred on May 5, and the third on June 2. My son also had a series of auto accidents each time another motorist either ran into the back of our automobiles or it was a hit and run. We coped with the situation, tended to our injuries and respond to the association each time they made demands. My daughter's car was towed several times from our parking pace even though the decal for parking was affixed to the car. Each of those occurrences and demands cost us a lot of moneys including out of pocket expenses.

In October 1995 the condo association filed for foreclosure on our home. October was also the month of our final celebrations of UN50. Each time a motion is filed in the court, I showed up in court and or responded, depending on the action that was taken.

I would not have acted otherwise because I am civilized and am a law abiding citizen. I believed that if someone takes action in court against another person, it must be because the first party has some form of grievance. As a law abiding citizen I must respect the court's request to either respond and or show up so that the grievance can be heard and settled, so I conducted and governed myself accordingly. The cost of everything and having limited mobility was driving us to a breaking point. I underwent medical surgical procedures for my injuries and continued to take physical and rehabilitative therapy.

Sometime in June of 1996 the condo association attorneys, according to them, under the request of the association sent a letter to UNA-USA national headquarters in New York suggesting that I have been using the organizations funds and equipment and staff to conduct my personal business. The headquarters in New York contacted me and provided me with a faxed copy of that letter. But that was not all, our program director from the national office contacted me by telephone to inform me on what was taking place. An attorney from the firm hired by the association, and was handling the foreclosure, was constantly call the national office making allegations and innuendos. Our program director informed me that he instructed that attorney to cease calling the office because it was a personal matter. Needless to say the report of those behaviors was very irritating, but I kept focus on our work. To have done anything else would have burden our workload and distract us from our work.

My son graduated high school in 1996 and would be attending University of Central Florida that same year. In the summer of 1996 I drove him to Orlando to attend college. He was housed on campus. I was away for two days to assist my son with orientation and to see that he settles in. When I returned to Fort Lauderdale and visit my office I found a three days notice to vacate tacked on my office door. The three days had already expired because I was out of town for those days.

That issue was resolved, at least so I thought. I began to notice interference and interruptions with my financial cycles and statements. I continued to move forward but by now everything was taking a great toll on me physically, financially, and emotionally. I started to receive telephone bills with astronomical charges. There were long distance changes on the telephone bills for calls made to places that I have never heard of. It would be easy for anyone to assume that because we were conducting work for UNA-USA, it follows that we made telephone call all over the globe based on the work that we do. but that was not the case. Our resource center was our UNA-USA headquarters which was located in New York. We had no need to place calls anywhere else except to our national headquarters.

A review of our telephone bill and long distance charges showed a distinct pattern. Ninety percent of the calls were made to places that one can readily associate as areas of ill reputation. By that I mean those places were currently in the new media narcotic drugs targeted areas. From that I imagined that anyone looking at our telephone bills may conclude that because calls were made from our telephone number to those places, then by benefit of association we were involved with those things. Another scenario quite possible was because telephone numbers and calls to those places are shown on our telephone bills, then we could be targeted for investigation. We kept moving forward, toiling upward in the night, using our meagre resources, our creativity and innovation to press on with our programs. I have often asked myself the question, what manner of man would take the time to scheme, and contrive evil and deception, as a means of preventing ordinary law abiding citizens from doing volunteer work that benefits their community.

The telephone bills were astronomical. We had to pay the bills to keep our service on. We disputed the calls which required a lot of time to follow up. Some days we spent hours on the telephone waiting in queue to speak with the representative, only to have the call disconnected. To get the telephone company to work on the issue, it requires re-dialing, waiting in queue again and to start the process of explaining all over again. Natural conflicts and issues have a natural process of resolution because they are generic in nature. Manufactured issues and conflicts are never resolved easily simply because they defy all sense of logical reasoning and only the proof is in the pudding.

To prevent ever running into those problems again, we installed a new telephone system. On the new system we were able to print our bills for periodic review, and also we codes when dialing any long distance calls. My home telephone was also routed through the same system although the listing of home and business telephones were separate. We considered the move a proactive measure to protect our character and good reputation. That move was also a way of not having to pay any more long distance charges for call made to places that we did not know and that weren't made by any of our team members. We were working in a hellish environment and it was not easy, but our team spirit helped us to forge full steam ahead. I decided to file chapter 13 bankruptcy protections in January 1997 to protect my home and property.

My attorney who handled the bankruptcy proceedings thought it was a long shot considering that my assets exceeded my liabilities. However she thought that in view of everything that was going on, it would be a good strategy to protect myself and my property. The problems were not created by my creditors. They were brought into the equation as triggered by my Chapter 13 bankruptcy proceedings. The problems were created by those who were seeking to wear us down financially. I am not clear on what the motives were at that time. Some people suggested that perhaps it was jealousy because of the work that we were doing. My response to them was utter absurdity. There were too many organizations looking for volunteers, and furthermore we have always maintained an open policy and invited others to become team members. Suffice to say we had not evidence of why anyone would want to do what they were doing, and neither did we launch any investigation. We pressed forward and continue with our work.

On January 20th my daughter and I went to the office to retrieve some documents. On our way to the office we took time on our way to watch the Rev. Martin Luther King's Day parade. It was a holiday so we were not in any rush to reach the office. We were only going there to get the documents that I needed. When we reached the office I realized that I took the wrong sets of keys. Because of the parade we did not think we could go back for the office keys. We went to the office in my daughter's car. The parade was now at its peak and main roads were closed. There was a locksmith in the building across from our office. My daughter suggested calling him to see what he would charge to open the office. The cost for his service was reasonable so we had him open the office for us. My daughter took the bill from the locksmith and paid him while I pushed the door open and went into the office.

I went through the reception area into the main office and I discovered that our office was broken into. All of our files were displaced and a noticeable African violet that was sitting on top of one of our file cabinets was missing. We reported the incident to the police and to the landlord. Taking into consideration all of the other occurrences that we have experienced, it did not take us very long to make a decision to relocate. It was as if everything was a moving violation. There was no telling what was going to happen next. The landlord came to the office later that same day and we showed him the state of the office. We told him on that day that we will be moving from that office. He confirmed receiving the notice of our bankruptcy proceedings.

I kept making arrangements with the landlord to get my stuff at the office. Each time he gives us a time to meet him at the office location he doesn't show up. We make arrangement with the moving company to help pack and remove our stuff. Each time we arrange a time to meet with the landlord, we also make arrangements for the moving company to come and remove our stuff. The movers show up with their crew but there was no landlord anywhere on the property. After repeatedly making arrangements with the landlord and he was a no show, I contacted the Oakland Park Police Department for help. The Police Officers advised me to keep all of my receipts of the moneys that I paid the moving company for their time.

We made several attempts at contacting the landlord. We kept leaving messages. His wife took numerous messages from us and told us that the landlord would contact us, but he never did. We never saw the contents of our office again. All of our files, boxes of artworks from our Friends of the Future project, office equipment, office furniture, and everything that was in our office. Our computers, telephone system, photocopying machines, and personal items that were in the office, we saw nothing of our stuff since that time.

The condo association foreclosed on our condo. There was a flurry of court proceedings. We were still making payments to the condo association, to their attorneys. Our mortgage company joined the proceedings. Now we were faced with paying the attorney's fees and costs of our mortgage company. We were the only ones to have lost our home. We were like kangaroos, they kept bouncing us all over the place and we just kept hopping.

The new purchaser of the condo offered to rent us our home for one thousand dollars per month. Our original mortgage was four hundred and seventy eight dollars per month. When I purchased the home our down payment was more than fifty percent of the purchase price. This way we had a small and affordable mortgage payment. My two children could maintain that payment even with part time jobs if needs be. When condo association foreclosed on our home we had a balance of nineteen thousands dollars on our mortgage and we were three years away from paying off our mortgage.

Some time in the first week of August 1997 a notice was posted on our doors that gave us twenty four hours to vacate the premises. I contact our attorney and spoke with him and asked what should we do. I told him that the notice was seeking $5,000.00 and asked him whether or not we should pay it. He told us that it was perhaps better not to do so because we would probably wound up loosing that too. He did not believe that anything we that we did or can do will prevent all the stuff that was taking place.

Nothing made any sense; we discussed it among ourselves and decided that it was time to move from the community. We packed all night. One of my son's friends helped us packed. We organized our belongings in a way that the movers would be able to pack the large items easily. We parked our car overnight at my son's friend home. We feared that it might be towed at the critical moment when we need it. It was just the way things were at the time. We were tired, overworked, and extremely harassed, but we continued to walk the straight and narrow with grace and dignity.

We began packing the small items taking it one room at a time. We went out and purchased additional boxes, and we figured these along with the ones we had in the storage room would be sufficient. If those were not enough the way we figured, we would go and bury some more boxes. The only problem was we would have to get a cab to go to where we parked our car and do the reverse when we get back. We did not know where we would be moving to yet, but we knew we have had it, and by the hook and the crook we were moving away from that community. We packed until the wee hours of the morning. Weird things were happening, and this has been going on for over two years.

We were tired of paying cab fares because our vehicle was taken from our parking space. Always at the end of everything when the vehicle was recovered, we were given some cockamamie explanation that was neither here nor there. The end point was that it was costing us in time and money, not to mention the physical toll and emotional ups and downs we were experiencing. It was a constant interruption of our lives. The half of all that was happening have never been told. What kind of person would serve a notice of the court on Christmas Eve concerning an already irritating situation, like the foreclosure of our home, as what has happened for the past two years. In spite of all that we held our head high, and moved on.

Now, it would not have been a human experience if I did not tell you that through all that many times I have considered throwing in the towel. Many times I have thought to quit my volunteer leadership and work in view of the price we were paying and the toll on my family. I have thought of taking on the enemy because they had planted their own mine fields. But to do that I would have had to give up leading our team of volunteers. I weighed the circumstances, balanced them and continued along my path. In situations such as the ones that I was experiencing, a good team leader soon recognizes, that in the words of Hannah Montana (Miley Cyrus) it is not what is on the other side, it is the climb. I guess if those bad people knew that their actions were fuel for the climb they would not have done what they did. I kept moving forward.

Kevin, Ceejae, and I packed as much as we could that night. The condo was two levels with three bedrooms, two and half bathrooms, a living room, a family room, a dining room, and a kitchen. At 8:00 a.m. the next day, we began calling moving companies from the Yellow Pages. We found one company that was willing to move us. The company provided us with a rough estimate over the telephone. The person on the telephone said that he could be there by 10:00 a.m.

We accepted his estimate with the condition that he would provide a written estimate when they get to our house. Kevin took us to get our car from Craig's house. We stopped at McDonald's to pick up breakfast for take out. The movers showed up on time, 10:00 a.m. on the dot. There were four men and a truck; the company was All American Movers. The leader of the crew was given a tour of the home. We sat down and went over the details. I provided them with instructions, and he began filling out the papers. I told him that we would like to have temporary storage of our stuff until we found a place to stay.

Shortly after they arrived, it began to rain heavily. He said that the weather would not hinder them because they will pack our contents while it is raining. When the rain ceases they will begin packing our furniture and boxes in the truck. We watched and listened to the leader providing instructions to his crew. He instructed them how to prepare the paintings and wall decorations for packing.

One of the men dashed out of the house and ran through the rain to the back of the truck. He returned with stacks of what looked like quilted blankets. The lead mover who said his name was Tony asked if I had special containers for the chinaware in the cabinet. I opened the buffet and pulled out the original cases that the china was packed in when I purchased them. He checked the drawers of the cabinet and pointed to the silverware. He asked me, "What about these, do you have containers for these too?' I said yes and retrieved those containers from the storage area.

He went through the house and began tagging items in different colors. He completed his paperwork and showed me where to sign. I signed the papers and gave him the requested deposit. He instructed us to remove all our sentimental stuff such as photo albums and valuables that were irreplaceable. Ceejae began packing our photo albums, family videotapes, and other collectibles in the large plastic containers. I had a supply of plastic containers.

I told him to pack all the videotapes of our UNA activities that were in the upper shelf of the wall unit. He asked about those videotapes of his football games. I told him, "Yes! Pack those in the plastic containers too." Tony told us not to worry; he and his crew would take care of everything. While Ceejae and Kevin kept packing our valuable and sentimental property, I began working the Yellow Pages looking for a temporary place to stay.

I called the local hotels within a fifteen mile radius from the listings in the Yellow Pages. The Days Inn on Oakland Park Boulevard West had reasonable rates and vacancy. I wrote the address down and left with a few boxes of personal items that Ceejae placed in the car. I drove to the hotel. I drove very slowly through the pouring rain. I had to be cautious because I could not afford to have any other situations on my hands. I put the windshield wiper on the maximum speed. I was soaking wet from going back and forth to the car.

I pulled up at the front office of the hotel. I took my pocketbook and went inside to check in. I checked into a double room on the second floor. I paid for one week. The attendant asked how long we planned on staying. I told him I did not know how long, but we would be sure to let him know when we were ready to check out. In the meantime, he could use the credit card on record for any future payments beyond the week that was already paid for. I paid for the first week with cash. I was given two sets of keys, our room number and my receipts.

I moved the boxes into the room, looked around for a minute, and then got back into my car to drive back to the condo. I stopped on the way to pick up lunch for Kevin and Ceejae. The rain slowed down a little, so I was in and out of the car without having to use the umbrella. I bought a bucket of KFC for lunch. I had drinks at home, so I did not have to buy any. There was enough to feed everyone back at the house. I figure that the movers perhaps were hungry as well, so there was enough food for every one.

I arrived at the house. I told everyone that there was a bucket of KFC. We took time out to eat, then it was back to packing. The rain stopped for a while, and the sun was out for a brief moment. I thought that was great because it gave me a chance to put some more small boxes in the car. I took a box and was heading out the door when one of my neighbors came by to ask if I was moving. I told here yes it was a quick decision.

Heather lived two doors down from us. Their condo unit 52 and ours was 56. She had two daughters, Holly and Sarah. Holly and I had a special kind of friendship. She was six years old. She was a very pretty little girl. We first started speaking about two years ago when her mom moved to the community with both of them. Holly did not speak to anyone except her mom and her little sister.

One day we met on the landing in front of her house. Holly and I started a conversation about Barney. Her mother was very surprised to see the two of us talking. That was when Heather informed me that Holly has never spoken except her and her little sister. She told me that Holly would not even speak to her classmates or her teacher in school. She did not know the reason why Holly did not speak to anyone, but she became ecstatic when she found Holly and me in conversation outside the door of the house. From that day, Holly and I became friends. Her mother told me that sometimes Holly would make special requests to visit with me. I told her it was no problem, I would love to visit with Holly from time to time. All she had to do was to call me and tell me when it is that she would like to visit. Holly gave me a number of artworks that she told me she made especially for me in school.

She gave me drawings of herself and other neat pictures that she drew in class. She made a nice hanging basket out of paper plates with ribbons hanging from the pocket. I hung them on the wall in the hallway on my second floor. When I saw Heather in the parking lot and she asked if we were moving, I told her yes, it was a quick decision thing, but I did not know quite how to break the news to Holly. It was just about that time when Holly came running out of her house. The big moving truck was in the parking lot in front of the condo, so it was no secret that I was moving.

Heather and I were worried about breaking the news to Holly and how it might affect her. There was no place to sit because the lawn and pavement were soaking wet from the rain. I crouched down low enough so that I would be on face level with Holly. By the look in her face she knew that something was up. It broke my heart to tell my friend that I was relocating. I gently broke the news to her, and I told her that I am taking her pictures with me. I also told her that I would visit her, her mom and Sarah after I moved. I told her that whenever she wants to speak with me her mom will call me on the telephone. Heather rested her hand on Holly's shoulder. I saw the disappointment in Holly's face. Then the tears began to roll down. I could not hide my tears either. I gave her a reassuring hug. We said good-bye with another hug.

Her mother gently steered her into the house with her left hand on Holly's back. As they walked away, the gentle tears became a loud crying. Heather was reassuring her that I would come back to see her. I heard Holly sobbingly say, "Sylvia is my friend, and she is leaving." I welled up with emotions as I picked up the box from the paved sidewalk in front of the condo and placed it in the trunk of the car.

As I continued to place more stuff in my car, I wondered if those people who did what they are doing knew the impact that they were having on our lives. I could not help but to wonder if they had families or friends. I wondered if they have ever heard of the "golden rule"; the one that says "treat others as you expect to be treated". I thought to myself no! they couldn't have, because if they did there was no way that they would have place a false claim for $300.00 and kept that tab running amounting to over twenty thousand dollars in legal fees and other costs, not to mention the physical and emotional toll it has taken on our family. They must have been children of a lesser god and from another planet.

We continued to pack boxes in the car that contained things that we would need right away. Things such as my son's college stuff, shoes, clothing, and other things that we need to take with us to the hotel. The car was filled with boxes in the trunk of the car as well as in the backseat and the front passenger seat. The rain had stopped for a while, so we decided that I should take those things and leave them at the hotel, and then come back and get the containers with our photo albums and irreplaceable things.

I left to take the things to drop them off at the room at the hotel. It took me about an hour and a half because I was doing all the unloading by myself. The hotel was about fifteen to twenty minutes away. I unloaded the stuff, making several trips back and forth to the car and the hotel room. There were many small boxes and a few plastic bags. I finally got it all into the room. I rested for about ten minutes before heading back to the house. I was feeling some sharp pains. I was aggravating my injuries from the repetitive movements and the stress of moving under the conditions those conditions. Everything was quick decision, we did not have time to plan our move. We were given only twenty four hours to vacate our home. I did not have any choice. I took two of the pain killers that I kept in my pocket book. I drank some water, then I headed back to the condo.

It started to rain on the way back to the house. It got heavier and heavier. The rain was pouring this time like there was no end to the supply of water in the heavens. I arrived at the house and told my son and Kevin that I was ready to take the plastic containers with our irreplaceable items to the hotel. Ceejae said it was no problem. He will put them in the car. The containers are in the family room. There were five huge plastic containers.

Our only concern was that I may have to make a couple of trips for those containers because only one at a time was able to fit in the backseat of the car and perhaps one in the trunk. It was no problem, we will do what we have to in order to make the containers fit in the car. We left upstairs and went down to the family room. There were no plastic containers, only boxes. It was not very difficult to move around because the movers had moved most of the heavy furniture into the truck when the rain had stopped.

We checked the living room, the kitchen, and other areas on the first floor, but there were no plastic containers. My son asked Tony, the lead mover, if he had seen the plastic containers. He told us the movers placed them in the truck. We told them we needed those containers because they had items that were not to be placed in storage. The rain was pouring heavily outside. He called the movers who were upstairs and asked them to get the containers from the truck. They told him that it was impossible to do so in that kind of weather because they would have to take out the heavy furniture to get to the containers because they put on the truck first.

There was nothing we could do at that point given the circumstances and the weather. According to the eviction notice that was posted on the door, we had twenty-four hours to move out. We continued packing and moving until around 7:00 p.m. when the last items were placed into the truck. Tony completed his paperwork, and I signed off on the time that the work was completed. The movers left with our property at about 7:30 p.m.; little did we know at the time that it was the last time we would ever see our personal property and the entire contents of our home.

We spent a couple of weeks at the Days Inn. While we were there, we worked the telephone looking for a place to live. I also put a lot of hours in contacting potential speakers for the conference. The conference was only two months away. Everything became critical. It was costing a lot to stay in the hotel. My son also decided that he did not want to return to University of Central Florida because of what was going on. He wanted to stay closer to me to make sure that everything was OK. God bless his heart. I cannot imagine what I would have done without him. My daughter did all she could, but she had to continue with her studies.

She was attending St. Thomas Law School. Her brother and I did not want her to become distracted with all the cantankerous things that were taking place. We also kept our cool to prevent any spill over on other family members or our team members. Her brother and I held the fort down.

And just as DJ Webster's song lyrics, it was like chicken noodle soup with a soda on the side. We let it rained then cleared it out.

While we stayed at the hotel, my son and I worked the local news papers trying to find a place to live. We found a listing of a house that was for rent. I contacted the owner at the number that was given in the local newspaper. We told the owner that we needed a place right away. He said that it was available. We made arrangements to go and see the property.

I visited the property on the evening of that same day. It was about dusk when I arrived to view the property. The house was occupied by a family with young children. The house was a lovely side split with three bedrooms and two baths. It also had a loft and a double-car garage. The house was situated on a water lot; the backyard sloped into the canal. The sliding glass door leading from the master bedroom and the one in the family room were covered with brown metal hurricane shutters. *Well!* I thought. *The hurricane shutters are on already, so I won't have to put them up in case there is a storm.* It was hurricane season.

I told the lady that I was going to look around the backyard. She stopped me from doing so. She said it was dark outside, and she did not want to risk my slipping into the canal because the backyard was on a slope. I suggested we turn the lights on in the backyard, but she said one of the bulbs needed to be changed. I did not press the matter and thought it made sense to do as she suggested.

The next day I contacted the owner of the property and told him that we will rent the house provided he had it painted and the carpet cleaned. He said that would be no problem. He told me how much he wanted for the rent and the terms of renting. I made arrangements to go to his place of residence in Pembroke Pines the next day to pay him the money for the first month and security deposits. He said that he will have the lease contract ready for signing when I arrived.

We rented the house. It was painted, and the carpets were cleaned. We moved in late August. We did not have too much things to move in with; we had only the items we took with us to the hotel. Our furniture and other contents of our previous home were in storage with the moving company. My sister gave us two mattresses that we placed on the carpet for sleeping until we could arrange to get our furniture from the storage company.

In the meantime, we concentrated on those things that were of a higher priority. I had a fax machine that I was using while at the hotel. We found a couple of boxes and empty crates in the garage; we used those to set up makeshift seating and a table in the kitchen. Our first priority was to visit the FIU campus to finalize my son's transfer from University of Central Florida. We were working against the clock. We did everything in person. We wanted to complete his transfer so that he would not miss anytime from college.

It took us a couple of days, but we were successful in having the transition completed. Over the next few days, he enrolled in his classes and was ready to attend FIU. During the same time we requested to have our telephone service transferred from the previous home to the new address. We also worked at getting the utilities set up at the new location. my son kept his part-time job at Fuddruckers. Our financial resource was near rock bottom. I poised myself for the challenges of getting my services transferred. I now have a mortgage foreclosure and a bankruptcy filing on my credit report. It did not matter that the bankruptcy was discharged because all that it was intended to prevent had taken place, or that in the foreclosure action every one of the parties were settled with the proceeds from the sale of my home.

The sale of the home took place before and immediately after the foreclosure. It is anybody's guess which of those transactions are legal. I kept moving forward. Every bit of costs, attorney's fees, court costs and all was paid from the proceeds of the sale of my home. There was even seventeen thousand dollars left over in the courts after all that. What became of that money is another story. Anyway, for now I had to concentrate on our immediate needs. I braced myself for the challenges in getting or utility services set up at our new location.

As I had expected we ran into problems getting our telephone and electricity services set up. Both of the utility services companies requested exceedingly high deposits before our services could be connected. The telephone company requested $1,200 deposit before they would connect the telephone lines. That was a tall order for us considering our expenses and costs were already ceiling high. We had just spent a huge amount of money for the first and last month's rent to secure the property. It was another dark moment but we kept looking ahead and continued to move forward.

I asked the telephone company's representative to give me the reason why such a large deposit was required before the services could be turned on. I was told it was because of pending unresolved disputes from our previous service. I agreed to pay the amount of deposit money the company asked for because we needed the telephone service. Bear with me, the plot gets thicker. I was beginning to feel like a hockey puck that is being slapped all over the ice. I knew that all that was going on just did not add up as the regular scope of personal business affairs, but I could not evidentiary support what it was I thought was taking place. The proof was in the pudding, so I took all at face value and kept moving forward.

We did not argue with the electricity company either. We paid the required deposit so that the electricity could be transferred to our name. The water was already running on the property, all that was needed was to go to the city of Miramar and have the account set up in our name. The next morning I took my son to his part time job at Fuddruckers. On my way back I decided to stop at the Miramar City Hall to set up the water account.

There was no one waiting to be served, so I walked up to the clerk at the counter. I told him what I was there for. He looked at the address on the current bill several times before he proceeded to transfer the account to my name. When he was through setting up the account, he presented me with a receipt for payment. As he did that, he looked at me boldly with a smile, he looked at the address again, then he read it as if to confirm the location, he smiled again and said to me "Good luck, Mrs. McLeod"

I took the receipt from the clerk and with a friendly smile I said thank you. I was thinking that the clerk was very friendly, and that it was so nice of him to be so receptive and welcoming to new residents. He even went as far as wishing me good luck. "More cities and utility companies should behave that way," I murmured to myself. I returned to the house to work on my speakers list. I called Wayne Smith to tell him that I have relocated. I provided him with my new telephone number and contact information. I was no longer living in a mailbox. When we first moved from the condo, I forwarded our mail to a P.O. Box that was set up temporarily at the Post Office. I called UNA national office to inform them where to send my mail. Jeff Laurenti asked me is I was now living in a P.O. Box. I was sure that he intended his comments to be taken as a joke, but my circumstances were very real.

I was standing at the kitchen sink holding my cup of tea in one hand and extracting the tea bag with the other. I glanced through the kitchen window occasionally looking at the neighbor's backyard across the canal. He had a real nice wooden deck with a small pier over the water. It is a nice place to fish from, I thought. I raised up on my toes and peered through the kitchen window to get a better view of the backyard. I saw a large brown object moved in the backyard. I thought nothing of it, except that it must have been one of the children's toys that the previous tenant left behind when they moved.

I moved away from the kitchen sink and sat down on one of our makeshift chairs. It was a crate that we took from the garage when we first moved in. It was turned upside down. I placed old newspapers on them for padding. I reached for the telephone which was hanging above my head and dialed the Center for International Policy. I wanted to get an update from Wayne as well as to give him my update on our speakers for the conference. We spoke for a while and we were both satisfied that we were on target with the time line for the event. I also spoke with Kelly the coordinator at CIP. She reminded me that we need to finalize our speakers. We also discussed travel arrangements for our speakers, the program draft and other things. I called Jim Mullins and provided him with my new contact information.

I had not yet received any commitments to speak from Otto Reich's office or Senator Menendez. I contacted the office of the Cuban American National Foundation to follow up on our invitation to have a speaker from the organization. The representative was very polite and cordial. He informed me that they received the information and passed it on to the person who handles speaking engagements, and someone would be in touch with me soon. Before I hung up the telephone, I reminded the representative that the conference was less than two months away, and I would really appreciate hearing from someone soon. He assured me that there was no problem, and I will receive a response from them.

I called Ethel, my sisters, and other family members to give an update of my resettling. My final telephone call for the day was to the moving company to make arrangements to have our furniture delivered to the new address. The movers told me that we should expect our furniture to be delivered in two days. He did not have a set time but told me to expect them in two days. It began to look like things were moving along fine.

I picked up my son at work later that evening. He brought me a hamburger for dinner. He already ate at work. "Fuddruckers burgers are huge" I said to my son as I unwrapped my burger. We talked about him going back to college as I ate my meal. We also talked about which of the rooms in the house he would choose and which one was for his sister. It wasn't much of a decision because there were only two other bedrooms besides the master bedroom. Both rooms were on the northern side of the house so it was either the one in front or the one in the back.

My son said he would like to take the loft. "It would be cool to be up there. I could play my music when my friends come over." We laughed, and I suggested that his sister may take the front room. By this time I have finished eating my burger meal and I was full. My son left to take a shower while I sat there for a little. I later took my shower then we sat around and talked for a while. The two mattresses that my sister gave me lay on the carpet in the master bedroom. That was our temporary sleeping area. My son laid on one of the mattresses and I on the other. We did not have our television sets because they were in storage with our other stuff. We talked about different things until we fell asleep.

We woke up early the next morning. The first thing my son did was to call his sister to tell her that we were o.k. He fill her in on our experience. While attending St. Thomas Law School, she had a summer job in Palm Beach County. She was unable to be with us while we were relocating, but we kept her up-to-date on what we were doing. My son and I had a quick cup of tea. Soon it was time to head out the doors to take him to his part-time job. My children are such great blessings. I cannot imagine what I would have done without them.

On my way back after I dropped my son to his part-time job, I made a quick spin to Ft. Lauderdale, to collect our mail from the P.O. Box. I tried to get back to the house as quickly as possible because I did not want to miss the movers who were bringing our furniture. When I walked into the kitchen I saw the fax machine receiving a document. It was from Kelly at CIP. I tore it off the machine and moved closer to the light by the kitchen window so that I may see what was on the document.

It was about 11:00 a.m. I looked out the kitchen window into the backyard. I could believe what I saw. It felt like my eyes were going to pop out of the sockets, they were opened so wide. I placed my hand over my mouth with my jaws dropped. I saw a huge creature ran at super high speed and dove into the canal. I thought it must have been an alligator. Then another one of the creatures did the same thing, it dove into the water at a high speed. And then there was yet another one. I dropped the paper and braced myself against the kitchen sink. What in the world? I said to myself. I waited and watched to see if anything emerged from the canal, but nothing did.

I really was not certain if it was a bunch of alligators, but I thought that they could be especially being so close to the canal. However with so many of them running around I thought that I had better be careful. I would not want to run into one of them in the house or anywhere on the property. I picked up the document off the kitchen floor. It was about three pages in length. My fax machine used the paper rolls so pages do not come out separately. The document was a rough draft of the program of the conference. It was incomplete because we had not yet finalized the speakers for the conference. The layout looked perfect. Before calling Kelly to provide her with a feedback of the program draft, I decided to go through the tons of mail that I had retrieved from our Post Office box.

While I was sorting the mail at the kitchen counter I kept glancing through the windows to see if anything was out there in the backyard. There was nothing out there so I kept on sorting my mail. After I sorted and separated the junk mail from the pile, I began working the telephone again. I called some of our board members and provided updated information on the conference. It was now past lunch time and I was getting a bit hungry. I did not have much in the house to choose from for lunch. All I had was some peanut butter, strawberry jelly, a loaf of bread, tea bags, sugar and water.

I made myself a peanut butter and jelly sandwich and sat down to eat it. I needed something to wash down my sandwich, so I got up from my makeshift chair to get myself a cup of water from the kitchen tap. I reached for one of the paper cups and followed my eyes into the back yard. That's when I saw the monsters. There was a whole host of huge lizards. It felt like one of them was watching me. I totally flipped out. I recognized the creatures. They were giant iguanas. There were all strung out in the backyard, some were across the canal on the neighbor's deck. Some of them, I swear with Scout's Honor, were about six to seven feet long from head to tail. They were no longer brown but now green in color. I must have swallowed the whole of my sandwich; it felt like something was stuck in my throat.

I turned to reach for the telephone and stumbled over my makeshift chairs. I lunged forward and landed in the carton box that was my makeshift table for the fax machine. Thank goodness the box was sturdy and placed squarely in the corner. If it wasn't it surely would have crumbled sending the fax machine to the floor. I picked up myself, grabbed the telephone from the wall and pulled the cord so that it could reach the kitchen sink as I resumed my position. The lizards have moved. They must have heard the commotion in the kitchen. I dialed the number for the landlord. He picked up the phone. "Was there something you forgot to tell me?" I asked him in a very brash way.

I could not believe that this guy hid the lizards from me. It was no wondering that when the woman showed me the house, she did not want me to go into the backyard. The shutters on the windows were not for hurricane protection. They were to prevent anyone from seeing the lizards. I was now getting very worked up and angry. This was a huge problem. I do not get along with lizards and those are the small critters that run around. Now look what I have to deal with, they are much bigger than me. "What are you talking about, is it the lizards?" his voice came over the telephone. "What do you think I am talking about?" I shouted at him. "Oh! They are harmless, don't worry about them. Some kid must have let their pet go, and they grew and multiplied over the years." He said. I told him that he has got to let me out of the lease. I have tried to keep a cool head in spite of everything we have been going through, but this one takes the cake. It was the straw that broke the camel's back. I could not take it any longer. I totally blew my stack.

I did not believe a word he was saying. I told him that there was no way my daughter would move into the house, and neither was I going to stay there. I requested a refund of my money. He was not agreeable to giving me back my money. I hung up the telephone facing another dilemma. I had to find a way of getting out of that house. I hung up the phone and sat down on the crate. *Good Lord!* I thought. *What am I going to do?* Everything was now changed.

I kept a baseball bat in the trunk of my car. I went into the garage to get it. I walked through the house with my baseball bat in my right hand. I planned to use it if I see one of the creatures in the house. The carpet is brown, so it is not going to be easy to spot them. They change their color to match the environment. The only place I saw them before was at the zoo. And even then they were not as big as the ones in the back yard.

I went from room to room with my baseball bat. I peered into all the nooks and crannies. I opened every cupboard, closet, and I looked behind every door. No place in the house was left unturned. I climber to the loft and checked there too. I then went into the garage and checked under the car. I also checked on top of every shelf. I did not go anywhere else. I would not go on the property.

I was dripping with perspiration from my tiring search but I satisfied that there were no iguanas in the house. I went back into the kitchen to see if they were back and lying in the backyard. They were there, they had returned. One of the lizards had its head turned in a position so that I was looking directly into its eyes. It was aware that I was looking at it. I moved a crate closer to the kitchen sink and climbed up on it so that I could sit on the sink area to get a closer look. I had a very good view of the lizards from where I was sitting. I was looking down on them. They knew I was looking at them.

One of them looked older and was about seven feet tall. It had powerful big limbs. It must be the grandfather of them all. I could see he was the leader of the pack. He had a giant of a tail behind him. There were large ones about six feet in length. The others were large but smaller, perhaps five feet or more. There were a whole bunch of smaller ones. *My goodness!* I thought. The property was infested with lizards.

I was about to call the city to file a complaint when it occurred to me that they probably knew about them already. I remembered when I went to the city of have the water account transferred into my name. I remembered how the clerk looked at me, then he looked at the address on the bill and smiled at me. I also remember when he said "Good luck". I was now beginning to wonder if he knew about the lizards. Perhaps other tenants have complained before. Perhaps that was the reason why he wished me good luck. He probably knew the challenges that awaited me at that address. I wondered how the previous tenants managed to live there with young children. She told me that she was living there for over one year. Now I did not believe one word she told me. She too must have wanted to get out of that house badly.

I met our next-door neighbor a few days after I moved in. I was looking at some of the shrubs at the side of the house when she said hello to me. I went to the side of the house to check the electricity meter before I had our service turned. Her husband joined her and we formally introduced ourselves. She was a native of Trinidad and he was from the Netherlands. I say hello from time to time when I see them in the front of their home. But they were always looking at me through the corner of their eyes whenever I walked away to continue doing what I was doing. I thought it was their custom. Their backyard resembled a tropical forest. It was literally fill with tropical flora. I had wondered why they did not take the time to cut down the forest. I thought perhaps it would allow more light in but I shelved that thought because it was none of my business. It was their backyard. Now that I know that the lizards are out there somewhere, I wondered if they slept or perhaps lived in the neighbor's backyard.

I picked up my son from work later that day. He saw the baseball bat beside me and asked what I was doing with the bat. I told him that it was to defend myself. He asked me from what. I told him he was not going to believe what I was about to tell him. I told him about the lizards on the property. I told him what I saw and thought was a toy blowing in the wind was no toy but it was one of the giant lizards. He asked me if I was for real. I asked him if he thought I would make up such a story like that. He said no, he believed me, but he couldn't believe that it was for real.

I told him that it was for real. He asked me if I called the landlord. I told him that I did, and the landlord said that they were harmless. My son said "Sure, Mom, they are harmless. We have to move from that house, who wants to pay rent to live with lizards.

When I got into the house I checked every room to make sure that no lizards were in the house. It was now a challenge to sleep on the mattress on the carpet, especially knowing that those lizards were around. I was not sure if they could find a way into the house. I slept very lightly and was awakened by every sound. Even the wind against the window disturbed my sleep.

The next day I took my son to his new campus. He was going to be there all day. Ceejae was not new to this FIU Campus. We visited his sister on that campus numerous times during her undergraduate years. My son had an interest in playing college football. The one setback in attending FIU was that at the time the college did not have a college football program. He had begun his training on the University of Central Florida football team. He was a member of the St. Thomas Aquinas High School football team. I went to all of their games at home and on the road. I wished him well at his new campus, but I was a bit disappointed for him because FIU did not have a football program. But there was talk of one in the works.

After I dropped my son off at his new campus, I rushed back to the house. I did not want to miss the movers. They said they would deliver the furniture in two days. This was the second day. I was having a predicament however, because now that I know the place was infested with lizards I did not want to stay in that house. I had not thought that far ahead so I did not contact them to stop them from delivering the furniture.

I reached the entrance of the subdivision where we lived. The traffic backed up to the subdivision. It looked like an accident was up ahead. With my luck it would have something to do with the movers with my furniture, I said to myself, but I quickly dispel that thought for fear it would materialize. That is what is referred to as "goat mouth" in the Caribbean. It is a way of predicting misfortune or failure. I tapped on the wood of my car to correct the thought but realized that my dashboard was plastic.

The traffic began to flow and I moved along to the top of the line. Sure enough, it was what a thought it was. I saw flashing lights and police vehicles. It was an auto accident. There was a big white truck parked in front of the house. There were a number of cars parked along the side of the street. Many people were standing around. It was quite a commotion going on. I drove up as close as I could and parked on the side of the street. I could not get in my driveway. With my baseball bat in hand, I walked up to my driveway.

A gentleman who was speaking with one of the officers approached me and asked if I lived there. I asked him who wants to know. He said he was there to deliver some furniture. The truck had no company name written on it. No one would that it was a moving and storage company. When they first move my furniture it had the name "All American Movers" written on both sides and the back of the truck. I told him that I was expecting a delivery. He said he had the furniture in the truck. I told him to wait a minute. I entered the house and put down my purse and the baseball bat, then I went back outside to speak with him. I asked him if the truck was in an accident. He said, "Yes, it collided with a car around the corner. I asked him to open the truck so that I may examine the condition of my furniture. He refused to open the truck, and before I knew it, he went in the truck and drove off without unloading the furniture. The whole thing appeared to have been staged. I did not believe he had any furniture on the truck. I did not believe a "goat mouth" had anything to do with the matter either. I checked the time of the accident. It had occurred long before I uttered those words. So much for knocking on wood or better yet knocking on plastic.

I went indoors and made a telephone call to the moving company. I told the manager what happened. He said he would call me back when the driver returned to the office. I settled down and began working on the conference materials. There was too much stuff happening. Working on the conference kept me calm and focused. I waited but never heard anything from the moving company. I continued to move forward staying on the straight and narrow. I decided to do some research on the lizards.

I went to one of our local library to look up information on the iguanas. I did not know much about them. The closest that I have ever seen big lizards was at the zoo. Those at the zoo were not as big as the ones in my backyard. I read that they were primarily herbivores and that they were active during the days. The information I found also suggested the lizards lived near water and were excellent swimmers. I found out that if they are threatened, they will leap from a branch of great heights and escape with a giant splash in the water.

I continued to read the information about the monsters. I found out that they have strong jaws with razor-sharp teeth. The more I read the more I discover bad news. It did not sound too good for me living in a house that is on a property that is infested by those creatures. I thought of closing the book and leave, but I couldn't because the more I know about the creatures the better I am able to defend myself if they attack me. They have sharp tails that make up half of their body length. I did not doubt the information because it confirmed everything that I saw.

I discussed the problem with Ethel. God bless her heart. After listening to what was happening, Ethel suggested that the lizards were perhaps more afraid of me than I was of them. I told her that fear was no longer an issue; it was a question of survival. I could always count on my team member for support. She always provide a unique perspective on things, one that boost strength and courage. Besides my grandmother, she is the only person I know who encourages the heart with her soft words and answers. She is a wise woman.

I shared with her how in my younger years I was intimidated by those four-inch critters, the ones that ran all over the place. I always shoo them away with branches when I see them, but the ones in the backyard were too huge, they could not be shooed. Her telling me that they may be more afraid of me than I was of them was reassuring, but that did not last very long. I need to move out of that house as quickly as possible. I need to find a place first, and I also have to continue my work on the conference.

I could not afford to deal with anymore destabilization. It has been going on for far too long. It does not require a rocket scientist to figure out and understand how lives are affected when environments are destabilized. By that I mean that anyone even without any high degree of intelligence knows what it feels like to be harassed, forced to move from place to place, to loose money, to suffer personal injuries, and a suffer a whole host of other maladies. Through all that we kept moving forward. We continued doing our work and stayed on the straight and narrow path. My family and team members were depending on me so we moved forward.

I must have developed some form of psychosis because of the creatures. My conversations were often interrupted with thoughts of those lizards. I was always thinking up another strategy of dealing with them. They were annoying me. I could not take my mind off the lizards. Sometimes I would perspire real hard when I think of them. But where there is a will there is a way. I remembered a long time ago in our RCIA (Right to Christian Initiation for Adults) class we were discussing the topic of following one's thought during mass or during a prayer. The drift of it was that if ones thought is interrupted by drifting to something else, do not become alarmed. Followed the thought process and see where it will leads, it may just lead to the root of a problem or to a solution. I never shun my thoughts of the lizards, no matter when and where they surfaced. It was my way of being alert at all times because they were a threat to me. Hence my psychosis was a protective and defensive mode.

It would not have been so bad if the current state of affairs was similar to the one Ethel and I experienced when we visited Gainesville for one of our annual state meetings. Ethel and I were on our way to one of our annual meetings. Our state board meetings are usually conducted at the Langford Hotel in Orlando. The hotel is located in a very quiet setting with tons of Spanish moss hanging from the trees. It is one of the older communities in Orlando. It is centrally located and provided easy access to some of the historic and cultural centers of the city. We go there for board meetings at least four times each year. Whenever our Orlando Chapter host our annual state meeting it is held at the Langford

Hotel. However, the meeting that Ethel and I were attending on this occasion was our state annual meeting, hosted by our Gainesville Chapter.

We normally go the route of the Florida Turnpike or I-95 whenever we attend any UNA-USA meetings in Central Florida region. This time we decided to go via Alligator Alley. Ethel and I shared the driving; she drove her car up and I drove it back. I had never driven that route before so I was looking forward to the trip. It was a chance to see different scenery. On our way up, I had the pleasant opportunity of see the gators in their natural habitat. I saw tons of them along the road. I had a good view of the alligators for miles and miles. I was in the passenger seat so I could look out of the window as much as I wanted. Sometimes my excitement of seeing the alligators got the better of me and I shout my exclamations out loud.

Ethel sometimes get caught up in the excitement. I told her to keep her eyes on the road for safe driving. I reminded her that on our way back she will get a chance to look out of the window when I am driving. There were all sizes and shaped of alligators. There were big ones, little ones, and those in between. There were also real dark almost black one, brown ones, and some of them were green.

Wow! I said to Ethel, "I have never seen so many alligators on the same day ever in my life, what a wonderful experience". Ethel said she could not wait to see them on our way back. We continued on our trip. We snacked on peanut butter and banana sandwiches that Ethel made for us. I opened one of the can of pops that I brought for the trip, and placed it in the cup holder for Ethel. Then I popped one open for myself. We snacked and chatted until we reached our destination.

We arrived in Gainesville after our long drive. We had a bit of difficulty finding our way to Sue's house. We made an error by taking the opposite direction to her house. We pulled over, reviewed our directions, turn around and headed straight to Sue's house. We had plans of staying overnight at Sue's place. She invited us over for the night. Sue was a UNA-USA member in our Gainesville chapter. Our annual meeting starts the next day.

We arrived at Sue's home before dark. She welcomed us with open arms. She said she hoped we did not have too much difficulty finding her place, and was very happy that we arrived safely. Likewise, Ethel and I were happy to see her. We told her we took the wrong direction otherwise we would have arrived much sooner. Ethel, jokingly, tried to blame me for taking the wrong directions. I concurred because she was driving and I was the one reading the map. I told them the fact that I have a Bachelor's degree in geography does not necessarily mean that I am good at directions. There is a big divide between theory and applications. The three of us cracked up laughing.

Sue showed us to our rooms where we would spend the night. We fetched our overnight bags from Ethel's car and placed them in our rooms. We were then hurried up by Sue to see her property before it gets too dark. She gave us a grand tour of her property. It was a very nice spread. There were lots of tall trees on her property and they were spaced out very nicely. After we toured her property, we settled down around the kitchen table for tea and cheesecake. We chatted at great lengths about everything one could imagine.

Ethel raised the question of gators. She asked Sue if there were any gators in Gainesville. Sue replied "Sure, we have tons of them,"

"Well great! Where can we see them?" I asked. "In the swamp" Sue replied. Ethel told Sue that it would be nice if she and I could see the gators before we return to Miami. Sue provided us with the directions of where we will find the gators. She told us we would find them in the swamp. The next morning we were up early. Ethel and I wanted to set out for the annual meeting to make it to our first board meeting on time. We also wanted to give ourself sufficient time so that we could see the gators on our way. Sue was to follow later. She said she had to pick up a few things for the meeting. We thanked Sue for her hospitality and a nice evening, then Ethel and I headed on our way to University of Florida. We followed the directions that Sue gave us. We looked for the swamp with the gators, but we saw none.

We arrived at University of Florida, registered for the meeting, and checked into our room. Ethel and I shared a room because we are able to share the cost of the room. We were on time for our breakfast and the board meeting. The presidents and vice presidents of all our chapters in Florida were present, and so too were the officers the officers and board members of our Florida division of UNA-USA.

After our business meeting ended, Ethel and I went back to our room. We talked for a while all the time wondering where the gators were.

Ethel was a bit disappointed that we did not get a chance to see the gators on our way to the University. On the final day of our convention before dinner, I opened the patio door and stepped outside for some fresh air. We have been very busy for the past two days. Since we arrived for our meeting we have been indoors, so it was a good time to step outside and get a bit of sunshine. As I stepped through the sliding glass door, I was greeted by a maroon-red structure high in the air. I looked at it, turning my head to get a better view. On the huge circular mushroom top of the structure, I saw the word *swamp*. I thought for a moment. *It could not be. No, it couldn't be.* I leaned on the balcony rail and called for Ethel to come outside.

Ethel walked out onto the patio. I pointed to the structure and asked, "Do you thing that is what Sue is referring to?" Ethel was silent for a moment. I watched her facial expression change as she burst out laughing. We hugged and laughed ourselves to the point of coughing. "Well! Well!" exclaimed Ethel. "Are there gators in Gainesville?" We were laughing so hard we could not stop laughing. The three of us—Sue, Ethel, and I—spoke for over an hour about the gators. We discussed the reptiles without a hitch in our conversation. Could it be that we were talking about something entirely different? Go figure.

I wish I could do the same about the lizards but I couldn't. They looked awfully scary and threatening. There was nothing I could do except to move from that house. The information that I found on the iguanas was helpful because it gave me a sense of control but it did not help a whole lot. It was very difficult having to live with the iguanas, and especially at a time when my attention was focused on the Cuba conference. I was not sure which of the two was giving me more anxiety, the lizards or the conference.

Any activity that involves public outreach and public awareness requires careful planning and considerations. There was an awful lot of consideration not only in developing the event but with information management. It was great that I was not doing this alone and that we had a very good and capable team working on the program. Any detour from the project or to take on any other issues may make the conference more controversial that it already is. So I tried to remain calm about the lizards even though it was a big challenge.

The haunting iguana experience was so bad that even when I was at the conference, and I was having a conversation, my thoughts drifted to the lizards. In the reception at the conference, Admiral Saunders and I were talking about how we put the conference together. Without realizing what I was doing, I changed the conversation from speaking about the conference to speaking about the lizards. That must have appeared totally off the wall. I knew that the lizards gave me some form of psychosis. It was the way life was, living in an iguana infested house.

My family and I paid a big price for doing volunteer work. Developing the programs and conducting the activities were TAAL orders, but we did not expect to loose all of our property, our business, and our all of our moneys. Gone! everything was gone, and we were left with nothing! nada!. We were slapped all over the place with lawsuits, then we were forced into the streets. Our home and all of its contents, our business and all of its contents, automobiles, and everything we owned. We were left only with the shirts on our backs. What manner of man would invite such serious consequences of volunteer work on anyone. I simply cannot imagine who would ever do such ghastly things. But in spite of the challenges, we continued moving forward.

Our team members were depending on us so we had to move forward. We have never been political, and we have never taken any political platform. We were strictly nonpartisan, and ordinary citizens from all walks of life. All of our programs were designed for public outreach, were educational, and intended to increase public awareness on the issues that were presented and discussed. Our youth programs were designed to encourage students' participation in the celebration of UN50.

Our conference in October 1997 was one of the most challenging of or programs. Perseverance and persistency was our greatest challenge and our greatest advantage. Although the foreclosure action on my home began in 1995, it came to a head in 1997 which was the time we move out of our condo. It was very difficult to continue working on that conference while looking for a place to live, sharing space with iguanas, and suffering such a devastated financial collapse. Personally, all that I worked for all my life was gone, everything; but we kept moving forward with our programs.

We have suffered tremendously but nevertheless we completed all of the programs that our board approved. Every one of our team members inclusive of all our sponsors and corporate partners had a vested interest in the development, execution, and management of our programs. Hence, the integrity of our programs and activities were reinforced by the cross functionality and the strength of our teamwork and efforts.

It would not be fair if I did not share some of our personal experiences. We did not live in a vacuum. Our team members are people two, and like others we were exposed to the hazards in our society. Those hazards could have prevented our programs from continuing, but of teamwork, team spirit and team members ensure the continuity of our programs thus achieving our goals and objectives. My hope in sharing our experiences is that it will inspire other volunteers not to give up when the going gets tough but to press forward to the finish line because there is a light at the end of the tunnel. It does not matter what modality or method of work, keep moving forward. Team work is a good way to go because it helps to lighten the load.

Between 1995 and 1997, we had numerous automobile accidents that led to bodily injuries; in fact, I had three automobile accidents in less than two months. I could not understand how after all my years of being a licensed driver; suddenly I am attracting all sorts of hit and run drivers and other motorists who kept on rear ending and damaging my vehicles on the road.

It was almost as if I was constantly being body checked with other automobiles. Not to mention being slap shot in my financial affairs. I had no personal conflicts with any one. All my life I have done volunteer work. I was never a political person. I was simply doing volunteer administrative work of which everything was publicly disclosed.

Everything is a matter of public record. The lawsuits that were slapped on me and my family were unconscionable. Thank goodness all of our work was a team effort, without team spirit and dedicated team members we could not have completed all of our programs successfully.

The condo association placed a lien on our home for $300. It was a never-ending process of having to respond to the courts and motions. It cost an awful lot of money to hire attorneys and to work through the process. It was even more frustrating and aggravating when the motions and court dates coincided with those dates on which activities were planned. Even though we were paying the costs on all levels, it was also devastating having to resort to filing for chapter 13 bankruptcy as a way of protecting our home. That did not help because we still wound up having to move from our condo.

The condominium was not our first home ownership. Since 1980, we had purchased and owned four residential properties at different intervals. Our first home was purchased in 1980. As the family matured and needed more space, we sold and bought a bigger home. We started out by purchasing a small home. We built equity in our property by making improvements. It was also a time when property value appreciated based on market values. We sold and bought others properties as our needs changed.

It may appear that I am unduly speaking about the loss of our home. Well, it is intentional and there is a reason for this. For many people, purchasing a home is the single most valuable investment during our lifetime. It is also the one goal that every member in our society aspire, owning a home. A home foreclosure is remedial process in our society, but it certainly isn't when used for other purposes. It took two years of fighting the foreclosure on our condo to realize that in fact we were not dealing with a foreclosure issue. I had no idea what the underlying issues were. But we left the condo and hoped that someday we will be able to purchase another home.

As time went by we thought about our experiences and wondered what might have happened. We considered whether or not we may have overlooked any internal conflicts which may have contributed to our personal woes. There was nothing there, no internal conflicts. It is not that we did not have conflicts among our team members because we did. Our conflicts, however, were constructive in nature. It helped us to hone our programs and to work better as team members.

The experiences in my personal life were by no means unique. All of our team members in their personal lives were experiencing natural challenges as well as challenges brought on by others because of the work we were doing. Those challenges were also not unique to our Greater Miami chapter but to all of our chapters in our division. Some presidents in other chapters in our division ran into para military challenges and activities. Through shared experiences we offered solutions and suggestions of how to improve working relationships.

Personal conflicts among our team members were few. We were all volunteers, and we did not have a lot of time to engage in personal conflicts. Each time that we met, it was down to business. We socialized in the context of what we were doing as members of the organization. We did not get involve with the personal lives of our members. We had a code of respect for each other and valued the time and dedication of each one of our members, irrespective of general membership or board members.

Bear with me while I continue discuss the possible method to madness. We considered the possibility of our personal experiences being related to bad business decisions. But that did not fit. Firstly, in the work we were doing, there are no competitors. We were already working as team members with all of the organizations who may have any interest in our area of work.

It was very unlikely that it was any bad business decision on our part because the condo was not the first home that we had purchased and owned. It was our fourth primary residence which we owned. Our home ownership began in 1980. Since that time we have acquired knowledge and knew the value of home ownership. Our financial interest in our home was having more than 50 percent equity. We have lived in our home for more than 5 years. Our home had a market value of more than $90,000.00, which perhaps to some people was not a lot, but to us it was, it was our million dollars. There was only three years to pay off our mortgage, not to mention the intrinsic value of having a home; a place to live, a place to sleep, a place that we called our castle.

Now which home owner would stand by and allow his or her home to be taken away in a foreclosure action, and not even by the mortgage company but a condo association and their attorneys. Go figure!. It did not add up, which lead us to believe that our experiences had nothing to do with payments or financial decisions in the normal sense, but with some other motive and factors of external influence.

The use of the terms internal and external environments are not unique. Those are the terms that are used by business professionals when assessing strengths, weaknesses, opportunities and threats. Those occurrences were executed by an external environment. It had nothing to do with any business decision, nor did it have to do with any personal conflicts, and it did not have anything to do with any regulatory environment or competitors. There was nothing to be gained from the work we were doing except the knowledge that we have met our obligations of increasing public awareness through public outreach programs. We were a volunteer organization doing volunteer work.

There was another personal element in coping with the personal experiences. It had to do with spiritual and emotional well being. In July of 1997 I returned from consultation with an attorney. Her was already handling legal matters for other residents in the condo community where we lived. One of the documents that I took to him was a copy of a letter that was written by the condo association through their attorneys, and sent to our national office. My impression of that letter was a veiled threat to the organization. In the letter I was accused of using the organization's funds, office, and equipment for my personal use. The national office faxed me a copy of that letter. The national office knew better that the accusations in the letter.

I was very hurt by what I read in that letter. I was already going through enough and still have much more work to do. I could not understand why those people were doing what they were doing. It just did not add up, but I could not afford to become distracted I had to keep focus on our work.

The organization already knew that the reverse was true. It was my office, my equipment, my staff, and my personal funds that covered the overhead cost of the operation of the local chapter. It was the same group of people who were wearing me down with the foreclosure action on my home who sent the letter to the national office. It would have been easy to engage the default position. I am a black female, playing the racist card would have been very easy. It was very likely, quite possible the case, but to follow that process may have very likely be a distraction and derailment. We continued to move forward. The sum total of our teamwork was more than each single unit.

The letter was addressed to John C. Whitehead, the chair of our organization. I received the copy of that letter in 1996 that was when it was written. I kept it in the file with the documents. The attorney asked for copies of all documents relating to the foreclosure, so a copy of that letter was given to him with all the other documents. It was three o'clock when I unlocked the entrance to the condo and entered. The wall clock began to chime as I entered. I placed my car keys on the table in the foyer and went upstairs to my bedroom. I put the envelope that had all copies of my documents on my desk.

I took off my suit and put on more comfortable everyday clothes that I wore around the house. I then picked up the telephone to call Jim Mullins. I did not carry through with placing the telephone call, instead I unplugged the telephone cord from the wall. I had a previous arrangement to contact Jim later that day to discuss our choice of venue for the conference, but after returning from the attorney's office, I really did not feel like speaking with anyone else for the day.

I knew I had entered a systems-down mode. I prefer to use the term *systems-down mode* instead of *feeling down*. I was determined to manage every aspect of my experience in such a way that I would not cultivate negative feelings which in the long run, would affect my well-being. Yes, there were bodily injuries and great financial challenges. We were spending money to cover costs that did not result from our own doing but from the actions of other people. I lay down for a while to let the moment pass. I need to wade through the waters to purge any negative thoughts that were taking roots. I had to be strong for me, my children, and my team mates. I was not about to adopt any altered state of being that are being imposed by external forces.

I lay across my bed with my hands and arms outstretched on both sides of my body, turning my head to rest on the right side and dangling my feet off the edge of the bed. I lay very still closing my eyes and began the journey with my thoughts. I was prepared to go wherever my thoughts were leading me. With my eyes closed, I knew I would maintain control of my emotions. I told myself that I will not enter the hate zone. I have hated situations but never people. It was a dark and light zone issue, and it is always the darkest before the crack of dawn.

I knew where I was. I was sitting in a sea of grass. It was a bright and sunny day. I love rose apples, the golden fruit with the rich aroma. The blossoms filled the air. The gentle breeze rushed through my hair. The cane fields lay smoothly in the distance, a beautiful shade of green, as the Plantain Garden River wound its way through the plains. Beyond the plains was the coast, a single stack high in the air puffing away, the gray smoke rising to the skies, a lone ship stood in the harbor.

Down below, the quiet plain a picturesque landscape like a masterpiece lay snuggled between the crevices of the mountains and framed by the horizon. I was captivated by the southern view as I sat there, on the grass with my legs curled under my skirt. I slowly turned the pages and began reading "The Creation" by James Weldon Johnson. With my eyes closed, I read the words. "And God stepped out on space." I continue reading to the end of the poem. I thought about it for a while, and said, "That's good."

I closed my book and picked up another one. Rudy Wiebe was written boldly across the bottom of the cover. *Peace Shall Destroy Many* was the title. I was about to open it when the shadows began to move in. I looked up; dark clouds were everywhere. I wondered if I could make it to the cafeteria before the rain. I should have used the tunnel and that way I would not have to get wet, I thought to myself. Dark clouds were everywhere. There was a sudden gust of wind. It began to swirl picking up dust and debris as it twisted across the courtyard. I tried to put the book in the bag that hung at my side.

My barrette flew off and was caught up in the wind. I turned a full three sixty, there was no point in going after it because it was gone in the wind. My book fell, I stomped on it to hold it in place and prevent it from blowing away. I bent down to pick it up from under my foot. My blazer blew over my head. It was blocking my vision. I felt for my book with my hand. It was under my foot, I knew it was there but I could not see it. I felt for it and found it. I snatched it up and held it tightly. I have to read it for my next class. I stood up and was about to rush for the building. I became aware of their presence as I stood up.

They were standing all around me. I did not know who they were. I could not see their faces. It was a mass of contortion. I tried to pass them, but they would not let me. I heard their laughter. I saw a space between two of them. I darted, thinking I was through the circle, but I was still there. I just could not get through. Like a bouncing ball, they tossed me from person to person. The laughter got louder. I still could not see their faces, but they were there. I felt the presence of their thoughts. I did not know who they were or what it was they wanted with me. I could hate them for what they were doing, but I could not do so. They were very ugly and so were their ways, it would have been easy to hate them but I choose not to do so.

I felt their anger and hate because of the bad things they did to us. I do not know why because we have done them no wrong. Perhaps it is in their nature to hate, I do not know and I do not see why, or perhaps they do not know how to love and respect others. I lay across the bed with my eyes closed as they tossed me from person to person. One of them grabbed my book bag. I pulled it with just enough force to let it go. Like a slingshot, the book bag with its long straps boomeranged, and he fell.

The clouds were getting darker; there were more of them than I first thought. It grew darker and darker; the darker it got, the more the pressure mounted. I kept on saying no with strong conviction. Hostility was everywhere, but I was un-responsive. I will not accept the seed of hate rage; I resisted the hatred with every essence of my being.

It was at that moment while still holding my breath that I felt a warm glow came over me. It was a huge starred flag; it covered the entire house. It was there; I knew it was real. The faces were pulling back into the walls from which they came. I have to see for myself. I got off the bed quickly. I felt dizzy at first, but I steadied myself and ran down the stairs. I ran outdoors to see the U.S. flag draped over my house. It was bold with a resounding presence. I knew then that it was no longer in my hands. I did what I could, but they would not listen. It was totally out of my hands. It was now between them and God. The gnats bundled, flying furiously away finding no place to go.

I went back into the house. I stopped in the living room and hit a few keys on the piano. I walked into the kitchen and wondered what to prepare for dinner. It was almost time for my son to come home from work. He was getting a ride from his friend Kevin. I opened the freezer and took out a couple of steaks. It was Friday, July 4, 1997. *I will fix some steaks; when my son gets home, after dinner, we will go and watch some fireworks,* I thought to myself. I placed the steaks in the sink to thaw. I checked the time on the stove clock; *it is only 4:30 p.m. It is the crack of dawn,* I said to myself. I turned on the kitchen tap to let warm water flow over the steaks so that they thaw quickly.

I turned on the stereo. I pulled the *Hooked on Classics* album from the rack. I put on the album and turned up the sound. I sat back in the couch with the album cover in my hand. My daughter gave me that album in 1990 for my birthday. I had a front-row seat to the Royal Philharmonic. I sat in the couch, curled my legs, and listened to the sounds. I merged with the music as the sounds fill the room. I got off the couch and grabbed a ladle; for one moment, I was the music director. I turned up my collar, ruffled my hair, and raised both arms with the ladle in my right hand. I was off to another world.

I went through the processes of responding and attending hearings in the courts. It was tons of paperwork, but I followed through. I have never met the adversaries. They continued their attacks, and I let them. I focused on what I was doing. I knew it would be a long road for my children and me, but we kept our faith. It was more than we could handle by ourselves.

In one conversation with one of my attorneys, there were many of them working on different issues; the attorney mentioned the term *scorched earth policy*. I wondered what he meant by that. He could not have possibly been referring to me because I had no earth to be scorched. He later explained that it meant the destruction of everything so that there was no reminder. He kept giving me papers to keep just in case they were nowhere to be found later.

I continued with the processes knowing very well that it was a long road ahead. My telephone bills were escalating. I contacted the telephone company and lodged complaints. My bills were showing long-distance calls to places we never called. The telephone numbers that were shown on my bills were to places one would assume that we placed the calls. Telephone calls to every corner of the globe, but we did not place those calls, and none of our team members would have done such thing. We knew our team members they were just like us.

Our telephone bills were slammed. We kept paying the bills to keep our service on. It was a drain on our financial resource. It was a bandwagon, and just about everyone hopped on for the ride. It was already the crack of dawn; I knew full well that soon, and very soon, that what ever was done in the dark, one day will be shown in the light of day. It was no longer in my hands. I continued to resist entering the dark alleys and instead kept focus on what I was doing.

Whenever the going became tough, I transformed. I found a new way of doing whatever it was that I was doing. Creativity and innovation became my manual of procedure. I was centered even though it was very difficult, it became a learning experience. I examined and studied each transaction and course of action. I was aware and present at all times. The evil forces could not have known that I was present.

The degree of the pressure, harassment, and annoyance was sufficient to drive anyone out of their mind, but there was a larger force at work. I knew everything would take time, but he was the creator and master of time. It was no longer in my hands. We took no prisoners because it was not our battle.

We fought to keep focus and stay on track. Perhaps we knew all along that our journey would be riddled with forces of derailment. Perhaps it comes with the territory.

I should also mention here that while I was going through all that I was also being audited by the IRS. It was totally a state of being. Anyone who has ever had an audit knows the demands of such a process. Imagine having to do all that when nothing is stable. Try getting documents that are required when every body else have all of your stuff. It was an absolute nightmare.

I have always been organized in what ever it is I am doing. I kept records and I love good record keeping. For as many years as I can remember I have always take time to go over my personal records. Whenever I take the time to review my personal records it gives me a sense of connection. It allows me the opportunity to measure my progress. I can see where I was, how far I have come, and what areas needs to be improved for growth and development. So my papers and documents are very important to me. They are part of my inalienable package.

I am not just making that up. Others before me with greater minds felt the same way. If you do not believe me take a look at the fourth amendment in the Bill of Rights. I like having my personal papers in my possession because they are mine. They are my stuff and my personal history. I feel like a fish out of water without them.

So when the auditor asked me how I lived and I gave her the response that firstly "I breathe oxygen, and thank God that was free, and next I exhale carbon dioxide which along with the sunshine helps the plant to produce the food that I eat" I really wasn't being facetious. I simply escaped to one of my "rain in Spain "moments. Every thing that was happening to us was a moving violation. It was very difficult to explain anything coherently when everything is constantly changing.

I ran out of ways to rationally explain what was happening to every one. I did not know what was going on either. It was all changing by the minute. When things change like the way they were and especially while dealing with real life situations, it is apt to make one look like a liar or that one is out of control. If it sounds or seems that we were under attack, we were. My grandfather told me many, many years ago, that if it walks like a chicken, clucks like a chicken, looks like a chicken and smells like a chicken, then for Pete's sake it is not a cow but it is a chicken.

I was dealing with an attorney who was handling the house issue, another one was handling the accidents issues, and another was handling the bankruptcy issue. The costs were adding up. It looks crazy to have so many attorneys but the issues did not happen all at once. One attorney specializes in one field and so on. Each time that other issues sprouted up I had to find another attorney with a specialty in the field of the newly sprouted issue. Those were circumstance beyond my control; I was just dealing with them as they occurred.

The impact of the external forces on my personal life is testimony that there was no way that I could have delivered the programs successfully by myself. The success therefore must be attributed to a greater force at work. That force is called team dynamics. We embraced and engaged teamwork as our grand and foundational strategy. Teamwork creates positive synergy among our team members. Thus, when one of our team members is under attack, the initial structure of team leadership and teamwork reinforces our actions, providing a framework that assures our work cannot be derailed or interrupted.

In order to dismantle and derail the processes of teamwork, external forces would have to attack team members individually. And even so, it would be very obvious and may cause a refueling and passionate reaction of full steam ahead of the team members. Our board members entrusted me to share our experiences in writing. The purpose is to serve as inspiration to others who are faced with similar tasks and challenges. It is also a way of encouraging the continued valiant work of voluntaryism.

We had full time occupations but nevertheless we volunteered our time and resources to help make our community and world a better place. We figured that with the information provided in this book, others will use it as a source of information and be inspired by it. Some people may want to draw on our experiences which may help them in charting their way in planning, developing, and executing their projects and programs. And yet still, others may simply find it entertaining. But more importantly I hope that it will demonstrate the power and dynamics of teamwork.

It took me many years before I could sit down to pen this book. It was intentionally done for many reasons. Firstly, the personal experiences and the attacks left my family and I wounded and hurt. Our financial foundations had crumpled and we were barely scraping to survive. We were also fill with anger. I was in no state to communicate the experiences of our team work, and I did not want to transmit the anger I was feeling. So in its true form, I am now sharing our experiences in this book.

CHAPTER 13

THE CRACK OF DAWN

W E LABORED AND toiled for over five years working as the foot soldiers for a larger cause. We were ordinary people doing extra ordinary things. Where there were no resources we innovate and became creative. And in our own little corner of the globe we let our light shine illuminating the vision of a brighter, better, and more peaceful world.

As a chapter of UNA-USA we were not unique because there are hundreds of chapters across the U.S.A. doing similar work as we were doing. Our harsh and crushing personal experiences exacted by external forces left us bruised and damaged in several aspects of our daily lives, but we forged ahead, moving forward as a team. We believed that we have helped to lay the foundation of a sustainable peace.

As a team, there was never one single moment or need to question our being or our ability to participate in the processes that affect our lives. We felt proud to share with our community and in helping to increase the awareness of members of community by providing our educational and public outreach programs. All of our team members recognized and value the authority that has been instilled in our leaders to make policies that governs us; but we were also aware of the part we played in helping our fellow citizens to become aware of those policies and issues. It is our inalienable right and has been a tradition and cornerstone of our great democracy for over two hundred years.

In conducting ourselves we followed the rules. Robert's Rules of Order was one of our guiding posts. It was nothing new, and it has withstood the test of time for many generations. Labor unions, business leaders, 4-H clubs, student councils, scouts and guides, churches, schools, debating clubs, social clubs, for-profit organizations, non-profit organizations, governmental organizations, non-governmental organizations, just to name a few, have used those organizational tools, principles and procedures for many centuries. It is a way and a system of getting things done while at the same time encouraging inclusivity and participation.

We have been there before, since our youthful days we have been walking the walk and talking the talk just like those who will follow. Everyone deserves to be heard and there is a system that allows that to take place. We operated and conducted our meetings with a fixed order of business. Our basic steps following the Robert's rules of order were as follows:

1. Calling our meeting to order and observing a moment of silence
2. A roll call of our members, recording those who are present and absent
3. Reading the minutes of our last meeting and making any corrections that are needed to the minutes of our last meeting
4. Officer reporting from our president, secretary, and treasurer
5. Committee reporting from all our committees chairpersons
6. Discussing special orders that are important matters that were previously discussed and were designated to be discussed in the current meeting
7. Concluding unfinished business
8. Discussing new business
9. Hearing announcements
10. Adjourning the meeting

Each of our team members had their own personal lives. Some of us had children who were still attending school or college. We also had full time jobs. We could not afford to allow our time to be consumed by volunteer work, even though it was important work. We had to balance our time, and having a way to conduct our business was one aspect of our teamwork.

As a local chapter, we embraced the mission of our national organization to inform the American public about the United Nations and the issues on its agenda and to mobilize public support for constructive U.S. participation in the U.N. UNA-USA carries out its action agenda through a combination of public outreach, policy analysis, and international dialogue.

Through a nationwide network of chapters, divisions, and affiliated organizations, UNA-USA reached a broad cross section of the US public. The association provides information and educational services on the work of the UN and on other global issues for students, scholars, Congress, and the media, and each year it coordinates the observance of UN Day (October 24) in hundreds of communities across the nation. UNA-USA conducts policy analysis and international dialogue through the Global Policy Project.

Effective international organizations are essential to deal with a host of global issues, peace and security, the environment, sustainable economic development, the scourges of disease and narcotic drugs, and the wise use of resources that touch the lives of every US citizen. Just as concerned citizens work to improve government at the local, state, and national levels, they should also understand the importance of international institutions and work to make them even more effective. UNA-USA believes that the UN has an essential role in addressing international issues and that it has a commendable record of achievement.

But like all human institutions, the UN has problems and could do its job even better. The association acknowledges these problems and offers constructive solutions. Thus, while the association supports the UN, it is not an uncritical supporter. Rather, UNA-USA is a constructive critic, providing balanced information and realistic recommendations for a stronger United Nations system. The association is a nonpartisan organization, drawing its leadership from both major political parties. Support for an effective UN should not be identified with only one political viewpoint.

UNA-USA seeks leaders and members of all ages, from all racial and ethnic groups, and all economic and social backgrounds. We take pride in our reputation as a credible source of objective information serving several different audiences: students, academics, the media, governmental and business leaders, and the general public. In addition, UNA-USA takes a position: we call for constructive and creative U.S. participation in cooperative efforts with other nations and with nongovernmental organizations to realize the ideals of the United Nations Charter.

We seek to be constructive critics of the U.N., likewise we offer constructive criticism of the policies of our government, and we encourage the United States to use multilateral approaches (that is, cooperative action by several governments) whenever possible to achieve its foreign-policy objectives. Those were the objectives of our chapter and team members over the past five years. And who among our fellow citizens would seek to prevent us from achieving those goals.

At the crack of dawn of the new millennium, we did not have a lot of money, but we had will power, commitment, and the desire to make a difference. Our small local chapter at Greater Miami embraced our mission and set forth in the darkest hour before the new millennium, engaging teamwork through creativity and innovation to achieve our noble objectives. It costs money to develop our programs. We did not have the money to foot the cost; therefore, our best alternative to having money was building on teamwork, creativity, and innovation.

We ventured into unknown territories and uncharted waters, as the leader of our local chapter, and as I have discussed earlier, I did not know anything about any of the organizations when we started the journey. All we needed to know was it is our world, we are stakeholders. We girded our loins with courage, raised high our banner of enthusiasm, opened our books on democracy and engaged fruitful dialogue. Charging into the twenty-first century we embraced each other in teamwork, and cultivated an engine of team spirit.

We considered our challenges and crossed those bridges when got there, and there were a lot of them. Even though we were boxed in time and again we never abandon our programs. Whenever, individually, one becomes worn and tired, a squirt of energy from other team members fired us on our journey. We engaged teamwork in intra-organizations and inter-organization because it was all we had to work with. We were seamless in our cooperative efforts across non-profit and for-profit organizations. We did not simply seek sponsorship of organizations; we invited and enlisted team work.

Our works involved interaction of over 190 different cultures, a wide range of organizations of different structures; and peoples from all walks of life, of different age groups, of different ethnic groups, of different socio-economic backgrounds, of different religious affiliations, and of different genders. For those of us who had the opportunity, it was that one moment in time; yes, we were there. At the crack of dawn of the new millennium, when the role called for a TAAL order, which was *thinking and acting locally*, the Greater Miami Chapter of UNA-USA answered, present.

PEOPLE, PLACES, AND THINGS

263

Frank Calzon   Prof. Anthony Roque   Prof. Joa

INTE

274

283

Alfredo Duran   Sylvia McLeod   Ralph Fernandez   Nicolás Gutiérrez

290

291

293

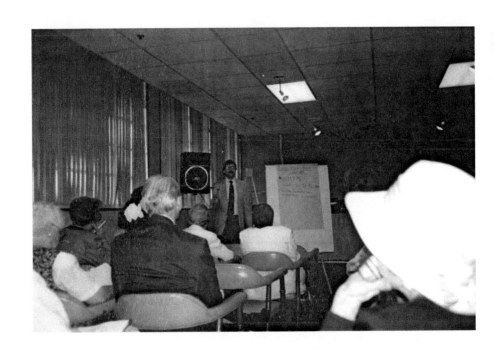

311

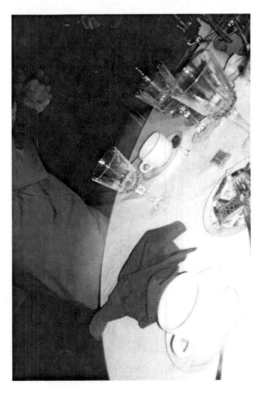

RALPH CWERMAN

329

331

337

347

348

95 10 27

362

CPSIA information can be obtained at www.ICGtesting.com
Printed in the USA
LVOW130024071112

306181LV00001B/1/P